THE WARS OF THE ROSES

THE WARS OF THE ROSES

MATTHEW LEWIS

AMBERLEY

First published 2015

Amberley Publishing
The Hill, Stroud
Gloucestershire, GL5 4EP

www.amberley-books.com

British Library Cataloguing in Publication Data.
A catalogue record for this book is available from the British Library.

ISBN 978 1 4456 4635 0 (hardback)
ISBN 978 1 4456 4636 7 (ebook)

Typesetting and Origination by Amberley Publishing.
Printed in the UK.

Contents

Introduction

Civil wars are among the most insidious forms of an always unpleasant side of the human condition. Glory can be mined from the defence of a nation or protection of the innocent from unjust aggression or, in the medieval era, from enforcing a just claim on foreign soil. War that pitches neighbour against neighbour and divides families will always be devoid of magnificence and splendour.

The cruellest trick of any civil conflict is to ask an apparently simple but inherently complex question that insists upon an answer: Stephen or Matilda? Catholic or Protestant? Royalist or Parliamentarian? North or South? The demand in the second half of the fifteenth century became equally unambiguous: Lancaster or York?

The period referred to by the misleading umbrella term of the Wars of the Roses is almost universally recognised as erupting in 1455 and imploding into the tranquil warmth of the Tudor dawn in 1485. The label is a convenient construct to house the sprawling and unwieldy social, political and international upheaval; this would be packaged more neatly by the Tudors to advertise their bold salvation of the floundering nation of England, for which all should be indebted to their dynasty.

In the mid-fourteenth century King Edward III, judged by many to be the perfect medieval king, had reached the summit of his Arthurian dreams by laying claim to the throne of France. In spite of early successes, it was the initiation of the Hundred Years War that would define the fortunes of a nation and by turns bring unrivalled glory and immeasurable misery. The ungainly nature of foreign war across the seas made progress difficult and stuttering.

Hot on the heels of the outbreak of this chivalric adventure came the savage onslaught of the Black Death, which would decimate national populations across Europe. Racing across the mainland from Italy in an insatiable expanse, the disease barely hesitated at the English Channel before taking ship and finding land again in England's green and pleasant land. Darkness arrived as the disease fell, shredding the fabric of English society. Without respect for class, occupation, age or location, it devoured human life wherever it went. Death rates varied, but in places entire villages were obliterated and abandoned. To the medieval mind there was only one possible explanation; the Great Plague was punishment from God for the sins of man.

The last years of Edward III's rule were blighted by his ill health. At least one and possibly more strokes withdrew him from public life and the country was run, less than successfully, by his sons. Predeceased by his oldest son Edward, the Black Prince, Edward was succeeded by his nine-year-old grandson, Richard II. The Peasants' Revolt followed heavy taxation. The Black Death had created a labour shortage that those who worked the land sought to exploit to improve their lot. Forced back down by restrictive legislation, the third Poll Tax was the final straw. Aged fourteen, Richard negotiated with the rebels, granting their demands in return for peace, only for his promises to be broken.

Growing into tyranny, Richard II was deposed by his cousin, Henry of Bolingbroke, son of John of Gaunt, Duke of Lancaster. With the accession of Henry IV the House of Lancaster took command of England. Richard II was quietly done away with, but Henry IV was plagued by rebellions and unrest throughout his reign. He was succeeded in 1413 by his son Henry V, who would lead the famous Agincourt campaign and prove so successful in France that he was named heir to Charles VI. Henry V died of dysentery on campaign in 1422 just months before the French king, leaving both thrones to his nine-month-old son, Henry VI, the only man to be crowned king of both England and France. His minority would be long and troublesome on both sides of the

Channel. A man disinterested in his father's wars, Henry watched both of his kingdoms crumble, and when trouble reached home shores it would threaten civil war. Failure to avert conflict ensured that hostilities were ushered in.

From 1399 onwards there was unsettlement around the throne of England. Men and women came to realise that change, uncertainty and conflict meant opportunity for those willing to seize it. The Wars of the Roses is the story of these men and women, whose motives are sometimes hard to discern and shifted as the political landscape changed. The contents of protagonist's minds cannot be known for certain, in response to which possibilities should be evaluated but conclusions will always, necessarily, be subjective and personal, leaving room for the kind of discussion that keeps the fires of this period of English history burning brightly.

1

The Most Despised Man in England

As the warm spring sun rose on the morning of 2 May 1450, it cast a pale glow upon a grisly sight on Dover beach. As the waves lapped at the sands of England's south coast, they must have looked as though they recoiled from the horrific spectacle deposited there. A headless corpse lay limp on the sand, dried blood staining the ragged wounds around the butchered neck. The shadow cast over the body came from the pale head that lolled atop a pole driven into the beach. The vacant eyes of William de la Pole, 1st Duke of Suffolk, gazed out over the sea upon which he had lost his life, a fate many believed that he deserved to have met at the king's own hand. At fifty-three years of age, William had taken his family to new heights of power from the humble beginnings that caused much of the odium that surrounded his name. After a lifetime of service and veracious climbing, his fall was complete and devastating.

Another William de la Pole, the great-grandfather of this duke, had been a wealthy and successful wool merchant in Kingston upon Hull. Under King Edward III in the mid-fourteenth century William had been able to loan money to the crown, bringing his family into influence. William briefly served as Chief Baron of the Exchequer, but it was his sons who were to reap the rewards of their father's work. The eldest, Michael, was appointed Lord Chancellor to King Richard II in 1383, with his younger brother Edmund securing the lucrative and prestigious position of Captain of Calais.

Richard II led his first military campaign to Scotland in 1385 and marked the occasion by making several promotions. Two of his uncles became dukes and Michael was elevated to the earldom of Suffolk. It was irregular to make these appointments outside of Parliament and it marked the beginning of trouble for the eighteen-year-old king. The de la Pole family's star was firmly in the ascent, but was now so closely aligned with that of Richard II that when the king's popularity slipped the de la Pole's fortunes necessarily tumbled alongside him. Michael in particular was at the sharp end of criticism as the leader of Richard's government. At a time when direct criticism of God's anointed king, no matter how unpopular or unreasonable he had become, was not an option, it was the closest advisors and figureheads of the king's policies that took the brunt of public and aristocratic hatred.

In 1387 Richard II was subjected to an embarrassing enforcement of terms by the Lords Appellant, a group of the most powerful nobles in the land, led by his uncle Thomas, Duke of Gloucester, who was joined initially by Thomas Beauchamp, Earl of Warwick, and Richard Fitzalan, Earl of Arundel. They were later joined by Thomas Mowbray, Earl of Nottingham, and the king's cousin Henry Bolingbroke, Earl of Derby, who would later seize his cousin's throne and rule as King Henry IV, the first Lancastrian king. The result of this was the Merciless Parliament of February 1388, which oversaw the executions of eight of Richard's closest associates and the dismissal of over three dozen of the king's household in an attempt to reform his government. Suffolk and the others were condemned as 'false traitors to and enemies of the king and kingdom, perceiving the tender age of our said lord the king and the innocence of his royal person, so caused him to believe many falsities devised and plotted by them against loyalty and good faith'. It was claimed that these men did not allow anyone else 'to speak with nor approach the king, properly to counsel him, nor the king to speak with them'. A few of Richard's favourites managed to flee the country before the parliament sat, including Robert de Vere, Duke of Ireland. Michael de la Pole escaped to Paris, but died there the following year, an exile, at the age of sixty.

The earl's son, another Michael, the father to our duke, was just twenty-two when his father died. The Merciless Parliament had stripped the family of their lands and titles and the young Michael was more closely aligned to the Lords Appellant than the king.

When Richard again took control, Michael was out of favour. For a decade, he fought to restore the family's position, finally being allowed to take the title 2nd Earl of Suffolk in 1398, just a year before Richard II's cousin Henry wrested the crown from the king's grasp. Although Michael rose at the Duke of York's call to arms to defend Richard II's kingdom, like almost every other man of influence in the land, he quickly embraced the cause of the first Lancastrian king.

When Henry V set sail for France on his legendary campaign, Michael was with him, but the earl died of dysentery in September 1415 during the siege of Harfleur, not quite fifty years of age. The de la Pole family's fortunes would be redefined in the mud and blood of the English kingdom in France. Michael had been blessed with five sons and three daughters. His heir, yet another Michael, became the 3rd Earl of Suffolk aged just nineteen. He had travelled to France with his father and the king and on 25 October took the field at Agincourt. Only a month after inheriting his earldom, Michael lay dead in the sucking mud of a French field.

William de la Pole became 4th Earl of Suffolk on his brother's death. He was to spend most of the next two decades fighting for the English cause in France. After Henry V's death he continued to try to preserve the gains in the name of the infant Henry VI. A babe of nine months, there was an inevitably long minority to be endured, with all of the problems that would bring. None could accuse the de la Pole family of shirking their responsibility to the new king. William led the English forces at the Battle of Jargeau in June 1429, the first battle with a France resurgent under the fervent offensive inspired by Joan of Arc. Jargeau was the first encounter with the Maid of Orleans' forces and it was a crushing defeat for the English. Among the heavy losses was William's brother Alexander. William himself was captured and held prisoner. In the same year another brother, John, died in a French prison, and by 1433, when Thomas de la Pole perished while acting as a hostage for his brother William, the de la Pole brothers were reduced from five to one. The family had sacrificed blood and sons to King Henry VI's cause.

When he finally returned to England, William was nearing forty, a veteran warrior, his family scarred by the struggle to hold on to hard-won territory. Henry VI was now heading toward adulthood but appeared not to share his father's martial character. Henry V was remembered as the lion of England. His son was likened more to a lamb. It would be interesting to know what this old soldier who had dedicated his adult life to fighting for a teenager who had no interest in the war perpetuated in his name made of his sovereign. Whatever their differences, Suffolk was to grow close to the king. In a repeat of his grandfather's fate, Suffolk was to find his fortunes tightly bound to those of a king who was not going to be popular.

Suffolk's first major contribution to his new political role in England was to make arrangements for the king's marriage. In 1444, when Henry VI was twenty-two, Suffolk was instrumental in the selection of Margaret of Anjou as the king's bride. It was a decision that would define both Suffolk's fate and that of Henry's kingdom. Outrage within England was immediate. The king's last surviving uncle, Humphrey, was dismayed that Suffolk planned to ignore an existing contract for Henry's union to the Duke of Armagnac's daughter. The Tudor chronicler Grafton wrote that 'Humphrey Duke of Gloucester, Protector of the realm, repugned and resisted as much as in him lay, this new alliance and contrived matrimony: alleging that it was neither consonant to the law of God nor man, nor honourable to a prince, to infringe and break a promise or contract'.

Margaret of Anjou brought with her little discernible benefit for the crown. Matches with foreign princesses were political exercises in the increase of power, influence and wealth, made for advantage. Margaret's father, René, Duke of Anjou, was the brother of the Queen of France. Although Margaret's blood was not of the finest royal pedigree, the match might have been reasonable if it would serve to bolster the English position in France or provide a powerful ally in the war to maintain a quickly weakening grip on hard-won territory.

Suffolk proceeded in spite of Gloucester's objections, taking a lead in the negotiations that was to leave him open to absorbing the blame when things went wrong. Baker wrote in his *A Chronicle of the English Kings* that 'in the meantime the Earl of Suffolk, one of the Commissioners for the Peace, takes upon him beyond his Commission; and without acquainting his fellows, to treat of a Marriage between the King of England, and a Kinswoman of the King of France, Niece to the French Queen, Daughter to Rene Duke of Anjou styling himself King of Sicily and Naples: In which business he was so inventive, that it brought an aspersion upon him of being bribed.' Despite René's fabulous array of titles, he owned virtually nothing. He had paper claims to his kingdoms, within which he included the title King of Jerusalem, but he had bankrupted his family in unsuccessful bids to make them a reality.

The Treaty of Tours, signed on 22 May 1444, concluded the marriage arrangements. Two days later on 24 May, the King of France was present, along with Margaret's aunt the queen, when Suffolk stood as proxy for Henry VI in a ceremony betrothing the English king to the fourteen-year-old Margaret. It was a further year before she travelled to meet her husband, and when the time came for her to make the voyage into the unknown, it was the no doubt comforting presence of Suffolk that accompanied her on the frightening journey. On 23 April 1445 she finally married Henry and a little over a month later, on 30 May, she was crowned Queen of England at the age of fifteen. The nobility of England were unimpressed that Margaret brought with her no dowry. The two-year truce agreed at Tours was viewed as an admission of weakness by the faction at court that campaigned for renewed hostility, led by the king's uncle Humphrey. Closely tied to this group was Henry's cousin, Richard, Duke of York, a man of wealth and power in his mid-thirties.

What was widely known of the Treaty of Tours was causing friction at court. That which had been kept secret was incendiary, and could not remain hidden for much longer. A fuse was burning and Suffolk would shoulder the blame for lighting it. A separate set of negotiations had taken place behind the scenes at Tours. Henry, who loathed war and wanted peace but knew no way to even begin seeking it, had agreed through Suffolk to a devastating set of concessions, and the French were impatient for their spoils. Henry handed over the vast territories of Maine and Anjou, a swathe of land that accounted for around a quarter of the French territory held by the English crown. With the stroke of a pen, land won with English blood was simply handed back. For his part in the arrangements Suffolk was further elevated to Marquess of Suffolk, but powerful men at court were outraged. Men who had bled on French soil felt betrayed. Families who had settled in those lands at the crown's request were suddenly homeless. There would be a reckoning for this.

After the death of the king's father in 1422, his eldest uncle, John, Duke of Bedford, had served as regent in France, continuing his brother's work efficiently and with a deft hand. Constantly deprived of men and money for the defence of the territories they had won, Bedford had ridden out Joan of Arc's offensive and was as respected by his enemies as by his own men. With Bedford's death in 1435 and the emergence of the king's personal distaste for war, the campaign in France ground to a halt. It is possible that Suffolk's personal exposure to the realities of the English kingdom in France led to his realisation that the war could not be won if the king was unwilling and the requirement now was damage limitation. English occupation of France had been faltering since Henry V's death, unable to replenish the funds and soldiers soaked up by the effort. Suffolk had seen this at first-hand, in the eye of the storm, and endured personal loss because of it. Marriage to a niece of the Queen of France would bring Henry the peace he craved. Giving back Maine and Anjou was judged as a signal of weakness and bad council, yet this may not be the whole story.

By the end of the 1420s England controlled a large area of the north of France, stretching down in the east to meet the territories of their Burgundian allies. Gascony in the west was a lone outpost of English dominion. As impressive as this feat had been, it had produced a stalemate. Starved of men and finances, the English effort could not push any further forward while fighting the sporadic fires that broke out behind their own lines as French confidence was first restored, and then began to swell. The meandering front line was massive and virtually unmanageable. It highlights the incredible job that Bedford had done with the available resources, but Suffolk, from personal experience, may have judged the situation unsustainable. The English crown had a centuries old claim to the Duchy of Normandy. Gascony was a valuable wine-producing region that England had successfully held wherever else land was lost in France. Retaining Brittany completed the domination of the north coast, thus protecting England's own south coast. There were good strategic, economic and political reasons for retaining these territories.

The neighbouring regions of Maine and Anjou to the south of Normandy were perhaps deemed less vital. The English council, though Suffolk was to eventually assume the full blame for the decision, may have concluded that returning these lands, securing a marriage and a two year truce would allow them to take a breath and strengthen their grip on an unmanageable portfolio of foreign duchies. King Henry had no interest in war. If his mind could not be changed then it was only a matter of time before France began to push back. The sacrifice of Maine and Anjou may have been considered necessary in order to preserve any hope of keeping control of the remaining English kingdom of France. Henry VI is the only monarch in history to have been crowned king of both England and France. Bedford had pushed for a coronation in France in 1431 to bolster support in the face of French resurgence. Allied to Bedford's long-term plans for continued expansion, it made perfect sense. With Bedford gone, and with him the appetite for aggression, it created a huge problem that would dog Henry's desire to cease fighting. Once crowned, he could not be uncrowned. The English kingdom of France would have to be lost in war with the accompanying loss of honour and, in the case of many, personal wealth.

If the return of Maine and Anjou was an attempt to buy time to reorganise and tighten control of what remained, it failed. The effect was to offer the French not only a glimpse of England's panicky weakness and unwillingness to fight for what they had won, but also to kindle within them a renewed desire to drive their enemy from France altogether. Suffolk would be blamed for opening the door through which England was driven from France until nothing remained of Henry V and John Duke of Bedford's gains. Only Calais, a fortress outpost won by Edward III early in the Hundred Years War, remained in English hands.

The king's uncle, Humphrey, Duke of Gloucester, died in 1447. He had withdrawn from public life after his second wife, Eleanor Cobham, had been accused and found guilty of using witchcraft against the king to bring power to her husband. Gloucester was stained by the charges. An educated humanist with an interest in literature and learning, Gloucester was popular among the people, not least for his firm stance on continued war in France. He and Bedford had frequently been at odds, with Humphrey impetuous and Bedford more measured, but both had been utterly committed to the fulfilment of the aim their oldest brother had given his life for. Humphrey's death marked the end of an era. Rumour began to spread that Gloucester had been murdered, with Queen Margaret presumed to be the driving force. Humphrey had been arrested for treason on 20 February 1447, but died in custody just three days later. He may have suffered a stroke or heart attack, but a sinister report sprang up that he had been poisoned before he could defend himself. One anonymous chronicler explains that 'Many now recollected how stoutly the duke of Gloucester had stood up against the surrender of those provinces from which the king of France had made his attack'. Whatever the truth, the people knew what they believed.

Shortly after Gloucester's death, Suffolk was promoted once more to the title of Duke of Suffolk. As his power and authority grew, so did the odium and suspicion about him. His ascendancy was complete. In four generations, the de la Poles had been transformed from wool merchants to dukes. Suffolk's rise brought with it enemies, and now, as Henry's foremost advisor, he was the focus for any dissatisfaction with the ineffectual rule of Henry VI. The same anonymous chronicler further accuses Suffolk 'of plotting to get the English crown into his own Family, by marrying his infant ward, Lady Margaret Beaufort, to his own son; she being, they observed, the presumptive heiress of the royal house of Lancaster, as long as the king had no children'.

Margaret Beaufort was the most eligible heiress in England at the time she was betrothed to William's son John. She was the daughter of John Beaufort, 1st Duke of Somerset, himself a grandson of John of Gaunt, Duke of Lancaster, Henry VI's great-grandfather. John had, following the death of his second wife, married his long-term mistress Katherine Swynford, with whom he already had a brood of illegitimate children. They took the name Beaufort, probably from John's French castle in which they were all born. The other Beaufort children included Henry, Cardinal Bishop of Winchester, a towering figure of Henry VI's minority government who almost singlehandedly financed the stuttering efforts in France, and Joan Beaufort, who would marry Ralph Neville, Earl of Westmorland, and pass the link to John of Gaunt on through the Neville line to some of the key political figures of the coming decades. John of Gaunt had petitioned his nephew, Richard II, to legitimise his Beaufort children. This had been done just before Richard lost his throne, though a clause specifically restricted any Beaufort from ever claiming the throne. This legitimisation was later reissued, but the caveat remained.

Margaret Beaufort was not Henry VI's heir presumptive. This, it was universally but tacitly accepted, was a position filled by Richard, Duke of York until such time as Henry and Margaret produced a son. The accusation that Suffolk sought to place his own son on the throne through this union seems flawed. The unlikely scenario of her accession to the throne suggests that the attraction of the match lay in Margaret's vast wealth, the same financial consideration that saw Henry VI annul the marriage in 1453 and give Margaret to his newly emerged half-brother, Edmund Tudor.

As the year 1450 began, Suffolk found himself caught in a mire. He had made powerful enemies, including the Paston family of Norfolk. The Pastons kept a huge amount of their personal and business correspondence and it has survived to offer an invaluable insight into the politics and daily life of the time. The Pastons were at odds with Suffolk, who it was felt was using his position to bully those in surrounding lands out of their possessions to strengthen his own position. The parliament that had opened in November 1449 returned from a Christmas break on 22 January 1450 as planned, but one matter was to dominate this second session. The Commons demanded that Suffolk be tried for treason. In answer, the duke requested the right to plead his case before the king in Parliament. Less than a fortnight earlier, on 9 January, Adam Moleyn, Bishop of Chichester, had been murdered. Relieved of his position as Keeper of the Privy Seal and no longer required in Parliament or government, Moleyn had been killed in Portsmouth by Cuthbert Colville, a soldier waiting to embark for France. Moleyn was perhaps the first scapegoat for the government's failure, but he was not to be the last. Now, the Commons went for the jugular.

On 26 January, the Commons asked the Lord Chancellor, John

Stafford, Archbishop of Canterbury to have Suffolk arrested and placed into custody. The request was debated by the king, his lords and the judges the following day. It is a mark of Henry's unwillingness to proceed against his closest friend and advisor that they refused, at least until some specific charges were laid against the duke. Undeterred, the Commons tried again on the 28th, offering the required charge by claiming that 'the realm of England is about to be sold to the king's enemy of France'. Baker summarised the charge against Suffolk, writing that 'he had traitorously incited the Bastard of Orleans, the Lord Presigny, and others to levy war against the King to the end that thereby the King might be destroyed; and his son John who had married Margaret, daughter and sole heir of John Duke of Somerset, whose title to the crown the said Duke had often declared, in case King Henry should die without issue, might come to be King'. After Suffolk's involvement in the handing over of Maine and Anjou, it is perhaps unsurprising that the Commons should, in seeking out a plausible charge against him, suggest that he was now plotting to invite the French king over the Channel into England itself. This was enough to see Suffolk placed into custody. It also saw Stafford sacked as Lord Chancellor and replaced with John Kemp, Archbishop of York.

A long list of general and very specific charges was laid before the Commons on 7 February. On 12 February, the charges were read before the Lords, who decided to refer them to the judges for an opinion. None were willing to condemn the king's favourite as a traitor. Henry stepped in to have the matter shelved until he decided that it should be dealt with, but by 7 March it was again before the Lords, who decided that Suffolk should answer the charges. On the 9th, the Commons sent to the Lords a further long list of damning accusations against Suffolk. It was clear that Henry did not want the matter taken any further, but it was equally clear that the Commons had the bit between their teeth and had no intention of letting go of their prize. The king and the Commons were dangerously at odds. It had become a battle of wills for the life of one man.

On 9 March, and again on the 13th, Suffolk was brought from the Tower to answer the charges laid against him. The Parliament Rolls record that Suffolk, 'kneeling before the king and all the said lords, answered himself to each of the said articles of treasons, which were eight in total, and all those which touched high treason to the king's person he denied completely and said, saving the king's high presence, they were false and untrue'. William offered evidence to refute the charges that related to specific dates and locations, but he must have known that he was never going to prevail. Suffolk had, however, allowed one door to remain open to him. The Lord Chancellor reminded the duke that he had not insisted upon trial by his peers, probably because he knew that they would be hostile to him, happy to extricate themselves from any blame by seeing Suffolk shoulder it all. Again, Suffolk denied the 'great and dreadful charges', telling them that 'he took his soul to everlasting damnation if he ever knew more of those matters than the child in the mother's womb'.

As it became clear that no defence could save Suffolk, Henry intervened, using the door Suffolk had kept ajar. Henry exercised his prerogative to deal personally with the matter in a final, desperate bid to save his favourite. On 17 March the Lords Spiritual and Temporal then in London were called, not to Parliament, but to Henry's own apartments. Here, the Chancellor, in a tone the Parliament Rolls recorded as almost unwilling, told the duke and the gathered Lords that 'the king commands me to say to you that regarding the great and dreadful charges contained in the said first bill, the king holds you neither declared nor charged'. To mitigate any backlash from this decision, Henry did find Suffolk guilty of some of the minor crimes of which he was accused. The Chancellor was keen to confirm that Henry did this 'by his own advice and not resorting to the advice of his lords, nor by way of judgment for he is not in a place of judgment'.

King Henry passed a sentence of exile against his favourite, commanding him that 'from the said 1 May until the end of the next following and fully complete five years you shall refrain from living in his realm of France or in any other lordships or places which are under his obedience'. The sentence was probably designed to save Suffolk's neck. It seemed unlikely that the Commons, who were not at the sentencing, would acquiesce quietly and Suffolk would be at risk of mob justice. Henry must also have realised that keeping Suffolk by his side was no longer a viable option. Perhaps with the passage of time he might return, rehabilitated, but right now Suffolk was toxic.

On leaving Henry's apartments, William was hassled and jeered at in the streets as he tried to return to his London residence. Driven from the capital by a crowd baying for his blood, Suffolk retired to his manor at Wingfield to prepare for his impending exile. William's only son, John, was now eight years old. Fearing that he was destined to miss out on his heir's formative years, Suffolk penned a letter to the young boy instructing him in the ways that he should behave at home, at court and in his dealings with the king and other men. The letter is filled with the kind of fatherly advice that Shakespeare's Polonius would employ to his son in *Hamlet*. He counselled John thus;

My dear and only well-beloved son,

I beseech our Lord in heaven, the Maker of all the world, to bless you, and to send you ever grace to love Him and to dread Him; to the which as far as a father may charge his child, I both charge you and pray you to set all your spirits and wits to do and to know His holy laws and commandments, by which ye shall with His great mercy, pass all the great tempests and troubles of this wretched world.

And also that wittingly ye do nothing for love nor dread of any earthly creature that should displease Him. And whereas any frailty maketh you to fall, beseech His mercy soon to call you to Him again with repentance, satisfaction, and contrition of your heart, nevermore in will to offend Him.

Secondly, next Him, above all earthly things, to be true liegeman in heart, in will, in thought, in deed, unto the King, our elder, most high, and dread Sovereign Lord, to whom both ye and I be so much bound; charging you, as father can and may, rather to die than to be the contrary, or to know anything that were against the welfare and prosperity of his most royal perity of his most royal person, but that so far as your body and life may stretch, ye live and die to defend it and to let His Highness have knowledge thereof, in all the haste ye can.

Thirdly, in the same wise, I charge you, my dear son, always as ye he bounden by the commandment of God to do, to love and to worship your lady and mother: and also that ye obey always her commandments, and to believe her counsels and advices in all your works, the which dread not but shall be best and truest for you.

And if any other body would steer you to the contrary, to flee that counsel in any wise, for ye shall find it nought and evil.

Furthermore, as far as father may and can, I charge you in any wise to flee the company and counsel of proud men, of covetous men, and of flattering men the more especially; and mightily to withstand them, and not to draw nor to meddle with them, with all your might and power; and to draw to you, and to your company, good and virtuous men and such as be of good conversation and of truth, and by them shall ye never be deceived nor repent you of.

Moreover, never follow your own wit in any wise, but in all your works, of such folks as I write of above ask your advice and counsel, and doing thus, with the mercy of God, ye shall do right well, and live in right much worship and great heart's rest and ease.

And I will be to you, as good lord and father as mine heart can think.

And last of all, as heartily and as lovingly as ever father blessed his child on earth, I give you the Blessing of Our Lord, and of me, which in his infinite mercy increase you in all virtue and good living and that your blood may by His Grace from kindred to kindred multiply in this earth to His service, in such wise as after the departing from this wretched worlde here, ye and they may glorify Him eternally amongst His angels in Heaven.
Written of mine hand,
the day of my departing from this land,
Your true and loving father
SUFFOLK.

Leaving his wife and son behind, Suffolk took ship and sailed into exile on 1 May 1450, the date his king had appointed for the beginning of his five-year expulsion. As he crossed the Channel, a huge ship of the royal fleet sailed into view on a course that would intercept the duke's boat. *The Nicholas of the Tower* had been used by Henry V as one of his flagships when he set off on his famous Agincourt campaign. Did Henry have one last message of comfort for the favourite that he had been forced to punish? Was Suffolk to be saved from his exile by a last-minute reprieve? If William's heart soared at the sight of *The Nicholas*, it soon sank again.

William Lomner wrote to John Paston on 5 May, telling him how the crew of *The Nicholas* had boarded Suffolk's vessel and rounded on the duke as 'the master bade him, "Welcome, Traitor," as men say'. Lomner goes on, no doubt to Paston's delight, to describe the duke's fate, continuing, 'And then his heart failed him, for he thought he was deceived, and in the sight of all his men he was drawn out of the great ship into the boat; and there was an axe, and a stoke, and one of the lewdest of the ship bade him lay down his head, and he should be fair faired with, and die on a sword; and took a rusty sword, and smote off his head within half a dozen strokes.'

Beheading by the rough hacking of a sailor's rusty blade was an ignominious end for a duke, a man who stood at the apex of his family's power and who exercised an authority second only to the king's. It is hard at this distance and with the evidence so heavily stacked against him to determine whether William acted solely out of greed or well-meant service, doing what he deemed to be in the best interests of crown and country in spite of the consequences. The truth probably lies somewhere in the vast grey area in between. Suffolk had acted as scapegoat for an unpopular government, and the job for the king and his advisors now was to use this sacrifice as a fresh start, to move forward with the king liberated from an evil advisor and able to rule his country as he should.

As that sun rose over Dover beach, it rose on a new chapter for England, though not the one the country might have hoped for. There were rumours that the king's cousin Richard, Duke of York, had organised Suffolk's assassination, dissatisfied with the outcome of the trial. Still more accused the men of Kent of the murder of a man that symbolised the cause of their county's suffering. As his empty eyes gazed out over the Channel to the land where his family had been broken and made, William would never again look upon the country that had turned its back on him, nor see his son grow to heed a lost father's advice. His place at Henry's side was swiftly filled by Edmund Beaufort, 2nd Duke of Somerset. Bitter rivalry and personal hatred were allowed to fester and breed as King Henry VI pressed his hands together in prayer, oblivious to the chaos churning all about him.

War was on the horizon.

2

The Man Who Set England on Fire

One man rode the tidal wave of seething discontentment that permeated almost every level of English society as the reign of King Henry VI entered its thirtieth year. This man went by several names, but no-one seems certain who he really was. His identity grew with the rebellion that took his name and became lost as it overtook and consumed him. Jack Cade set England alight, harnessing a country desperate for a firm hand. Perhaps the loss of his true identity was no mistake.

William de la Pole was dead, murdered at sea. Rumour spread throughout Kent that Henry and his queen intended to exact revenge on the men of that county, holding them responsible for the assassination. Added to this, the social fabric of southern England was pulled taught and ready to split. *Stow's Chronicle*, compiled toward the end of the Tudor era, sums up the mood, explaining, 'A general agitation pervaded the nation. At each arrival from Normandy or Guienne, the discontent increased: the wildest charges against the court were circulated; and the people were everywhere threatening to reform the government by force.'

England was losing control of what constituted the English kingdom of France. Soldiers were flooding back into Kent and the southern ports, unpaid, penniless, hungry and with no work to occupy them. It was a recipe for trouble. Suddenly, as if from nowhere, a man emerged as the leader of this disquieted rabble. He brought control and purpose, transforming 'general agitation' into organised protest. Jack Cade also used names including Captain

Amendall and, most significantly, John Mortimer. The importance of this last name is easy to overlook but, in the context of the time, is intriguing.

In May 1450, the month that had begun with Suffolk's murder, men began to gather in numbers throughout Kent and the surrounding counties. Parliament was in session at Leicester when news reached the king, and Henry and his lords moved swiftly back to London. The protesters could count merchants and landowners alongside hardworking labourers and destitute soldiers. This was the largest uprising since the Peasants' Revolt against Richard II in 1381, but at least Henry VI had a template from which to work. Richard II's brave meeting with his rebels and intimations of sympathy with their cause had dispersed the immediate threat.

Cade's group mustered at Blackheath just to the south-east of the walled City of London. Estimates of the size of the rebel force by this stage range from around 20,000 to the 46,000 *Gregory's Chronicle* credits him with. A document was sent to Parliament, entitled *The Complaint of the Poor Commons of Kent*. The paper declared Kent's innocence in Suffolk's death and bemoaned the rumoured plans for vengeance against the county. They spoke of the king being forced to live off his people while the Crown's estates were given away to corrupt men and that these corrupt men surrounded the king to the exclusion of better councillors – those of his own blood. The document berated the loss of the king's lands in France and the effect upon the soldiers now returning, complaining too of the excessive taxation of Kent above other counties and of the oppression of free elections.

As with all such criticism at the time, it was not levelled against the king himself. Instead, the condemnation was directed at those who surrounded and advised the monarch. Although Suffolk was gone, the remainder of the unpopular advisors still had a stranglehold on power around the weak king. The reference to others of the king's blood was a clear allusion to Richard, Duke of York. The crowd's demands seem to mirror the grievances of York himself. The duke had been Lieutenant in France and had overseen the last days of any semblance of strength there. Now he was Lieutenant of Ireland, a role that was vital and prestigious but considered exile for the man who represented the antithesis of the peace-loving king.

The Kentish rebels were beginning to sound like York's mouthpiece, and this led to heightened fear among the royal party. The rebellion would take on a new level of threat if it was connected to the rich, powerful and popular Duke of York. Some were whispering that York had been behind Suffolk's assassination at sea. Was he now instigating a full-scale revolt? One of Cade's names added fuel to this smouldering cinder of mistrust.

King Henry and his nobles returned to London to face the threat, gathering men as they rode. Cade had promised that his men would await the king's reply before moving again and his word proved good. His men had been well controlled and disciplined as they awaited Henry's response. By the time the court arrived in the capital, Henry had mustered around 20,000 men and a second missive had arrived from the leader of the Kentish force. This document was conspicuously entitled *The Requests by the Captain of the Great Assembly in Kent* and marked a change in tone from a force either growing frustrated, more confident or nervous as the large royal army approached. It is telling too that this was no longer a list of grievances from a county feeling the weight of injustice. It was now a list of demands from their leader.

Cade's proclamation was still careful to begin by identifying those gathered at Blackheath as 'the King's liege men of Kent', but went on to condemn those surrounding their king as 'insatiable, covetous, malicious, pompous and false'. Cade quoted Latin scripture, warning, 'Ve vobis qui dicitis bonum malum et malum bonum'; 'Woe to you that call evil good, and good evil.' This document bears some closer examination, since it details in full the grievances of the commons against their lords, providing a rare insight both into their perception of the land in which they lived, and of just how easily they believed their king could repair the damage they saw.

Cade provided twenty-one articles of complaint, beginning with the accusation that 'they say that our sovereign lord is above his laws to his pleasure, and he may make it and break it', contending that the 'contrary is true' according to the king's coronation oath, during which he had promised to uphold the law. Next, the proclamation berated the king's false advisors for claiming that the Kentish men intended first to destroy those councillors, then to remove the king himself so that they could place the Duke of York on the throne. The rebels pointed out that they convinced the king of these slurs 'so that by their false menace and lies they make him to hate and to destroy his friends, and cherish his false traitors'.

The new set of grievances complained that 'they say' the king should live from his commons, meaning that he should levy taxes to meet his financial needs rather than managing his estates more efficiently, that the greed and corruption surrounding the king prevented him from taking proper control of his own possessions and called for a remedy to the way in which access to the king is restricted unfairly.

Two articles point out the unfair treatment of the Duke of Gloucester, the king's uncle, blaming his mistreatment firmly on Suffolk, on whose word alone, it was claimed, Gloucester was impeached, only to be murdered before he could present a defence. When Suffolk was similarly called to account by the will of all England, he escaped any punishment beyond exile. The rebels demanded justice for those who had contributed to Gloucester's fall.

The faltering of the rule of law occupied several clauses, voicing concern that 'whom the king wills shall be traitor and whom he wills shall be none', for 'the law serves nought else in these days but for to do wrong' and 'no remedy is had in the court of conscience'. The men of Kent paint a dire picture of England, pleading with the king to see that 'his false council has lost his law, his merchandise is lost, his common people destroyed, the sea is lost, France is lost'. This was made worse by the fact that Henry 'owes more than ever any king of England ought'. Other articles of the proclamation offers specific details of abuses that should be ended, including extortion, corruption of legal officials, the seizing of wheat and grain without recompense, requesting honest officers to put an end to the 'traitors and bribers' and for the king to take their property, keeping it for himself to improve his financial situation, to pay off his debts or to pay for an army to return to France.

Cade insisted that although they are called traitors, 'they shall be found the king's true liegemen and best friends', for they pray daily that God will take vengeance upon the true traitors that surround the king. The document points out that the Kentish men do not blame all of those who surround the king, but primarily the remainder of Suffolk's faction. They seek justice only against 'such as may be found guilty by just and true enquiry of the law'. The intention of the uprising was not to cause trouble, and the rebels promised that once their grievances were remedied 'we will go home'. On this basis they called for the support of all good, honest men, 'for who is against us in this case, him will we mark, for he is not the true king's liegeman'.

The core of their demands and their hopes are summed up in two of the articles. King Henry should rid himself of the remainder of Suffolk's party and 'take about his noble person his true blood of his royal realm', specifying 'the high and mighty prince the Duke of York, exiled from our sovereign lord's person by the noisings of the false traitor the Duke of Suffolk and his affinity', also citing 'the mighty prince, the Duke of Exeter, the Duke of Buckingham, the Duke of Norfolk and his true earls and barons'. If Henry were to realise this, he would, Cade claimed, 'be the richest king in Christendom'.

Finally, the proclamation pleads that once all is remedied, none about the king should be permitted to take bribes on pain of death, offering a final appeal that if King Henry were to do all that was required, 'he shall have so great love of his people that he shall with God's help conquer where he will, and as for us, we shall be always ready to defend our country from all nations with our own goods, and to go with our sovereign lord where he will command us, as his true liegemen'. It is a touching sentiment that carries a note of desperation for a king worthy of his subject's love and devotion.

This document doomed Cade's Rebellion the instant it was dispatched to Parliament because it is possible to read into the proclamation darker sentiment than the hopeful pleading it appears to announce. The rebels make it very clear that they will only go home once their grievances are settled. The reference to defending their country 'from all nations' is also dependent upon their success and there is a perceivable implication that they will not offer such support if they are denied their requests. In the early thirteenth century, barons rebelling against King John had invited Prince Louis of France to lead them and seize John's throne. After John's death and the accession of his son, the nine-year-old Henry III,

England came very close to falling into Louis's hands completely, saved only by the mighty efforts of the legendary William Marshall. It was perhaps not lost on the government of Henry VI that a king who came to the throne young, after losses in France he failed to reverse, had suffered such a threat. Henry VI was an adult now, but Charles VII was rampant as France was revived, and it must have worried all parties that in the shadow of his success lurked a tempting notion to look over the Channel. The men of Kent perhaps offered a thinly veiled threat to the government that as things stood, they might not resist such a challenge.

Even without the darker undercurrents of the document, it could not succeed. Henry had only three choices. He could accept the validity of the rebels' demands and see the wrongs set right. In doing so, he would win the affection of his commons but risk losing their respect, and he would be forced to divest himself of all those close to him within weeks of being forced to part with Suffolk. As much as the commons might support such a move, with at least tacit approval from the likes of York, Exeter, Buckingham and Norfolk if they were indeed feeling pushed aside, those surrounding Henry would fight bitterly against it. If he were ever to hope to become an effective king, Henry could not allow himself to be dictated to by a rabble of his disgruntled subjects. If that tactic were to work, London would be besieged daily by new mobs.

The second course open to Henry was the same moderate route employed by Richard II. He could present himself to the mob as their leader and champion, diffusing some of the animosity and sucking the wind from the rebels' sails. He could offer investigation of their charges and perhaps some concessions, appearing horrified and sympathetic to abuses he was at arm's length from without joining the condemnation of those close to him. A similar approach had served the teenage Richard II well, yet his government's later reversal may have made the Kentish men wary of such a strategy and would necessitate placing the king's person in a risky situation to which he was unlikely to be well suited. Richard II had demonstrated a personal bravery that seems to have been lacking from Henry's makeup.

A final path was available to Henry. A demonstration of power would show that such uprisings would not be tolerated and that the king would not be bent by the demands of his commons, particularly when they were made with force. The attractions of this method were clear, but so would have been the risks. The use of a royal army to subdue a commons voicing, to their collective mind, legitimate grievances was an act of tyranny from which there could be no way back. It would open a door to civil war that it was a king's duty to keep firmly locked. Yet it was this route that Henry chose. His only hope of salvaging the situation lay in swift and complete success with minimal bloodshed.

The Parliament Rolls record a commission, given on 6 June as Parliament was brought to an abrupt end, requiring the Duke of Buckingham and the Earls of Arundel, Devon and Oxford to act 'against the traitors and rebels in Kent and to punish and arrest the same'. It was clear that Henry had no intention of riding out alone to face the crowds. The royal army of around 20,000 rumbled out of London to drive the rebels from their camp at Blackheath and crush the uprising.

News of the royal army's approach had reached Cade and he had made a tactical withdrawal from Blackheath to Sevenoaks, about twenty miles to the south-east. It is unclear whether this is evidence of panic at the size of the well-equipped force approaching or of the rebels' genuine desire not to fight their king. Henry and his advisors appear to have decided that it was the former. In a move that can only mean they believed the rebellion was undone by the threat of the royal army, a small force was sent forward to disperse whatever lingered of the rebel force and restore order. Sir Humphrey Stafford and William Stafford were despatched toward Sevenoaks to complete the rout.

Neither of the Stafford brothers returned. Cade's force was not spooked. The withdrawal had been an organised tactic and the small force led by Sir Humphrey proved no match for the Kentish men, whipped up into a fury that their king would send soldiers to hunt them down. In the forests of the Weald of Kent the rebels ambushed the Staffords among the trees on 18 June. This fraction of the royal force was put to flight, the Staffords were slain and it was enough to sow panic in the remainder of the royal camp. The soldiery began to speak openly of their sympathies with the Kentish rebels' grievances. The king withdrew to Greenwich but London was beginning to seethe, dangerously close to boiling over within the kettle of its own walls. Lord Saye, a man deeply unpopular in his seat in Kent, and his son-in-law William Crowner, the hated undersheriff, were placed in the Tower. Although this was most likely done for the men's own protection, word was put out that they were to be tried for treason.

Trouble was not restricted to the capital, nor even to the south-east any longer. On 29 June, William Ayscough, Bishop of Salisbury was dragged from his residence in Edington, Wiltshire, and murdered by a mob. His only infraction was that he had, five years earlier, performed the marriage ceremony between Henry VI and Margaret of Anjou. With Bishop Ayscough's pronunciation of the royal couple as man and wife, almost half of the English kingdom of France was handed back without an arrow being cast in its defence. Whatever the political reality of that decision to the common man it was a dishonour and they saw an opportunity for restitution.

London's temperature continued to rise and the atmosphere in the capital became stifling. The soldiers brought in to protect the king and the city were at the very brink of revolt. A decisive move was needed. It did not come from the king. His advisors, no doubt wary of what might follow, had Henry spirited back to the Midlands and he took refuge at Kenilworth Castle. The king was hiding from a rabble of ill-equipped, poorly trained commoners behind the walls of one of his most stout fortresses. It was all the encouragement the men of Kent needed. Cade made the decisive move. He returned to Blackheath on 1 July.

Gregory's Chronicle makes an interesting note at this point. The Londoner writes that 'upon the first day of July, the same captain came again, as the Kentish men said, but it was another that named himself the captain, and he came to Blackheath'. This raises the possibility that Jack Cade, in the incarnation that had mustered, gathered and organised all of these forces, had been killed at Sevenoaks and a replacement found to keep the rebellion alive. Perhaps the matter had gone beyond what the Kentish man who began things could handle and a more suitable leader was drafted in. Perhaps the new leader was even sent to aid the uprising as its threat swelled. Gregory appears to be the only source to claim that there was a change of leadership at this point. If true it mattered little, a testament to the almost ethereal personality of Jack Cade. He captured the hearts, minds and strong arms of the south of England, yet none knew who he really was. Perhaps it didn't matter. What mattered was what Jack Cade represented and what he could win for the people.

On 2 July, the mob pressed forward into Southwark. Cade took the White Hart Inn on the High Street as his centre of operations. It is perhaps no more than a coincidence that the white hart was the heraldic badge of King Richard II. Nothing remains today of the inn as it was destroyed in the Great Fire of Southwark in 1676, but it lay just outside the walls of the City of London and marked another step forward by the rebels. It is impossible to know whether the events of the following day were born of negotiation or fear, but on 3 July Jack Cade marched his men over London Bridge, cutting the drawbridge ropes so that it could not be raised.

Gregory was clearly outraged by the arrival of 'the multitude of riff raff' into London, claiming 'many a man was murdered and killed in that conflict' that saw Cade march triumphal over the Bridge and into the City. It is hard to believe that a large portion of London's citizenry did not openly welcome the rebels as men who shared their grievances and offered a glimpse of the possibilities of their correction. Cade swore to keep his men under control and to retire to Southwark, outside the City walls, each evening to reassure the capital's inhabitants of their peaceful intentions. This was a shrewd move that won over many of the no doubt dubious residents and offers another glimpse of the intelligence, control and political astuteness demonstrated by Cade that give lie to the angry thug he was painted as.

On entering the City, Cade, surrounded by an ocean of followers, struck the London Stone with his knife and roared 'Now is Mortimer lord of this city!' The meaning of this action is lost somewhere in the mists of time. What remains of the London Stone can still be seen, a sad remnant of what had been a mighty pillar. The stone originally rested on the south side of Cannon Street, but today shelters in an alcove on the north side, protected from the further ravages of weather and traffic. Tudor antiquarian John Stowe records that in his day it was well fixed to the ground and protected by iron bars to prevent damage by passing carriages. The stone was moved in 1742 when it was deemed too great a hazard to traffic and was placed against the wall of St Swithin's church on the opposite side of the road. Today, modern buildings huddle protectively over this ancient artefact, only 43 cm of which remain above ground.

It was a thing of antiquity when the first recorded mention of it was made in the twelfth century and its origins remain shrouded in mystery. The most compelling theory of its purpose is that it was a central milestone of Roman origin from which all distances were measured, sitting as it does in the very heart of the City. It has also been suggested that the stone was used as a point from which public proclamation was made. When Cade struck it and made his claim, the message was clear enough. The use of that name would have raised eyebrows amid the crowd too.

The Mortimer family had a long and chequered history. Most notable among their ancestors was Roger, 1st Earl of March, who had been the lover of Isabella, Edward II's queen. He had headed the minority government of the young Edward III and fallen foul of the emerging man's desire to take the reins of power for himself and to be rid of a man he viewed as greedy. The family was eventually rehabilitated until Edmund's great-grandson, the 3rd Earl, who shared his name, was married to Phillipa, the only child of Lionel of Antwerp, Duke of Clarence, the second son of King Edward III. The Mortimers had married into royalty and Edmund's descendants were considered the heirs apparent to the childless Richard II. This blood saw them treated with suspicion by the Lancastrian kings. The vast Mortimer inheritance had passed, upon the death of the last Earl of March in 1425 – another Edmund, without issue – to Richard, Duke of York, whose mother, Anne Mortimer, was the last earl's sister. The name therefore alluded to York, adding to the suggestion that if the duke was not responsible for the uprising, then it was at least in his name that these men seized the capital.

There is, however, another possibility worthy of consideration. On 26 February 1424, a man was quietly condemned to death by Parliament. His crimes are unclear, the charges of attempting to escape the Tower and ferment rebellion offered as proven with minimal detail. The low profile was deliberate. The man's name was Sir John Mortimer. His crimes were an alleged intention to place Edmund Mortimer, 5th Earl of March, on the throne, shortly before the earl's death. Sir John's apparent escape attempt sealed his fate. Such a challenge could not be tolerated in the delicate beginnings of an infant's kingship.

Sir John's relationship to Edmund Mortimer is not recorded, but he was quietly sacrificed for the security of the new regime. A rumour sprang up that Jack Cade's real name was John Mortimer and that he was the son of this wronged scion of the House of Mortimer. If Cade were to play upon this, he would have been staking a claim to the throne itself, transforming his declaration that 'Now is Mortimer lord of this city' from local triumph to statement of national intent. Even if Cade was not a Mortimer himself the use of the name picked the scab from a wound that bled afresh. The rebels' sympathy toward the current Mortimer heir, the Duke of York, served only to add fuel to a fire that was threatening to engulf England.

Cade and his men were in London. The capital was theirs, but its residents now held a collective breath to see what they would do. Lord Scales, a veteran military man now in his early fifties, was in command of the Tower. Lord Saye was Constable of the Tower, but was, at least nominally, under arrest. Alongside Lord Scales on the ramparts of the Tower stood Matthew Gough, a Welsh soldier with a wealth of experience fighting in France. They watched as Cade's men spread through the narrow streets of the City like a tidal wave coming to crash against the Tower's walls. There was some resistance in the streets, but the momentum was with the rebels. The question for Scales and Matthew Gough was how best to deal with the threat.

As the last remnant of royal power watched on, Cade was stage managing the occupation with a consummate ease at odds with the king's reaction. As dusk fell, the Kentish men withdrew to Southwark, beyond the City walls, in an act designed to reassure the citizens of London that they were not the marauding mob they might have been. On the morning of the 4 July they seeped back into the City. Cade's control was so complete that Lord Scales was obliged to pacify the horde. He sent James Feinnes, Lord Saye and his son-in-law William Crowmer to face the Captain's justice. Crowmer, the undersheriff of Kent, was hauled, along with another man, to Mile End, where *Gregory's Chronicle* records that they were beheaded. In the afternoon, Lord Saye was taken to the Guildhall and subjected to a show trial before Cade. Feinnes demanded to be tried before his peers but he never had any hope of a fair hearing.

Lord Saye was removed to the Standard on Cheapside where he was beheaded. His gory head was placed, alongside Crowmer's, on a spike on London Bridge. Gregory records two other executions at Southwark on the same day. The Captain of Kent's grip on the capital was complete. He was holding court like a mighty lord. He gave a letter of safe conduct to one Thomas Cock, a London draper, writing that 'By this our writing ensealed, we grant, that Thomas Cock of London Draper, shall safely come into our presence, and avoid from us again at his pleasure, with all other persons coming in his company.' Cade signed the note, 'Subscribed thus, His Majesties loyal Subject, John Mortimer, Captain Mend-all.'

Cade sent Thomas away with instructions that 'You shall charge all Lombards and Merchant-strangers, Genoese, Venetians, Florentines, and others, this day to draw themselves together, and to ordain for us the Captain, twelve Harness complete of the best fashion, four and twenty Brigandines, twelve Battle-axes, twelve glaives, six horses with saddle and bridle completely furnished, and a thousand marks in ready money: and if they shall fail herein, we shall strike off the heads of as many as we can get.' The threat appears to have worked, as the draper saw the requirements met. This episode is interesting as a demonstration of Cade's power and authority, issuing safe conduct notes and demanding not insubstantial gifts of the foreign merchants in London, a group who were always eyed with suspicion. He showed his strength, upset no-one and was also now openly using the name John Mortimer.

On 5 July, Cade's men returned from their Southwark camp to the City once more, but it soon became apparent that Cade's iron grip on his legions of men was slipping. Gregory explains that on this day they 'began to rob' and London's residents were thrown into panic. Lord Scales and Matthew Gough spied their opportunity from behind the Tower's stout walls. As Cade's force moved out of the City over London Bridge, a force from the Tower, swollen by the mayor's men, local sheriffs and a now unnerved citizenry fell upon them. Gregory recorded a battle on London Bridge from nine o'clock that evening until nine o'clock the following morning, when Cade fired the Bridge. Casualties were high and it must have been a terrifying night of fierce fighting in the dark, narrow, cramped spaces on London Bridge, hemmed in by looming buildings. The howls and screams of men hacked down was broken only by the heavy splashing of innumerable bodies lost to the black chill of the Thames below.

As morning broke, it was the men of Kent who were driven back. London was quick to dispel them once their discipline faltered. Among the casualties was Matthew Gough, who had led the soldiers of the Tower. Edward Hall, a Tudor antiquary, noted that Gough was 'a man of great wit, and much experience in feats of chivalry, the which, in continual wars, had valiantly served Kings Henry the Fifth and Sixth, in the parts beyond the sea'. Having survived years of service across the Channel, he fell to his own countrymen in England's capital city. As London set about clearing the carnage and measuring the damage the Kentish occupation and the night-time battle had wreaked, wondering how they would retrieve so many bodies from the Thames and how many the current had already dragged beyond reach, the Lord Chancellor seized the initiative.

Cardinal John Kemp, Archbishop of York, rode out to the rebel's camp. He made them an offer that was designed to be too good to refuse. Kemp carried with him the promise of a full pardon for all who would return to their homes in peace. As their neatly packaged, well-presented campaign unravelled, it was probably the best result the rebels could hope for. It also served both London and the Crown to see this vast horde, drunk on their success, dispersed with the wind taken from their sails. The Kentish men accepted the terms and abandoned London in their droves before the offer could be withdrawn.

Cade's story did not end as he turned back south. On the way home he and some of his comrades raided Queenborough Castle. The constable was the absent Humphrey Stafford, Duke of Buckingham, a man the rebels nominally supported, but the castle had originally been built nearly a hundred years earlier by Edward

III on the Isle of Sheppey to protect the Medway estuary from attack. The circularly designed fortress was named Queenborough in honour of Edward's wife, Queen Philippa. It did not lie on Cade's route home, nor was it an easy target. Perhaps the attack was designed to show that resentment still smouldered for Henry's queen, Margaret of Anjou. Cade did not manage to breach the castle's walls and quickly abandoned the venture.

As the government tentatively retook the reins of control, there was a startling development. On 12 July a proclamation was read throughout the land that whoever could capture Jack Cade and bring him to the king, dead or alive, would receive a thousand marks, with a ten-mark bounty placed on the head of Cade's associates. Gregory explains this sudden change of heart by pointing out that although Cade had received his pardon in the name of John Mortimer, 'it was openly known that his name was not Mortimer, his name was John Cade, and therefore his charter stood in no strength'. Alexander Iden, a Kentish squire who would later rise to be High Sheriff, tracked Cade down and he was cornered, according to local legend, in a garden in Heathfield, East Sussex. In the scuffle, Cade was mortally wounded. He died from his injuries, but his body would not yet find peace. Stripped and thrown onto a cart, Cade returned to London with far less menace and in far less triumph. He stopped once more at the Hart Inn so that the lady of the house might identify him. It was vital that the authorities were certain they had the right man, but also that the country knew Cade was dead.

The corpse was displayed at the King's Bench for four days, after which the body was beheaded and quartered, placed on a hurdle and dragged throughout Southwark, across London Bridge and into the City, ending its ordeal at Newgate. Finally, Cade's head was placed on a pole on London Bridge alongside several of his associates. When Parliament met, Cade's fall was further reinforced. The Parliament Rolls recalled that 'although he is dead and destroyed, he has not yet been punished by the law of your said land', requesting that 'by advice of your lords spiritual and temporal assembled in this your present parliament, to ordain by the authority of the said parliament that he be attainted of these treasons'. The bill was passed and Cade was forever branded a base traitor.

Jack Cade may have been a simple Kentish soldier with the charisma to unite thousands in their anger. He may have been John Mortimer, a dispossessed man seeking to reignite his family's claim to power. Was he Cade masquerading as Mortimer to arouse the fear and passion that name could draw? Or was the Mortimer name used to promote the cause of Richard, Duke of York, a prince of the blood royal driven from influence? If this were the case, did it mean that York had instigated the uprising to test waters he suspected were warm to him, or was it simply a call to the king to use those who deserved a place at his side?

Although his true identity and motives may be lost, these are perhaps less telling than what the rebellion that took his name meant. Cade was a wolf in wolf's clothing, sent as a sacrifice to a lamb, yet the lamb failed to see it, fleeing in terror. Had King Henry stood before the rebels to deal with them and their grievances it might have marked a turning point in his rule. Jack Cade rode a wave that had been swelling for a long time, born far out at sea from the shockwaves of failures in France. His cruel end drove the problem back beneath the surface, but nothing had been resolved. England was ripe for rebellion. The clamour to pick the fruit was growing.

3

Deadly Rivalries

On 18 December 1452, Richard, Duke of York, pawned a white rose brooch believed to have cost around 4,000 marks when it was bought, probably toward the end of the previous century. It was certainly the most valuable jewel recorded as being in private hands in medieval England. It is described in the loan agreement as 'a brooch of gold with a great pointed diamond set upon a rose enamelled white'. A decade earlier, York had been the richest man in the kingdom, conspicuously displaying his vast wealth. Now, he was raising funds from Sir John Fastolf, a veteran knight who had been in France with York, at terms so harsh it is a wonder York accepted them.

In the wake of Cade's Rebellion, York had exercised a clause in his commission as Lieutenant of Ireland that allowed him to return to England in cases of national emergency. The rumours linking York to Cade's uprising had clearly had an impact on the court party. When York landed at Anglesey in early September 1450, intending to head for his home on the Welsh border at Ludlow Castle, he must have been disturbed to learn of rumours that King Henry had issued orders for him to be arrested as a traitor. In response, York began to raise men. He surely felt the need to protect himself but could not do so without appearing to be an aggressor.

Richard, Duke of York, had inherited lands and titles from two lines of descent from King Edward III. His father had been a son of Edmund, 1st Duke of York, the fourth son of Edward III. His mother was Anne Mortimer, the granddaughter of Philippa

Plantagenet, only daughter of Edward III's second son, Lionel of Antwerp, Duke of Clarence. Born in 1411, Richard's mother died shortly after and his father, Richard of Conisburgh, Earl of Cambridge, was executed for treason by Henry V, days before leaving on his Agincourt campaign in 1415. With the death of Richard's uncle Edward, 2nd Duke of York, at Agincourt, the title passed to the four-year-old Richard. When another uncle, Edmund Mortimer, 5th Earl of March, died in 1525, Richard inherited the Mortimer's vast Marcher lands and wealth too. Like King Henry, he had a long minority during which his estates were managed for him and he was in the care of Ralph Neville, Earl of Westmorland. Ralph had the right to arrange York's marriage, and had him wed to one of his own daughters, Cecily Neville, renowned for her beauty and called the Rose of Raby. Cecily had a link to Edward III herself through her mother, Joan Beaufort.

After Bedford's death in 1435, Richard had served as Lieutenant of France for several years. On his return to England in 1439, Richard does not appear to have been part of Henry's council, but when no peace could be agreed with France Richard was returned as Lieutenant once more with increased powers in 1440. Before York's return in 1445, John Beaufort, 1st Duke of Somerset, had been sent with a large force into France. These men had effectively been diverted from Richard's control. Somerset led a catastrophic campaign, mistakenly attacking a friendly town while ill and being forced to retreat. Disgraced, Somerset died shortly afterwards amid rumours that he took his own life. York's vocal disapproval of Somerset's actions was the beginning of a blood feud at the very core of the Wars of the Roses. Somerset's daughter, Lady Margaret Beaufort, was barely a year old when her father died and she held a lifelong grudge against the House of York because of Richard's part in her father's humiliation.

When the time came to re-appoint a Lieutenant of France it was John Beaufort's younger brother Edmund, 2nd Duke of Somerset, who was granted the prestigious post. York was handed a commission as Lieutenant of Ireland for a period of ten years, double the usual timescale for such appointments. Ireland was not a glorious place to be. It was nevertheless a prestigious role; Edward III's second son Lionel of Antwerp, Duke of Clarence,

Richard's great-great grandfather, had been governor there and Richard's familial links and large land holdings made him the natural choice. Whether Richard embraced it or viewed it as a form of exile, he ruled there with an even hand and fostered bonds that would serve the House of York for decades.

Whether York had a hand in Suffolk's murder, Cade's Rebellion, both or neither is unknown, but it seems from Henry's response to his return that the rumours were enough to cast a long shadow of doubt over the Duke of York that he would never shake off. Richard's very return at such a time of unrest has been cited as evidence of his desire to harness the turmoil to his own ends, but the very opposite is far more likely. Medieval nobility enjoyed unrivalled, and frequently unbridled, power, but with it came obligations and responsibilities that they were honour bound to observe. The notion of 'noblesse oblige', French for 'obligation of nobility', required a noble to behave in a manner befitting his rank and to exercise his power as a shield for those who lacked such means. If York saw popular discontent reaching boiling point and legitimate grievances being ignored, it was his duty to intervene. When such public feeling threatened the crown itself, he also had a duty to defend his king. He could do neither from Ireland.

Other political realities must also have contributed to Richard's return from Ireland. His personal wealth had been impacted by his service in France, for which he claimed he had gone unpaid by the crown. York had sold estates, most notably in Wales, throughout the 1440s in an unsustainable effort to support himself as revenue fell while he was forced to meet the costs of his position in France from his own funds. His finances were in no position to now maintain Ireland for the crown. He had also seen what happened to the men blamed for failure across the Channel and it seems likely that, similarly starved of men and money, Ireland was on the verge of bucking against Lancastrian control. On 15 July York had written to his brother-in-law Richard Neville, Earl of Salisbury, asking him to notify Parliament of the woeful position 'for mine excuse in time to come'. Parliament had already ended when Salisbury received the letter and it is possible that York returned at least in part to make his excuses in person lest he later be accused of costing the crown Ireland through negligence.

News that Calais was threatened with siege also greeted York's return. Capgrave, the contemporary writer of *The Illustrious Henrys*, bemoaned the state of the English navy, complaining, 'We who used to be conquerors of all nations are now conquered by all. The men of old used to say that the sea was England's wall, and now our enemies have got upon the wall; what think you they will do to the defenceless inhabitants?' He ended his tirade with a call that 'May God take away our reproach and raise up a spirit of bravery in our nation'. If this was York's aim he was surely dismayed to find that having returned to help, he was made a fugitive from the king the moment he landed.

Less than three weeks after setting foot on Anglesey, on 27 September, Richard was in London accompanied by a hastily assembled armed force of around 5,000 men. He barged into the king's private apartments, causing uproar, and demanded that Henry listen to him. William Wayte, a clerk to Justice Yelverton, reported that York 'visaged so the matter that all the king's household was and is afraid'. Was York trying to shock Henry from his apathy, attempting to force him to see the reality of a kingdom falling around his ears as he prayed? York had written to his cousin the king of the slanderous rumours which 'sound to my dishonour' and offering to face any accuser 'as a true knight ought to do'. He told the king that he should be punished 'as the poorest man of your land' if he failed to meet any who charged him thus, so long as any man who failed to prove his case against York be 'punished after his desert in example of all other'. He went on to list those who had tried to apprehend him in Wales, intending to 'take me, and put me into your castle of Conway'.

King Henry replied to this first letter by reassuring York that there had been no order to arrest him. In response to what Henry described as calls from many corners 'that you should be fetched with many thousands, and you should take upon you that which you neither ought, nor, as we doubt not, you will not attempt', the crown's officers were on high alert. York's 'sudden coming, without certain warning' had unnerved the officials and they had, Henry promised, understandably overreacted. As for an instruction to seize York, Henry assured him 'there was none such', ending his letter 'Upon this, for the easing of your heart in all such matters, we declare, repute and admit you as our true and faithful subject, and as our faithful cousin'. York represented everything that Henry was not, and that must have been unnerving for the king, and more so for those around him.

At the parliament that had already been summoned, Thomas Young, a Bristol MP who also happened to be a legal advisor to Richard, moved that York should be recognised as Henry's heir presumptive in the absence of a son. For his troubles, Young was thrown into the Tower and the motion was defeated. If York was behind the move, it was ill judged, forcing Henry to declare his official position regarding both the succession and the duke. Neither came down in York's favour. Perhaps Young had been put up to it, or perhaps he was simply over exuberant in his master's cause, but if York had misjudged the temperature of the political waters and damaged his own cause, it would not be the last time.

At the same time that York had returned, Edmund Beaufort, Duke of Somerset, had come back from France. The space at the king's side needed to be filled. York seems to have intended to place himself there, but Somerset slipped into the vacuum with comfortable ease. Somerset had not been particularly successful in France. He was to bring this unpopularity back to England with him and his presence at the king's right hand was to pour oil on the fire that already burned between the houses of York and Somerset.

The year that followed was one of building tensions across England, not least between the king and his most powerful subject. Although unpunished, York was in effective exile in his fortress at Ludlow, but he was not the only problem Henry had to keep an eye on. By September 1451, matters were deteriorating at an alarming rate. In the south-west, private armies stomped the fields settling their masters' scores. When Lord Bonville and the Earl of Devon argued over entitlement to the position of Steward of the Duchy of Cornwall they felt confident enough in the failing rule of law to settle it on the battlefield. At Lackham in Wiltshire, the Earl of Devon took an army to meet the Earl of Wiltshire, who supported Bonville, crushing him before turning back into Somerset to lay siege to Bonville at Taunton Castle.

At this point, York appeared between the two forces with his own army. Although Devon was generally sympathetic to York, the duke sought to force the two men to come to terms peaceably. Preventing further open warfare on English soil, York returned to Ludlow. It would not have been lost on all parties that these wild acts of disobedience had taken place on land belonging to Somerset. That York had been forced to march into his rival's territory to restore the king's peace in spite of his own less than favoured position speaks volumes both for York and for the state of Henry's England. Law and order was lost. Chaos threatened once more, escalated from the men of Kent to armies led by peers of the realm. Perhaps more than anything else, York's intervention demonstrates Somerset's failure to control his own lands. Henry's position was further undermined when he summoned York and Devon to answer before him at Coventry for their actions. Both men simply ignored the order. York was not thanked for enforcing the king's peace but was viewed even more warily as a threat, his ambition an unknown quantity.

In 1452, matters were to come to a head once more. York had been stewing behind the walls of his vast estates for almost two years as Somerset's star rose high, bringing the Beauforts power and influence. Just as Suffolk had done, Somerset attracted charges of corruption, undue influence over the king and poor government. On 9 January, York felt compelled by the continuing rumours against him to write to Henry once more professing his loyalty. Richard was concerned that the king was 'deeply displeased with me, and hath in me a distrust by sinister information of mine enemies, adversaries, and evil-willers'. York goes on to explain that he had called to him the Bishop of Hereford and the Earl of Shrewsbury to hear him swear an oath of allegiance to the king, offering to swear the same oath once more before 'two or three, such as shall please the king's highness'.

The letter did not have the desired effect. Convinced that those closest to the king, Somerset in particular, were whispering against him, York began to recruit men again. Henry withdrew to the Midlands and York marched on London. Finding the City gates barred, York skirted the capital to make camp at Dartford Heath. Henry brought his royal force back south, arriving in London on 27 February. A witness credited York with some 3,000 gunners, 8,000 men in his own retinue, 6,000 serving the Earl of Devonshire to the south and the same number at the riverside with Lord Cobham. Seven ships carried the vast horde's supplies. Henry's army at least matched York's, but once more York would not go on the offensive against his king, staying at Dartford to await the king's next move.

Several lords were appointed to an embassy from Henry to York. These men, 'my Lord the Bishop of Winchester, my Lord Bishop of Ely, my Lord the Earl of Salisbury, my Lord of Warwick, my Lord Beauchamp and my Lord of Sudeley', were dispatched to bring York to heel. Two of these men, Salisbury and Warwick, are notable for their later affiliation to York's cause. Salisbury was his brother-in-law and Warwick his wife's nephew but it is clear that they remained loyal to King Henry at this point. York told them that all he wanted was the arrest of Somerset and his removal from the King's Council. When the lords took the demands to the king, he accepted, ordering Somerset's arrest and sending word to York that it was done on 1 March.

The duke immediately disbanded his force and, no doubt pleased, made his way to Henry's presence. Whether the arrest of Somerset was ever genuine is uncertain. Perhaps it was a ploy, or maybe Queen Margaret, who trusted Somerset far above York, convinced Henry that he was wrong to bow to the duke's demands. Either way, when York entered the king's tent, he was shocked at the sight of Somerset standing free at Henry' right hand. He had been duped and was forced to accept an ignominious defeat. He entered London on 10 March riding ahead of the king's party like a prisoner. At St Paul's Cathedral he was forced to read a humiliating oath of loyalty, swearing that he 'shall not at any time will or assent, that anything be attempted or done against your noble person'. He swore to report any such threats against Henry immediately, pledging to 'come at your commandment whensoever I shall be called by the same, in humble and obedient ways'. He further promised never again to raise an army against Henry and 'whensoever I find myself wronged or aggrieved, I shall sue humbly for remedy to your Highness, and proceed after the course of your laws'. Richard was forced to swear all of this 'by the Holy Evangelists contained in this book that I lay my hand upon, and by the Holy Cross that I here touch, and by the blessed Sacrament of our Lord's body that I shall now with His mercy receive'. It was a humiliation his enemies among the court party must have revelled in and felt that he deserved. If York had been seeking to fulfil his noble obligations, to see Henry's authority restored and England well governed, this was sore payment indeed.

In Rome, the ending of the first half of the century had been celebrated as a jubilee. The Pope offered a general indulgence and pardon to anyone making a pilgrimage to the city. Not to be outdone, on 7 April 1452 the pious Henry VI offered a general pardon to all those guilty of disloyalty upon application to Chancery. Richard, Duke of York, applied for and was granted such a pardon on 3 June. It was no more than a thin bandage drawn over ugly scars. Henry had bolstered his position by promoting two half-brothers that he never knew he had. His mother had fallen for a handsome Welshman named Owen Tudor, a member of her household. The couple had children who had been kept secret from the young king. Now, his half-brothers were presented to him at court and he spied an opportunity to promote men tied to him by patronage as well as blood. Edmund Tudor was created Earl of Richmond and permitted to marry Lady Margaret Beaufort, the valuable heiress. His younger brother Jasper was made Earl of Pembroke. Things were going wrong in France again, though. May saw the loss of Gascony after three centuries in English hands, June the fall of Bordeaux. Trouble in France always meant unrest at home and Henry never managed this trouble well.

July 1453 saw the effective end of English power in France at Castillon. Queen Margaret had finally conceived a royal baby but this was only a faint ray of light in dark days. Nobles were once more settling private scores outside the king's laws and Henry was to make an enemy of one of history's most powerful, flamboyant and enigmatic men. In the north, ancient rivalries spilled into new bloodshed. In the West Country, Somerset was at odds with Richard Neville, Earl of Warwick, over an inheritance that both men claimed but which had been in Warwick's hands for a decade. Henry awarded the lands to Somerset and ordered Warwick to vacate them all. Warwick dug in at Cardiff Castle, one of the disputed properties, and Somerset began raising an army to prise him out. While York sat behind the thick walls of Ludlow Castle, Henry scurried west to try and resolve the problems that threatened to erupt into open warfare.

King Henry reached a royal hunting lodge at Clarendon in Wiltshire in early August 1453, and it was here that an unexpected disaster struck. The king was suddenly afflicted by an unknown condition that left him catatonic, 'so incapable that he was neither able to walk upon his feet nor to lift up his head' according to Benet. At a time when the king was the government and no arm of government could function without the person of the king it was an unprecedented catastrophe. The court party hid the king's condition as best they could for months. When Queen Margaret was delivered of a son, Edward, on 13 October, Henry could not be made aware of the infant presented to him for his approval. Until the king claimed his son, he was not a legitimate child, not an heir to the throne of England at a time when that might have been some slight comfort. Henry could not even give his people that. The physicians tried everything they could, bleeding the king and feeding him all manner of concoctions, but they could neither rouse him nor could they offer any indication of when, if ever, he might recover.

In November, Richard was called to sit on the King's Council. Parliament had been due to commence after its break on 12 November, but this had been postponed until 11 February the following year. The recall of York is perhaps a signal of the panic that spread throughout an establishment not designed to run without the person of the king, however ineffectual he may be. Presumably as a condition of York's return to court to settle the jangling nerves, Edmund Beaufort was arrested and placed in confinement in the Tower of London. Eighteen months after he initially believed that he had succeeded, York really did have Somerset where he wanted him. One woman was deeply unhappy at these developments.

As 1454 began with no sign of improvement in the king, the queen took the bold but ill-judged decision to claim the right to rule in her husband's place as his wife and mother to his son. The Paston Letters record the queen's advancement of her cause in January.

Item, the queen hath made a bill of five articles, whereof the first is, that she desireth to have the whole rule of this land, the second, that she may make the chancellor, treasurer, the privy seal, and all other offices of this land, with sheriffs, and all that the king should make; the third, that she may give all the bishoprics of this land, and all other benefices belonging to the king's gift; the fourth is, that she may have sufficient livelihood assigned her for the king, the prince, and herself; but as for the fifth article, I cannot yet know what it is.

Margaret had underestimated just how much her gender undermined her position. A queen consort, subservient to the king, was one matter. A woman exercising the power of a man was deemed unseemly. No lord would wish to be subject to a woman for fear of losing his honour, and no woman should want to wield such authority, for to do so was unwomanly. Margaret could not win, but she failed to see it before making her bid. The effect was to drive the Council to seek an alternative – a man who could grasp the reins of power and calm the runaway horse that thundered out of control toward certain disaster. The choice was as clear as it was stark: York or Somerset. With Somerset in the Tower, York's hand already on the tiller and the need urgent, there was hardly a decision to make. On 13 February, York was given a commission to hold Parliament in the king's name and it reconvened the next day at Westminster.

It was the death of John Kemp, Archbishop of Canterbury and Lord Chancellor, on the 22 March that forced the Council and Parliament to seek a long-term solution. The king's approval was required for any new appointment to either role. The secret of Henry's incapacity to make such decisions could not be maintained any longer. Parliament recorded the attempts of all parties to ensure that they were acting as correctly as was possible in these unknown waters. None wanted to be accused later of taking for themselves more power than was absolutely necessary. This must have been a real concern to York above all others, a man who had been forced so publically to swear his loyalty and future good behaviour. One wrong move now could prove fatal for the duke.

The Parliament Rolls very carefully detail the process undertaken. York, called 'lieutenant of his [Henry's] parliament', along with the bishops of Winchester, Ely and Chester, the earls of Warwick, Oxford and Shrewsbury, viscounts Beaumont and Bourchier, the lords Fauconberg, Dudley and Stourton and the prior of St John, designed a five-part communication that was to be delivered to the king, 'which message they shall read out if they find the king's disposition such that he can and will attend to the hearing and understanding of it, otherwise they shall only read out the first and second articles'. The first item was a plaintiff statement of allegiance to the king, assuring him that 'there is no earthly thing that they desire more, or set close to their hearts than to hear of his welfare'. The second part was aimed at ensuring the king knew that his lords, led by the lieutenant, were working diligently to keep Henry's government afloat 'for the repudiation of misgovernance'. These Henry was to hear whether he knew what was said or not. In this way, all of the men had Parliamentary record that they had made the king aware of what they were doing in his name.

Item three informed Henry of Kemp's passing, 'by whose death the said archbishopric is vacant, and his highness remains without a chancellor'. They would try to make Henry see that they needed his guidance and authority in 'how they should conduct themselves in providing the provision both for the church of Canterbury and the keeping of his great seals'. Next, the king was to be reassured that his seals were safe, having been 'enclosed in a chest and sealed with the seals of various lords and stored in his treasury where they remain in the keeping of his treasurer and chamberlain'. No one had authority to hand the seals to another, nor to use them without the express permission of the king. Uncertain what they should do, the lords had each witnessed their interment and sealing so that all could vouch that they were secure. Finally, Henry was to be asked about the composition of 'a learned and wise council' which he had promised to establish before his illness. The Commons had apparently asked twice already for details of the council and when it would be created. All of this was to be 'kept most secret' and was for the king's ears only.

On Saturday 23 March, these great men attended the king, though York himself did not go, perhaps to avoid a later charge of coercing the king. The Bishop of Chester was nominated to deliver the carefully constructed message. They arrived at Windsor to find the king at his dining table and waited until he had finished eating before the bishop began reciting the text. The first three items were read, but the king did not respond. Despite what had previously been agreed, the remainder was read out so that the king had heard all five articles, even though to none 'could they get any answer or sign'. The lords retired to take their own meals, giving the king time to think over what he clearly had not heard. They returned to receive a similar blank reception in spite of all of their efforts to obtain some form of response. When they asked that the king be moved to another room 'he was led between two men into the chamber where he lies'. Still they could not rouse him 'and therefore with sorrowful hearts they came away'.

York had stayed away from a meeting that would define his future. Parliament had little choice but to act now. York was asked to take up a post vacant since Henry had come of age. No doubt wary of later accusations of taking for himself power that was not his, York ensured that his reluctance was placed on record.

> Howbeit that I am not sufficient of myself, of wisdom, cunning, nor ability, to take upon me that worthy name of Protector and Defender of this land, nor the charge thereto appertaining, whereunto it hath liked you, my Lords, to call, name, and desire me unworthy thereunto;—under protestation, if I shall apply me to the performing of your said desire, and at your instance take upon me, with your supportation, the said name and charge, I desire and pray you that in this present Parliament and by authority thereof it be enacted, that of yourself and of your free and mere disposition, ye desire, name and call me to the said name and charge, and that of any presumption of myself, I take them not upon me, but only of the due and humble obeisance that I owe to do unto the king, our most dread and Sovereign Lord, and to you the Peerage of this land, in whom by the occasion of the infirmity of our said Sovereign Lord, resteth the exercise of his authority, whose noble commandments I am as ready to perform and obey as any his liege man alive.

After ensuring that the scope and reach of his authority was clearly defined and acceptable to all, York agreed to be appointed to the position of Protector and Defender of the Realm and Church on 3 April 1454. He was to rule in the position of the king for as long as Henry was too unwell to fulfil his obligations.

Only two years earlier, York was reduced to pawning his family jewels and appeared lost in the political wilderness, defeated and undone by a weak king to whom he had professed nothing but loyalty. When the very fabric of England was threatened, it was to York that the Lords Spiritual and Temporal and the Commons had turned. Fortune's wheel was turning, but it rarely stopped its fickle revolutions in those days.

4

Old Enemies, New Friends

If the Wars of the Roses were a Hollywood epic there is no doubt that York and Lancaster would be the stars. There is even less doubt that the Nevilles and the Percys would be fighting for Best Supporting roles. They would be fighting because that was what they did, over anything and everything. The royal houses may have taken the headlines, but these two ancient families demonstrated the breadth and depth of the fiasco that English law and order had become in the mid-fifteenth century.

Towards the end of the 1430s a notice was issued to several members of the Neville family requiring them 'upon their allegiance' to appear before the king the following Saint Hillary's Day 'wheresoever we shall be within our realm' in order to answer for a running private war between them. Ralph Neville, 1st Earl of Westmorland, had died in 1425 leaving an impressive brood behind him. By his first wife, Margaret Stafford, he had two sons and six daughters. When he remarried to Joan Beaufort, daughter of John of Gaunt and sister to John, 1st Earl of Somerset, the couple were blessed with nine sons and five daughters. Seven Neville men needed to be supported, or to support themselves, and eleven ladies needed marriages worthy of their birth. It is little wonder that the descendants of the prodigious Ralph were to be found shaking the family trees of England's greatest families in search of ripe pickings. Perhaps the richest fruit fell to Cecily Neville when Ralph obtained the care of the young Richard, Duke of York, ensuring his ward married one of his surfeit of daughters.

The Nevilles had a long history in the north of England. They were powerful and respected of old in places where the royal writ barely ran, yet they were at war with themselves now. On one side, three of Ralph's grandsons, Ralph, 2nd Earl of Westmorland, Sir John and Sir Thomas, were locked in a fierce quarrel with their grandfather's widow, the Countess of Westmorland, and two of her sons, Richard, Earl of Salisbury, born in 1400, and George, Lord Latimer. The notice from King Henry VI states that these two forces 'either against other by manner of war and insurrection have late assembled great routs and companies upon the field and done furthermore other great and horrible offences as well in slaughter and destruction of our people'. The north was running out of control, but it was the countess's branch of the Neville clan that was to emerge the stronger and to have the most incredible influence over English history. Two of her grandsons would be kings. But for now, the Nevilles were preoccupied with a new fight.

The Percy family were not unlike the Nevilles and their similarity, allied with their proximity, was perhaps the spark at the heart of the fire that burned between them. The Percy family was headed by Henry, 2nd Earl of Northumberland. He was born in 1393, the grandson of the first earl and son to Henry Hotspur, who had rebelled against King Henry IV, losing his life at the Battle of Shrewsbury in 1403. When the first earl was killed in rebellion in 1408, the Percy family lost everything. Young Henry grew up in exile in Scotland, but was granted the family title by Henry V in 1416. Their lands in the farthest northern reaches of England were almost a kingdom of their own. The royal arm did not reach that far. It was cold and wild and men there ruled their little kingdoms autonomously and absolutely. The problem for the Percys was the Nevilles. The problem for both patriarchs was a clutch of ambitious, unruly sons.

Henry Percy had six sons. Richard Neville had only four, but a broader extended family than Northumberland. With less than a decade's difference in age between them, their careers had already been long by the time trouble really began in the early 1450s. Northumberland had served in France with Henry V and been appointed to the minority Council of the infant Henry VI. Salisbury had also served in France for many years trying to preserve the king's lands there. When Northumberland resigned his post as Warden of the East March in 1434, it was given to Salisbury. With the heavy and almost impossible responsibility of protecting England's northern border from Scottish attacks, Salisbury found that he shared Northumberland's frustrations at being deprived of men and money for the task. When Salisbury quit the post the following year, Northumberland was re-appointed, holding the position until his death.

These two families were large and ambitious, but each stood in the other's way. They were constantly at odds, representatives of each family vying for the same appointments and offices, the loser always bitterly frustrated to miss out to their rival. A flashpoint came in August 1453. As King Henry headed west to resolve the feud between Somerset and Salisbury's oldest son, the Earl of Warwick, one of Northumberland's sons lit the fuse on war in the north too. It was perhaps news of these escalating problems that caused Henry's illness to surface. Surrounded, hemmed in and weighed down, it is little wonder a man unsuited to his lot buckled.

Ralph Cromwell, 3rd Baron Cromwell, was sixty, widowed and childless, so his inheritance would pass to his two nieces. A marriage was arranged between the elder niece, Maud Stanhope, and one of Salisbury's younger sons, Thomas. On 24 August 1453 Northumberland's second son, another Thomas, Baron Egremont, ambushed the Neville wedding party with around a thousand armed men. With Salisbury and Warwick both in attendance, the Nevilles were well protected. It was a rash move that could make or break the fortunes of either family. The reason that Egremont was enraged enough to risk open war was simple. Lord Cromwell had possession of lands that had once belonged to the Percy family before their fall from power. As part of the marriage settlement, these lands would pass into Neville hands, through Maud to Thomas. The notion of Neville hands wrapped around the deeds to Percy lands proved too much for Egremont to stomach.

Thomas Neville's wedding must have seemed the perfect opportunity, with all of the heads of the Neville clan in one place, off their guard, drinking, feasting and making merry. Egremont gathered around a thousand men and set off to intercept the Neville party. What Percy, or perhaps Percys, for it is unclear whether his father and older brother were aware of Egremont's actions, failed to realise was that the very presence of all the senior Nevilles was precisely what made this such a dangerous move. As earls, both Salisbury and Warwick were entitled to retain an armed guard of at least a hundred men and they would be the crack troops among the Neville following. With so many other guests and family there too, although the Percy force was probably larger, this was to be no pushover. The Battle of Heworth Moor on 24 August 1453 was probably little more than an angry exchange of unpleasant words. There were few casualties, some sources suggesting that there were none. The Neville party staged an organised retreat to their fortress at Sheriff Hutton nearby. The Percy force was compelled to call off the attack.

Like the private action at Lackham two years earlier, this skirmish is all but forgotten amid the fog of war that followed, yet the two examples are the early symptoms of a disease eating away at a kingdom without hope of a healing hand. York was still in the wilderness. Suffolk may have gone, but Somerset had filled his boots quickly and his personal rivalry with York was dictating government policy. These two eruptions of infection should have been lanced. York and Devon had ignored Henry's summons. Percy and Neville had similarly ignored calls to attend the king, answer for their breaches of his peace and come to terms. They were the visible sign of the disease that ate Henry's country away from under him. When a dirty bandage was placed over each, they simply festered, ready to erupt once more, even more violently, as fever gripped the kingdom.

The perfect storm of 1453 settled Neville fortunes for a generation. Henry would not, or could not, control the Percys or the Nevilles. Salisbury's son Warwick was in dispute with Somerset and was losing lands and titles simply because Somerset was Henry's favourite. Unlike York, who derived his wealth from the vast estates of his inheritance, Somerset had nothing of his own. He was utterly reliant upon royal patronage and grants of offices for his income, which was a fraction of the duke's, and it seems likely that Henry was keen to find in Somerset's favour in this dispute because it increased the Beaufort powerbase, as a counterbalance to whatever threat the king perceived from York. When Henry collapsed and the decision between York and Somerset became clear, there was only one side the Nevilles were going to take, thanks to Henry's treatment of them.

When York was appointed Protector the Nevilles gravitated to him and he was swift to install his wife's relatives at his side. Salisbury was appointed Lord Chancellor and York's sister's brother-in-law, Thomas Bourchier, was made Archbishop of Canterbury. Almost instantly there was a change of feel to the government. Those lords present at Parliament committed to send men and money for the reinforcement of Calais, the captaincy of which York took for himself from Somerset. Any lords who were not in Parliament would soon receive letters asking that they match the commitment. The Calendar of Patent Rolls recorded a 'Commission to Henry, viscount Bourgchier and others to negotiate loans to be repaid from tonnage and poundage granted in parliament for the transport of army for the safekeeping of the sea and the defence of Calais'. The threats to England's final continental outpost were finally to be taken seriously.

Within the kingdom, too, things were changing. York forced peace upon the north when he led an armed force into the region. Egremont and Thomas Neville clashed again and Egremont, along with York's son-in-law Henry Holland, Duke of Exeter, a volatile man who also could claim descent from Edward III, were arrested, fined and placed under house arrest. York's mere presence had caused the bickering to stop, in a way sorely and starkly lacking from Henry's constantly unanswered calls for the men to come to him. Law and order was being dragged back to the realm of England and Salisbury's decision to ally his family's fortunes to those of York was paying dividends.

The Duke of Norfolk laid charges of treason against Somerset and a date of 28 October 1454 was appointed for the trial. The date came and passed without a trial and Somerset languished on in the Tower. He must have been dismayed by the news that York was performing expertly and being well received. Queen Margaret was removed to Windsor Castle under what amounted to a comfortable house arrest. With the defence of Calais underway and the unruly reaches of the kingdom being brought back into line, York and the Great Council turned their eyes even closer to home.

England had been all but bankrupt for the whole of Henry VI's rule. Henry's great uncle, Cardinal Beaufort, had funded the government for years before his death. With the loss of lucrative French lands and those around the king monopolising offices for their own enrichment the situation had grown worse still. On 13 October 1454 a set of 'Ordinances for the regulations of the King's household' were drawn up that sought to correct these problems, with the aim of returning rules to Henry's household 'as were had and used of old time, and especially in the days of the most victorious Prince of blessed memory his father'. Putting the royal finances in order, stopping abuses and reducing the drain upon the general populace of taxes levied to fill the gap created was never going to be anything but popular.

The Ordinances defined very clearly how many people and of what rank should be about the king at any one time. Specifically named among a requirement for sixteen earls were the king's half-brothers Edmund and Jasper Tudor, whose signatures can be found among the twenty-nine members of the Council endorsing the document too. Their presence is a sign of York's even-handed approach. Those accused of abuse were removed from the king, but not those simply close to him, who might have made room for men more supportive of York. The Ordinances make allowance for a household of 120 to serve the queen and a further thirty-eight to be about baby Prince Edward.

Salisbury was heavily involved in York's government and reforms. The Council met frequently, six times in ten weeks between March and May, with more than twenty members at each meeting. York could not be accused of acting with autonomy and Salisbury, as Chancellor, was a key figure. His closeness to York did not grant him immunity from chastisement. Salisbury was among thirteen lords reprimanded for their failure to attend Council meetings, with a letter written to each nominally from the king, warning them that 'if ye come not it shall give us cause to entreat you in such wise as shall be thought unto us by the advice of our said Council according to your disobedience'.

York's power as Protector was to endure until Henry recovered or Prince Edward reached his majority. By the end of 1454, England seemed to be moving onto an even footing. *Benet's*

Chronicle wrote of York that 'for a whole year he governed the whole realm of England most nobly and in the best way'. As the court celebrated Christmas Day, the timing of what appeared to be a miracle could not have been lost on anyone as whispered rumour became excitedly proclaimed fact. King Henry VI had awoken from his dream and was renewed. The extent of Henry's vacancy during his waking sleep was revealed a few days later when the queen presented him with his son, only for the king to ask 'what the Prince's name was', as the Paston Letters reveal. Henry told the queen that he 'knew not where he had been while he hath been sick' and was shocked to hear of the death of Cardinal Kemp, who's passing 'he said he knew never thereof till that time'.

York's position was officially dissolved at a Council meeting on 30 December. Henry wasted no time in snatching back the reins of power. Over the next weeks, Salisbury lost his role as Lord Chancellor, Exeter was freed from his house arrest and, most telling of all, Henry was dismayed to hear that Somerset was a prisoner and ordered his release from the Tower. Edmund was also restored to the captaincy of Calais, which was taken back from York in spite of the seven-year term of his appointment. The political wilderness was beckoning York once more and this time Salisbury would join his new ally.

The Duke of Somerset protested vehemently at his treatment. He had been incarcerated without charge for more than a year. The date set for his trial had passed by without Norfolk appearing to present his accusations. Somerset was outraged but he should perhaps have considered himself another beneficiary of York's even-handed rule and unwillingness to act too extremely. Had York wished to, he could have dealt swiftly and mercilessly with his enemy and proceedings for treason against Somerset would have succeeded. That York did not rid himself of a thorn given the opportunity is either to his credit or condemnation. It was a decision that would define English politics for years to come.

With the revival of Somerset and Exeter's cause came a resurgence in Percy fortune that could only be to the detriment of Salisbury's Neville clan. Henry demanded that York and Somerset each offer surety of 20,000 marks to ensure they were committed to an arbitration process to settle the disputes between them, to be overseen by eight other lords whose judgement would be final and binding. York can hardly have been hopeful of equity and he and Salisbury must have foreseen the renewal of trouble. With his colours now firmly nailed to the mast of the House of York, Salisbury would have to accompany his friend on the long, dark voyage into the open ocean that was life cut adrift from the safe port of royal favour.

Over the following year, the country drifted back into old habits. York and Salisbury were excluded and frustrated to watch their good work swiftly undone. When a Council was called at Westminster, neither York nor Salisbury were summoned. When a Great Council was arranged at Leicester for 21 April 1455 York, Salisbury and Warwick were called to appear but seem to have been instantly suspicious. They began to raise armed forces, breaking York's oath at St Paul's never to do so again. The court party was on a collision course with the most powerful noble in the land. There seemed to be only one way that this would reach a resolution. Henry's feeble, ineffectual rule had let drift the ties that bound his nobility to him and as they cast about in the chaos they became snagged, snared or drawn to the causes of others, whether those others wished it or not. York, Salisbury and Warwick were bound together in their fate. If they were to rise or fall, they would have to do so together. York had strength in the Nevilles' numbers. Richard Neville, Earl of Salisbury, had many ancient enemies, but he now had one powerful new friend.

5

When Giants Collide

The date of the outbreak of the Wars of the Roses is consistently pinpointed at 22 May 1455, when the First Battle of St Albans drenched a small town in blood. Dedicated to the saint after whom the town was named, St Albans Cathedral remains the longest standing place of continuous Christian worship in England, built above the tomb of St Alban and predating even Canterbury as a centre of devotion and pilgrimage. The first battle fought here was perhaps a prelude to the Wars of the Roses, but was a very different kind of fight.

Throughout the spring of 1455 tensions within the kingdom of England were continuing to increase. Breaking point could not be too far away. The only question was which side would snap first. York, Salisbury and Warwick were deeply suspicious that the king's summons was a ploy by Somerset and the queen to trick and seize them. Henry, Margaret and Edmund Beaufort were doubtless equally put on edge by the three lords' refusal to heed the king's summons and their muster of an armed force.

On 20 May the rebel lords were at Royston, just south of Cambridge. From here York wrote to Archbishop Bourchier, the Chancellor, insisting that they meant no disloyalty. Since the Great Council had been summoned for the protection of the king the Yorkist lords were bringing with them 160 men each to add to the king's security. York pleaded with the Archbishop to inform the king of their continued and unfaltering fealty. Archbishop Bourchier dutifully sent the letter on to the king.

The following day York and his allies arrived in Ware, less than twenty miles south of Royston. They were not making particularly fast progress, suggesting that their intention was not to storm the capital or to catch the king by surprise. Concerned that no reply had reached them from the king, York, Salisbury and Warwick wrote another missive, this time directly to the king. Addressing Henry as 'Most Christian King, right high and mighty Prince, and our most redoubted sovereign Lord', York went on to complain of the harm done to his honour and his reputation by 'our enemies of approved experience, such as abide and keep themselves under the wing of your Majesty Royal'. He insisted that these evil advisors about the king conspired 'to estrange us from your most noble presence'.

York next advised Henry, or perhaps warned him depending upon the tone in which the letter is read, that 'We at this time be coming with grace as your true and humble liege men, toward your said High Excellence to declare and show thereto our said faith and allegiance'. The rebel lords insisted that they wished only the best for their king, unlike those currently about him who sought only to destroy him by their greed and corruption. The lords were offering themselves as Henry's salvation against his true enemies, asking that he did not 'give trust or confidence unto the sinister, malicious, and fraudulent labours and reports of our said enemies'.

Voicing concern that no response had been received to their previous letter, York explained that they had sent a message to the Archbishop of Canterbury detailing their position and commitment to the king, but could not be sure that the dispatch had reached Henry. To prove what they say, the letter mentions the inclusion of a copy of the note sent to the archbishop in case the original had not reached the king. If this were an ultimatum to Henry it was a gentle one and seemed to lay out York's intention to come before the king clearly. It appears more likely that the sentiment was genuine and that York, Salisbury and Warwick were despairing of their position. During the Protectorate great steps forward had been taken. Upon Henry's recovery the country had fallen back into darkness. York was certainly correct about one thing. His enemies were working to keep him away from King Henry. Somerset intercepted the letter forwarded by Archbishop Bourchier and this second one. They never reached Henry's eyes.

As the sun rose on the morning of 22 May it found York's forces, around 6,000 strong, outside the eastern gates of the town in Key Fields. Inside, King Henry was joined by the dukes of Somerset and Buckingham, Jasper Tudor, Earl of Pembroke, Henry Percy, Earl of Northumberland, and the earls of Devonshire, Stafford, Dorset and Wiltshire, along with the lords Clifford and Dudley and around 2,000 men. The royal forces inside the walls barricaded the three gates to prevent entry and there was a tense standoff for three hours, during which York once more sent word to the king, who had by now pitched his banner in the market square in St Peter's Street. The duke pleaded with the king to accept him into his presence as a faithful subject, swearing, in a description of the day found in the Paston Letters, that he was 'ready at all times to live and die with him in his right'. York called upon the mediation of St Alban to enable him to prove his loyalty, 'for God that is Heaven knoweth that our intent is rightful and true'.

However, this message did contain a firming of tone that must have, perhaps by design, shocked the royal party packed in behind their walls. York warned that they would no longer accept Henry's promise when it came to the removal of Somerset, for his oath had been broken once before on that very matter and it had cost York dearly. This time he wanted Somerset handed over, assuring the king that 'we will not cease for any such promise, surety, nor other, until we have him which have deserved death, or else we do die therefore'. York appears by now to have realised either that his pleas were not reaching Henry or that the king was ignoring them. Either way, he was now clearly threatening Somerset's life. One of them would die that day. York would accept nothing less.

Henry's reply was blunt and it is hard to know whether he spoke Somerset's words rather than his own. He warned that every man, regardless of his station and rank, should immediately 'void the field, and not be so hardy to make any resistance against me in my own realm'. The reply further insisted that if they did not follow Henry's orders 'I shall destroy them every mother's son, and they be hanged, and drawn, and quartered, that may be taken afterward'. It is not hard to imagine York's fury at the reply. His ultimatum had failed and he had left himself no way out but to attack. His rage must have burned hotter still if he suspected that Somerset was behind the threat rather than Henry.

The Paston Letters record York's impassioned call to arms to his men. He told them,

> The King our sovereign Lord will not be reformed at our beseeching … he will with all his power pursue us, and if been taken, to give us a shameful death, losing our livelihood and goods, and our heirs shamed forever. And therefore, since it will be no other way but that we shall utterly die, better it is for us to die in the field than cowardly to be put to great rebuke and a shameful death.

If York felt that he had done all that he could to avoid a confrontation, Henry was no doubt just as certain that he could not bow to the will of one of his subjects. Somerset was under no illusion that his very life was under threat and that the king was his only protection. Three hours of negotiation and standoff were at an end.

York, Salisbury and Warwick attacked with lightning speed that caught the royal forces off guard. The barricades stood strong, though, and the Yorkist push broke hard against them with heavy casualties. Lord Clifford, who was responsible for defending the barriers, was doing a fine job. Warwick industriously found a way to break into the gardens at the back of some buildings in Holwell Street, which had been overlooked when the defences had been set. The young earl's men swarmed through the streets toward the market square, where Henry, encased in his full armour, stood under his banner surrounded by the dukes of Somerset and Buckingham and a large force. They were taken completely by surprise when trumpets erupted and blood curdling cries of 'A Warwick! A Warwick! A Warwick!' echoed about the narrow streets.

There was fierce fighting, with Edmund Beaufort, Duke of Somerset, in the thick of it. He fell outside The Castle Inn, fulfilling a prophecy a fortune teller had once made that he would die beneath the castle. Having always feared that it referred to Windsor Castle, as he looked up, his vision blurring, Somerset may have finally understood the meaning as the inn's sign swung above his head. The trumpeters also panicked those at the barricades, who suddenly realised that there was an enemy force behind them as well as in front. Many fled and the sturdy defences were brought crashing down, Lord Clifford lying among the dead as York and Salisbury pressed on into the town.

In the centre Warwick had ordered his archers to open fire on those about the king. There was carnage, amid which the Earl of Stafford's hand was injured, the Duke of Buckingham was struck in the face and the king was caught by an arrow in the neck. He was convinced to take shelter in a tanner's house as the Yorkist horde poured into the square. Many of the common soldiery were spared as the slaughter focussed on finding the men of rank the Yorkists blamed for their predicament. Henry Percy, Earl of Northumberland, lay among the dead as the slaughter died out and it became clear to all that the royal forces had lost the day. All that remained to be seen was what the victors would do with the injured, vanquished king.

Henry was in the tanner's receiving treatment for the ragged wound to his neck when York, Salisbury and Warwick crashed in, bristling with armed menace and slaked in the blood of the king's men. *Benet's Chronicle* records that the victorious lords immediately fell to their knees and vowed their allegiance to their king, at which 'he was greatly cheered'. Escorted to the comfort of the abbey to continue his treatment, Henry was well treated, though dismayed to hear of Somerset's death. The Abbot of St Albans, John Whethamstede, recorded his shock at the carnage that littered the streets of his town. Although casualties were not high, with some estimates below even a hundred dead, it must have appeared greater in the claustrophobic streets rather than the open fields in which battles usually took place. The abbot wrote that walking the streets, 'here you saw a man with his brains dashed out, here one with a broken arm, another with his throat cut, a fourth with a pierced chest'. It must have been an unspeakable sight for the inhabitants of St Albans.

On the day after the battle Henry was escorted back to London. He rode in majesty, with York and Salisbury at either side and Warwick carrying the sword of state before him. Henry was, for all to see, very much still king, but those watching on must have also seen clearly under whose control he now was. In short order, York became Constable of England, an office of state previously held by his brother-in-law Buckingham, which gave him at least nominal control over the country's military affairs. Warwick now took the prestigious Captaincy of Calais and Archbishop Bourchier was given the Earl of Wiltshire's position as Treasurer. At St Paul's Cathedral on 25 May Henry received his crown from York, a demonstration that Henry's crown was not under threat and that he was still God's anointed king. Just like the entry into London a few days earlier, it cannot have escaped the attention of all who witnessed the ceremony that Henry had his crown now because York allowed him to.

The king, queen and Prince of Wales were sent to Hertford Castle as the Yorkists took control of the government in Henry's name. Parliament was summoned to sit and those lords who had aided the king at St Albans were, for the most part, dealt with. According to the Paston Letters Buckingham came to York and swore 'that he shall be ruled'. The Earl of Wiltshire, who Gregory quipped disparagingly 'fought mainly with his heels for he was frightened of losing his beauty', wrote from Peterfield to optimistically ask if he could return to the king's side. If he could not he requested permission to leave for Ireland to stay on his lands there. Lord Dudley was in the Tower, with Barker commenting 'what shall come of him, God knows' and the Earl of Dorset was placed into the custody of Warwick. Sir Philip Wentworth, who had born King Henry's standard at St Albans but, according to Barker, had 'cast it down and fled', was currently in hiding in Suffolk and 'dare not come about the King'. In a medieval battle the role of the standard bearer was to mark his lord's position for all to see, to act as both rallying point and encouragement. His duty was to die holding the standard high if it came to it. Wentworth's failure in this core duty may have contributed to the flight of a portion of the king's men from the field. If his banner were thrown down, it implied that he was dead or had lost the field. That Wentworth's actions were considered both cowardly and perhaps to have contributed to the loss of the battle can be read into Barker's comment that 'My Lord Norfolk says he shall be hanged therefore, and so is he worthy'.

Lord Egremont and the Duke of Exeter remained at large, but when Parliament opened on 9 July 1455, a ceremony for which Henry was present before returning to Hertford, it was very well attended, though John Paston points to a nervous membership who took their seats in the Commons, doubtless uncertain what to expect. 'Some men hold it right strange to be in this parliament, and me thinketh they be wise men that so do'. It would soon become apparent, though, that York meant to pick up where his Protectorate had left off. The Yorkist lords did ensure as best they could that their actions at St Albans, which undoubtedly amounted to treason, would not rebound upon them should they lose their position again by having it entered on the Parliament Roll that none of them should be 'impeached, sued, vexed, hurt or molested in their bodies, goods or lands' for their parts in the engagement. It is interesting that the rehabilitation of the reputation of the king's uncle Humphrey, Duke of Gloucester, was a major concern for this Parliament. It was perhaps a clear signal to all that York's government not only condemned his own treatment but also identified with Gloucester's popular agenda.

When the second session of this parliament opened on 12 November, the king was absent for what the Parliament Rolls record as 'certain just and reasonable causes'. Rumour abounded that the king's health had failed once more. This led the Commons to request the appointment of a Protector again and they awaited the Lords' decision before proceeding with their business. The Commons' delegation was headed up by William Burley, a man close to York, and there seems to be little real evidence that Henry was ill again. The Paston Letters record only that 'some men are afraid that he is sick again'. It seems possible that York felt too restricted without the powers a Protectorate afforded him and so allowed stories of a relapse to flourish, orchestrating a call for him to serve once more as Protector. Even if that was the case there was very little opposition to the move.

The Commons requested York's appointment specifically, entreating the Lords 'that considering the great nobility, gravity and wisdom of the duke of York, and the well-ordered governance and politic rule had in this land when he was last protector and defender of the land, he should now take charge upon himself again'. York made a show of asking that another be found, for 'he was not able either in wisdom or governance to undertake so great and burdensome a responsibility'. Although this may be no more than a show of unwilling for the record, it is also possible that York was somewhat genuine. He had assumed the mantel at their request once before and it had got him nowhere. In fact, it had left the stench of suspicion even stronger about him, resulting in open warfare with the king. York had dallied dangerously close to treason and may not have been keen to assume more of Henry's power now. If he did, and Henry recovered control, what might then befall York? Twice Protector and deemed to have done a better job of ruling than the king himself, a second Protectorate just might be the seal on his own death warrant.

This earnestly cautious view of York's response is backed up by his issuing of several conditions, to which he asked Parliament to assent before he would agree to act as Protector. Firstly, he wanted it known that he had not sought out the position, but the Houses had approached him with their request. He further required that they enrol a clear definition of his powers, making clear 'how far and how fully they shall reach and extend' and that they promise to support him in 'whatever may be to the honour, prosperity and welfare' of the king. York insisted upon the creation of a council of 'an adequate and appropriate number of lords spiritual and temporal' who were to be appointed 'not by favour or affection, but choosing those who are known to be of a virtuous and righteous disposition, men of reason, wisdom and impartiality'. He clearly wished to announce his intention to rule evenly and equitably again.

York also requested a suitable wage for himself as Protector and the payment of 2,000 marks owed to him from the last time he held the office and which was as yet unpaid. Although this was clearly self-interest it was legitimate, since meeting the costs of his position was not really his responsibility and may have been beyond his means after the problems of the preceding years. In addition, York also asked for the payment of a wage to each of those appointed to the council 'whereby they might be encouraged to attend' and requiring their attendance whenever possible. If they could not be present they were to inform the council in writing of their legitimate reason for failing to attend. Parliament agreed to York's terms and on 18 November 1455 he was appointed Protector and Defender of the Realm for a second time.

St Alban was the first recorded British martyr in the third century. During Roman occupation of Britain, Alban, believed to have been of Roman origin, offered shelter to a Christian priest. Alban was so moved by what the priest told him of God and Christ that he converted to Christianity and allowed the priest, Amphibalus, to stay in his home. When the Emperor ordered the persecution of Christians throughout the empire Alban's home was visited by legionnaires hunting for the priest. Alban swapped clothes with the priest to allow him to escape and so was arrested himself. During his trial Alban was ordered to show obedience by making offerings to the Roman gods but refused, affirming his belief in the one true God. Unrepentant, Alban was taken outside and beheaded. His sacrifice made him a saint and a martyr and the cathedral stands over the spot where he is believed to have been buried. This model of making the ultimate sacrifice to protect one another is perhaps a fitting parallel for the clash in Alban's town. No doubt York and Somerset both believed that they offered their lives to protect their king from persecution and evil.

The First Battle of St Albans was not truly the beginning of the Wars of the Roses. That term is used to describe a dynastic struggle for the throne between the houses of Lancaster and York. What occurred on 22 May 1455 had nothing to do with who was or should be king. If Richard, Duke of York, wanted the throne, he had only to finish the work an arrow had begun by widening the wound at the king's neck within the silent, unseeing walls of a tanner's house in St Albans. In fact, it was during the following Parliament under York's auspices that Henry's son, Edward, was created Prince of Wales, a move that effectively ended debate about York's own pretentions to be heir apparent. That was perhaps York's very intention, thereby reassuring the Lords, Commons and the nation that Henry was safe on his throne and that his son would succeed him.

This conflict was about other rivalries, every bit as bitter and spiteful as those to come. York wanted Somerset's blood, blaming Beaufort for the position he found himself in. Somerset would not allow York's letters to reach the king's ears, perhaps in the knowledge that Henry had no stomach for confrontation and would try to bargain a resolution. Both men wanted only one end:

the other's death. Both accused the other of trying to ruin the king and offered him salvation, but both could not be right. In truth, both simply wanted control of the weak king for their own reasons.

Similarly, the houses of Neville and Percy had scores to settle that had been straining at the leash for years. The patriarchs were both present, proud men at the head of proud houses. The opportunity to seek out revenge on the field of a legitimate battle fought in the name of others must have been too good to turn away from. Heworth Moor had been a mere dress rehearsal. Now they had a chance for the main event. There could be no backing down on any side.

York and the Nevilles were to win the day and all of the rewards of power that came with it. St Albans, though, did little to break the tensions that gripped England, only drawing them tighter still. Wounds were opened that day that would fester for years and contribute to the later brutality. Edmund Beaufort's nineteen-year-old son Henry was now 3rd Duke of Somerset and burned for revenge. Henry Percy's son, another Henry, took the mantle of 3rd Earl of Northumberland aged thirty-three. John Clifford became 9th Baron Clifford after his father's death just after his twentieth birthday, swearing that his father would not go unavenged. These men all had a common enemy in the Duke of York and those who attached themselves to his cause, particularly the ambitious Nevilles. They would bide their time, but they would never forget what they owed York.

6

A Great and Strong Laboured Woman

The second Protectorate of Richard, Duke of York, was brief. The Parliament Rolls record that on 25 February 1456, just three months after accepting the commission, Henry was in Parliament to advise York that he had been 'discharged' from the role. The king instructed York that 'we order you not to intervene at all in any further responsibility or charge', and concluded by reinforcing that 'we wish you to be completely discharged of the responsibility or charge and name of the aforesaid'. There was little room for ambiguity. Significantly no provision was made or mention given to what should put in place if the king were to fall ill ever again, which seemed a likely eventuality. Henry VI seemed finally resurgent, beginning a royal progress to dispense justice aimed at sealing the cracks that had appeared throughout his kingdom. York can have been under little illusion about what this meant for his cause. The wilderness beckoned to him once more. There was a new, confident force at work too, spurring Henry on and driving York further into the wasteland.

Margaret of Anjou was nearly twenty-five years old when York was removed from power for the second time. She had been Queen of England for a decade and while she had arrived in England under the escort of William de la Pole as a girl, she emerged from her enforced sojourn at Hertford Castle nothing less than a determined woman. On 9 February, a fortnight before York was officially relieved of his powers, the Paston Letters contain a note from John Boking to Sir John Fastolf describing how York and

Warwick had come to Parliament with 300 men 'all jacketed and in brigantines' in expectation of his discharge. He adds a note after discussing this that 'the Queen is a great and strong laboured woman, for she spareth no pain to sue her things to an intent and conclusion to her power'. A perception was developing of a new power behind Henry's throne.

Over the past decade Margaret had watched her husband's rule stumble and falter along. She had lost those closest to her in Suffolk and Somerset, and her husband, the king, had been powerless to prevent any of it. When she gave birth to a long-awaited child, a son and heir for her husband, he had been so lost to this world that he had not even noticed. She had eyed York with suspicion as his power grew and great lords drifted to his side, frustrated or disaffected by Henry. It was her son's position that she surely saw under threat next and if Henry could not be relied upon to protect his closest friends and supporters she could not be sure whether he could be trusted with her son. Margaret had applied to the lords of the land for power in 1454 and received her answer. This time she did not intend to ask.

Within weeks of St Albans King James II of Scotland had laid siege to Berwick. A combined force under the Bishop of Durham, the new Earl of Northumberland and other northern lords had driven the Scots back so completely that they left behind their ordnance and supplies, but James was not yet done. Edmund Beaufort, the Duke of Somerset slain at St Albans, was James's uncle and he used the family tie as a reason for his sudden aggression. It is more likely that the weakness he espied in his old enemy was the true cause of his boldness. The English fighting among themselves was simply too good an opportunity to miss.

On 10 May 1456 James wrote to Henry advising him that the current treaty between their nations was no longer acceptable, and threatening war if more favourable terms were not reached. The reply that James received came from Richard, Duke of York, in July, in the name of King Henry. It sneered at James and his posturing, assuring him that England did not fear his menace and that James was committing treason against his liege lord by his threats. England had long held claim to feudal lordship over the kingdom of Scotland, an assertion vigorously pursued by Edward I and never relinquished. The threat was turned back around and it is perhaps striking that York was the man selected to make it.

In the intervening time James had not been idle. In June he wrote to Charles VII of France urging him not to conclude a peace treaty with England but to join with Scotland to make the most of the disharmony there. Barely a month after Henry's reply, York wrote to James himself, rebuking the king for constant raids into England, from which he would retire immediately. York requested a meeting and told James that such actions were beneath one 'called a mighty Prince and a courageous knight'. The Scotch Roll into which Henry's official reply to James is entered contains a note that the English king did not approve of the reply nor of its tone, blaming it upon the Duke of York, who had been disrupting the rule of the country since Cade's Rebellion.

The contrast between the parties was becoming starker with each crisis that reared its head. There is little remaining evidence of government function during this period and the physical locations of the various factions might go a long way to explain this. King Henry was installed at Sheen Palace, nine miles downstream from Westminster on the south bank of the Thames. Queen Margaret was at her dower castle of Tutbury in Staffordshire, later withdrawing further to Chester. The Duke of York was at Sandal Castle near Wakefield in Yorkshire, at least in part to ward off a further incursion from the Scots, and the young Earl of Warwick was at his seat, Warwick Castle. The Duke of Buckingham was at Writtle in Essex. All power in England had evacuated the capital. The country seemed to hold its breath, waiting to see who would make the first move.

During this time, the only member of the nobility recorded as lodging with Henry at Sheen was his half-brother, Jasper Tudor, Earl of Pembroke. Jasper's brother Edmund, Earl of Richmond, was in Wales, putting down disharmony there. Edmund was to be captured by a man who would become the Tudors' rival in Wales, William, Lord Herbert. Herbert, whose father had been allied to Richard, Duke of York, was to capture Edmund and imprison him at Carmarthen Castle where the earl would contract the plague and die in November 1456. He would never see his son, Henry Tudor, who would be born to his teenage bride Margaret Beaufort in January the next year and who was destined to wear the crown that would settle easily upon no man's head.

Queen Margaret moved the royal court to Coventry, often using the mighty fortress of Kenilworth Castle, and had Henry join her there, clearly keen to secure the person of her husband behind the thick, stout walls of cities and castles deep in loyal territory. That York did not jump with both feet into the vacuum that surrounded the king for some weeks perhaps gives the lie to the assertion that he was hungry for the crown from the outset of this decade if not before. York made no move to seize Henry, his authority or his throne. York was certainly at Windsor, where Henry had taken up residence in July, to make Henry's reply to James II. Margaret may have tried to feed York enough rope to hang himself, preparing to swoop in from the north-west when he made his play. It may also be that Margaret simply dared not wait any longer and York felt that he had time on his side. Henry had proved himself incapable and unpopular more than once before. All York needed to do was wait and allow him to do it again. The alternative is simply that York did not harbour the covetous desires that the queen feared in him. Whatever the case, Margaret now had control of her husband the king.

Around Coventry the queen drew to her cause powerful and loyal men. Prime among these was the twenty-year-old Henry Beaufort, 3rd Duke of Somerset. The son of Edmund, the 2nd Duke, Henry had been wounded at St Albans and was among the next generation of royal lords burning for vengeance upon the faction under York. On 5 October 1456 Henry, Viscount Bourchier, was removed as Lord Treasurer and replaced with John Talbot, Earl of Shrewsbury. The viscount's brother Thomas Bourchier, Archbishop of Canterbury, was relieved of the Great Seal, which passed into the keeping of William Waynflete, Bishop of Winchester and new Lord Chancellor. The Bourchier brothers were maternal half-brothers of Humphrey Stafford, Duke of Buckingham, who must have been disturbed to see members of his family now being excised from court. He can only have believed that it was because of their associations with York and Henry, or at least that what was being done in Henry's name was treading a line dangerously close to alienating another powerful family just as he had the Nevilles.

The death of Edmund Tudor in November was a blow to Henry's cause. The closest thing that he had to family, his half-brothers had been promoted to bolster the king's faction and give breadth to the pool of nobility loyal, and indeed beholden, to him, just as the dukes of Somerset were. While Henry had been young their very existence seems to have been kept a secret from him. There is some debate as to whether their father Owen Tudor was legally married to their mother Catherine of Valois, the beautiful young widow of Henry V. When she became ill the news was broken to the young Henry that his mother had remarried and that he had several half-siblings. Little is known of another son, variously named as Edward or Owen, who is believed to have become a monk. It is possible that a daughter, Margaret, was also born to the couple but nothing is known of her if she did exist. Edmund and Jasper were embraced by Henry and created belted earls. Edmund was given the richest marriage prize in England, Lady Margaret Beaufort, who was to be widowed and pregnant aged thirteen.

Little is known of the governmental business of 1457, perhaps because it was conducted in secrecy as if by a war cabinet. It was a year which the country spent in a tense, coiled state of anticipation without knowing what precisely it was afraid of. Each side eyed each other with a suspicion that needed no fact to nourish it. They each knew what the other was up to. They were gathering armed men about them ready to strike. The only response was to recruit more men for protection. The tension rose to boiling point. On 21 April 1457 the Calendar of the Patent Rolls records a grant of an annual income to Richard, Duke of York, 'in recompense of the offices of the castles of Camarthen, Aberystwyth and Caerkeny, his estate wherein at the king's desire he has granted to the king's brother, Jasper, earl of Pembroke'. Henry and York had managed to remain on good terms personally after St Albans. York was still summoned to Council in Coventry in October 1456. It is likely that Margaret's hand was at work in this kind of manoeuvring. It served not only to strengthen a lord who stood prominently at her husband's side within his heartlands but simultaneously weakened York's position, taunting him, even, by flaunting the grant of his lands to Jasper. If it was meant to provoke York into the action that Margaret seems to have lived in fear of, it did not work.

Even in the mists of his shadow world, the atmosphere within the country did not escape Henry. He appears to have had even less grip on the government than ever before, happy to leave everything to Margaret and her advisors, but we can still glimpse his fervent commitment to peace and his hatred of conflict. Henry summoned a Great Council to meet in London, away from the queen's new powerbase. All of his lords were to attend and the sole aim was the burying of the various and tightly gripped hatchets that threatened Henry's beloved peace. Unless it were to further goad York, believing that he would not attend or try to seize Henry, it is hard to see Margaret orchestrating this return to a city where York was more popular than she, and perhaps even more popular than the king. York may have suggested the move to Henry, but it is hard to imagine Margaret allowing him the opportunity. Henry did issue a safe conduct to York to allow him to get to London without being arrested. It is almost unavoidable to conclude otherwise than that this was a desperate, strained, but determined demonstration of the king's will. As weak as his will may have been, Henry would try to bring his friends, who had become enemies to one another, back into a united fold. Doomed as the effort was, it is a touching glimpse of a man frantically trying to perform a function for which he had neither taste nor aptitude.

Inside the walls of the City of London, the temperature can hardly have been higher as the bristling entourages of sworn enemies packed themselves in uncomfortably close, itching for a fight and restrained only by the fragile will of a flawed king. York arrived with 400 armed retainers. Somerset arrived with 800. Salisbury brought 500 men and Warwick sailed over from Calais with 600, possibly including some of the professional garrison. Northumberland, his brother Lord Egremont and Lord Clifford could count 1,500 soldiers at their backs. The Yorkist lords and their men were billeted within the City walls while their enemies were found lodgings outside. *Fabyan's Chronicle* tells of the distress and panic caused within a capital doubtless nervous of a repeat of Cade's antics enacted by great lords with trained soldiers.

The mayor, for so long as the king and the lords lay thus in the city, had daily in harness 5,000 citizens, and rode daily about the city and suburbs of the same, to see that the king's peace were kept; and nightly he provided for 3,000 men in harness to give attendance upon three aldermen, and they kept the night-watch till seven of the clock upon the morrow, till the day-watch were assembled.

In spite of all of these precautions the lid could not be kept on such a pressurised cauldron. Northumberland, Egremont and Clifford tried unsuccessfully to ambush York and Salisbury as they travelled to Westminster one morning. Henry could not even restrain the blood lust of those who pleaded the greatest loyalty to him when they were trapped in such proximity to enemies upon whom they had sworn to take revenge. Margaret may have feared York's motives and intentions but he was slow to take any bait and did not pursue vengeance as openly as those about the queen. York displayed no great, overriding desire for the crown. Margaret may have instructed the bitter young lords to take their revenge, but if she did it served only to make York appear a pillar of reasonable restraint while she was unable to control her most powerful allies.

Two months of negotiations ensued, led by the king himself and Thomas Bourchier, Archbishop of Canterbury. It is hard to imagine the tension contained behind closed doors and the barely restrained tempers bottled tightly within hot-blooded, angry men as their king forced them to sit down and find a way to become friends where no amity could ever be cultivated. It was on 24 March that the final arrangements were announced. Henry believed that he had his peace. Recorded in the Calendar of Patent Rolls is a jubilant entry devised 'to avoid certain controversies between Richard, duke of York, and Richard, earl of Warwick, and Richard, earl of Salisbury, and other children of the earl of Salisbury, of the one part, and Eleanor, duchess of Somerset, and Henry, duke of Somerset, her son, and other children of the duchess, and Eleanor, countess of Northumberland, and Henry, earl of Northumberland, her son, and other children of the countess, and John, lord Clifford, and his brothers and sisters, of the other part'.

The agreement took the form of reparations for the deaths and destruction wrought at St Albans. Henry 'arbitrated and decided' that York should pay the widow of Edmund Beaufort and her son,

Henry, the new duke, 5,000 marks. Half was to be provided for the duchess and her other children and half for the duke. However, York was permitted to simply reassign some of the wages owed to him by the crown as Lieutenant of Ireland for the payment, effectively passing on a credit note which he was unlikely ever to see realised anyway. The House of Somerset would have recompense and it would, in reality, cost York nothing. The Earl of Warwick was instructed to pay Lord Clifford 1,000 marks and Salisbury was ordered to cancel fines levied against Northumberland and Egremont during their family's feuds earlier in the decade. The Yorkist lords were also required to endow St Albans Abbey with £45 a year to purchase prayers for the souls of those who had died in the battle.

For their part, the queen's party got off lightly. Lord Egremont, possibly deemed the chief cause of aggravation between his family and the Nevilles after his attempted attack at Heworth, was bound over to keep the peace with all of the Neville family for a decade and had to provide 4,000 marks as a bond. The agreement, if any party to it truly agreed, no doubt pleased Henry's need for peace and tranquillity. He felt that his job was done. The settlement clearly laid the blame for the battle that had taken place at St Albans at the feet of York and his allies, yet there is no record of any objection on their part to the penalties imposed upon them. Still York would not be goaded, if that was Margaret's aim. The likelihood of a kind-spirited truce between the Percy and Neville clans enduring once they ventured back north, beyond the reach of the crown, was faint, if it existed at all. Although York does not appear to have baulked at the agreement, it clearly placed him in the wrong when he would have believed himself in the right.

It is perhaps to the credit of his faction that they were still willing to agree to Henry's stipulations. They had always insisted in the strongest terms that their anger was aimed at those who gave the king bad advice rather than the king himself. This offers further proof of those claims. Whatever York and Salisbury thought of Somerset, Northumberland and others now gravitating toward the queen, they were still willing to be ruled by Henry. It is difficult to credit the royalist faction with the same commitment to peace. It was they who attempted to ambush York during the negotiations and it was their party who had come out of the settlement better. Even if York and Salisbury felt aggrieved, they acquiesced with better grace than their rivals.

On the same day as the agreement was announced a solemn procession took place through the streets of London to St Paul's Cathedral. King Henry led wearing his crown and was followed by Queen Margaret and Richard, Duke of York, holding hands. Next came Richard Neville, Earl of Salisbury, with his hand in that of Henry Beaufort, Duke of Somerset; behind his father, the Earl of Warwick strode, holding hands with either Henry Percy, Earl of Northumberland, or Henry Holland, Duke of Exeter. There is uncertainty in the sources as to precisely who was beside Warwick, but the message was as clear as it was false. Henry had his public display of mended fractures, orchestrated by the king as the liege lord of those who had been at war. Henry was the one common thread with any hope of uniting his noble subjects, but it required more than just will. Men so far apart needed a firmer hand to draw them back together than Henry was capable of bringing to bear. The men, and perhaps most significantly the one woman, walked dutifully, with an outward appearance of reconciliation, but it is not hard to imagine the deep discomfort each felt at such close contact with their mortal enemies. There was surely gritting of teeth, irritated squeezing of hands and uncomfortably sweaty palms.

John Lydgate composed a poem to mark the occasion, comprehensively entitled 'Upon The Reconciliation Of The Lords Of The Yorkist Faction With The King And His Adherents', which dripped with hopeful praise of the work that the king had done. 'For love hath underlaid wrathful vengeance; Rejoice England the lords accorded be.' The poem goes on to laud the peace and to threaten France and Brittany that, with England reunited, they would soon turn an eye across the Channel once more. The festivities and forced amity of what became known as Love Day was described more cynically, with the application of hindsight, by Grafton just over 100 years later.

As by this cloaked Pageant, and dissembling Procession, hereafter shall plainly be declared. For their bodies were joined by hand in hand, whose hearts were far asunder: their mouths lovingly smiled, whose courages were enflamed with malice: their words were sweet as sugar, and their thoughts were all envenomed: but all these dissimulating persons, tasted the vessel of woe, as the wise man said: and few or none of this company were unblotted, or undestroyed by this dolorous drink of dissimulation.

Whether any party beyond the king himself believed that the Love Day had been a success is doubtful, but all had put on a good show for their king and it must have seemed, at least to those outside the conflicts that writhed just beneath the smooth veneer presented for the king and the people, that the future was bright once more. What they were not permitted to see was the brinkmanship, the cold war that continued to thaw. The queen's primary, insurmountable problem was her gender. A strong woman defending her incapacitated husband and infant child might well have been applauded in another time. In Margaret's day it was terrifying. A woman was not supposed to behave like a man, but Margaret could not rule without doing just that. No man would lower himself to serve a woman, even a queen. Although there was no legal bar to its occurrence, a woman wishing to rule was incomprehensible to medieval English society.

As the queen drew the sons of St Albans about her a repeat of recent history cannot have seemed too far away. York appears to have remained on good terms with Henry, but the king was no longer the true power in his own kingdom and Margaret's suspicion of the royal duke only grew, nurtured by the warmth of her burning fear. She was no longer the girl who had entered England a decade earlier. She was a wife, a queen and a mother. She would not give up any of these easily. Queen Margaret was itching for a fight. Her excuse would not be long in coming, even if her husband believed for one day that all was well within the kingdom of England.

7

War Begins

Before the end of 1458 Richard Neville, Earl of Warwick, was summoned to London from his base at Calais to answer charges of piracy against the Hanseatic League, a trading block with whom England had no axe to grind. Almost as soon as Warwick arrived, trouble broke out. He claimed that one of the king's servants had attacked one of his men and a scuffle quickly expanded into unrest. Warwick and his men fled to their ships and made for Calais. He was ordered to return again but refused to obey. As the New Year began, all parties began their preparations for what was becoming unavoidable.

The tension that had been building throughout the spring and summer of 1459 broke in the autumn in spectacular style. Queen Margaret was still based in the Midlands, recruiting gallants to her personal cause as well as to the king's. Richard, Duke of York, installed himself within the stout walls of Ludlow Castle, a mighty fortress on the Welsh borderlands known as the Marches, and issued a call to arms. Richard Neville, Earl of Salisbury was in his Yorkshire heartlands raising the substantial Neville affinity. His son Richard Neville, Earl of Warwick, was in Calais, having held on to his captaincy there, but he too was busy gathering a force based around the Calais garrison. Both sides could plead the need to defend themselves from the other, meaning neither would appear to be the aggressor.

At a time when the king, and therefore the country, did not maintain a standing army, the crown was completely reliant upon the feudal system of loyalty. When the king needed an army he instructed his nobles to raise their retainers. Nobles and knights would indent to provide and pay a number of men-at-arms and archers, frequently providing more if they could afford to as a measure of their commitment to the king and of their available wealth. In turn, these nobles and knights would call upon those who lived on their estates to give their service to make up the required numbers. The system had worked well for centuries, but it relied on a strong king controlling loyal, well-rewarded nobility. Without these restraints, there was nothing to prevent powerful men from raising private armies for their own ends. The Calais garrison was a standing force employed by the crown to defend the last piece of English soil beyond the Channel and, as such, was the nearest thing to a professional army in the kingdom. Not until Henry VII created the Yeomen of the Guard as his personal bodyguard would there be another professional fighting force in the pay of the crown.

Each side gathered men and waited to see who would make the first move. Maintaining a large army ready for battle was an expensive business and the standoff could not last forever. Eventually, in September, it was Salisbury who moved first, marching south-west to join up with York at Ludlow. Queen Margaret was in Cheshire when news reached her that Salisbury had left Middleham. She had been handing out silver swan badges, the symbol of her husband, to those who pledged support to her. The queen summoned James Tuchet, 5th Baron Audley, who had served in France and who brought with him somewhere between 6,000 and 12,000 men – estimates of the sizes of many armies of this period vary widely, but it was understood that Audley had at least twice as many men as Salisbury, who must have been marching with 3,000 to 6,000 men. Margaret gave instructions that Audley was to bring her Salisbury dead or alive.

On the morning of Sunday 23 September, St Tecla's day, Lord Audley arranged his force on Blore Heath, near the border between Staffordshire and Shropshire, as Salisbury approached. The royalist force contained a large number of mounted men among its numbers, so the broad, open space of the heath was the perfect terrain for Lord Audley to make the most of his advantage. As

Salisbury approached, his scouts reported the presence of the huge army blocking their way, attempting to hide behind a hedgerow. A military commander even more experienced than Lord Audley, Salisbury set about deploying his own limited force to his best advantage. Not unlike Henry V at Agincourt, the earl dug wooden spikes into the ground to guard against an enemy cavalry charge. His left flank was shielded by dense woods but his right and rear were open. Facing a much larger force and with rumours of more of the queen's troops less than ten miles away, Salisbury had a broad trench excavated at his rear and arranged the baggage wagons into a protective barrier known as a laager to his right. The two armies faced each other, just outside the range of their longbows, separated by a narrow but deep brook, a feature Salisbury had ensured divided them.

The earl was all too well aware that he had no hope of winning in a toe-to-toe melee. As Audley's men advanced, archers on both sides opened fire, causing a handful of casualties on Salisbury's side but killing around 500 of Audley's men. As the archers fired, Salisbury's men harnessed the horses to the baggage wagons again and drew them apart. His men fell back in a managed withdrawal under the cover of the hail of arrows. Audley fell back under the weight of the attack, but soon spotted the Yorkists' retreat. Jean de Waurin, a Burgundian soldier and chronicler, recorded the battle, possibly based on eyewitness testimonies, though he got some details drastically wrong, including referring to Salisbury by his son's title Warwick. Waurin had been at Agincourt on the French side, so the parallels would not have been lost on him.

Waurin describes how Audley 'retired to around maximum range for an archer, but shortly afterwards charged again impetuously'. Salisbury's retreat had been a feint. As Audley's cavalry forded the stream the earl turned his men on them ferociously. Waurin places royalist losses at around a hundred to only ten of Salisbury's men, and it is possible that Lord Audley himself fell in this charge. Lord Dudley, Audley's second in command, 'considering that they were winning little honour and less profit on horseback, dismounted with around 4,000 men who returned to rejoin the battle'. Dudley pushed the army forward over the brook again, 'where they fought hand to hand for a good half hour, hoping to be helped by their allies who were still mounted', but the remaining cavalry, unimpressed with the progress their comrades had made so far, failed to engage; some – Waurin points to one unnamed knight and his 500 men – defected to Salisbury's side and began to attack their former allies. Finally, Dudley was routed, 'his troops were discomfited, and from their number, according to their heralds, there died 2,000', including Lord Audley. Many of the royalist forces were cut down in the brook, others tripping or stumbling and being drowned in the press as their own soldiers tried to retreat past them. The brook supposedly ran red with the blood of the fallen for miles downstream for three days after the battle.

There is a legend, which cannot be wholly corroborated, that Queen Margaret watched the Battle of Blore Heath from the steeple of Mucklestone Church, which lies about a mile north-east of the site of the fighting. She was certainly at Eccleshall Castle, a short distance south-east of Blore Heath. The story tells that Margaret took her six-year-old son Edward to the top of Mucklestone Church to watch her gallants crush the impudent Yorkist rebels. She may have wished to see an army raised in her own name do its work. She could not lead them onto the field of battle, but watching Salisbury being crushed and York losing a key ally might have been too much to resist. She had instructed Audley to bring Salisbury to her dead or alive, so it is not impossible that she was keen enough to see the outcome, and perhaps confident enough of victory, to risk getting this close. If she was there, she did not see what she had hoped for. The legend continues that as Margaret fled in panic she pulled her horse up outside a blacksmith's workshop, instructing him to reverse the shoes on their horses to disguise their escape. The blacksmith was then supposedly put to death to ensure his silence. It is not clear whether Margaret did take the bold and dangerous step of placing herself and her son so close to danger. Perhaps she thought the boy needed the exposure his father had always avoided, or maybe the chance to witness Salisbury's fall overtook her caution. The story may relate to an envoy of the queen's sent to relay news of the battle, but has become wrapped around Margaret's ever more formidable reputation. What is certain is that her army lost the field.

With the king's men reported to be nearby, Salisbury needed a way to cover his movement toward the safety of Ludlow Castle. Gregory tells how he left one of his cannon behind and paid 'a Fryer Austen', who 'shot guns all that night in a park that was at the back side of the field, and by this mean the earl came to the Duke of York'. The ruse must have worked, disorientating the king's army and sending them searching in the wrong direction for a battle that had long ended. 'And in the morrow they found neither man nor child in that park but the fryer, and he said that for fear he abode in that park all that night'.

Salisbury's bedraggled column of men was delivered to Ludlow by their commander's experience and resourcefulness, but they can have been under no illusion now as to their master's position. He had been attacked by a royal army and had killed its leader. None could have believed that this was the last they would hear of it. News arrived that two of Salisbury's sons, Sir John and Sir Thomas Neville, had been captured while chasing the fleeing forces of Lord Audley, and it seemed likely that the executioner's block awaited both men. Within a few days of Salisbury's arrival his son Warwick brought his own force, including a large portion of the Calais garrison, into Ludlow. The garrison soldiers were led by Andrew Trollope, a famed soldier who had been in service in France since the 1420s. Alongside his reputation for military ability stood one for piracy, accosting not only French shipping in his role as Master Porter of Calais but also allied and even English ships. It is perhaps Trollope's influence that had led Warwick into those areas of activity unbecoming of an earl that had seen him summonsed to London.

Also at Ludlow were York's own family. He had two grown sons. Edward, Earl of March was seventeen years old and stood six foot four inches tall, a giant of a man for the times. Edmund, Earl of Rutland, was just a year younger. Both had been belted earls since before the Battle of St Albans and might well have been excited at the muster of such large armies in their father's name. York and his duchess, Cecily Neville, also had two other sons and three daughters. Anne, the couple's oldest child at twenty, was married to Henry Holland, the Duke of Exeter, who had sided with the Percy family against York in the north. Elizabeth was fifteen, a year younger than Edmund, and had married John de la Pole, son of William and now Duke of Suffolk, the previous year. Margaret was just thirteen and as yet unwed. The two youngest children were George, aged nine, and Richard, who was six. The couple had lost at least six other children in infancy too.

As the threat of war grew, York had Cecily and his younger children moved from the family's traditional seat at Fotheringhay Castle to the security of Ludlow Castle, deep in his Marcher heartlands. George and Richard had been raised at Fotheringhay with their sisters in the care of their mother's household. It is possible that this was the first time they had met their older brothers. Certainly it is the first time that they are recorded in the same place at the same time. If Edward and Edmund were excited by the prospect of war, it could have been as nothing to the unbridled awe of the two younger boys at seeing the town bustling with soldiers, watching men practice at arms in the castle's outer bailey and looking up at their giant oldest brother in reverence. They were young enough for the threat behind the muster to be lost in the fields of men, armour and weapons.

York decided, as he had done in 1452, to march his men to London and protest his loyalty to Henry in person. His son and namesake, Richard, turned seven on 2 October and his birthday must have forgone much celebration in the hustle and bustle. The Yorkist columns left Ludlow heading south, keeping out of reach of the queen's strongholds in the Midlands and planning to swing east toward London. When they had just marched past Worcester, news arrived from York's scouts that a vast royal army was approaching to intercept them. Reliable estimates of the numbers on each side do not exist but it was clear that the royal army vastly outnumbered York's own, perhaps being twice the size. Salisbury had beaten such odds at Blore Heath, but there was another reason York was unwilling to attempt a repeat.

King Henry VI rode at the front of his vast host, wearing full harness and displaying his royal banners. This changed the game so completely that York was stunned. He fell back to Worcester. At the cathedral he swore an oath of allegiance to the king before the bishop, had the oath committed to velum and sent it to Henry. The only reply that came back was an offer of a full pardon to any who abandoned York's cause immediately. The situation was becoming desperate. Precisely how much control Henry was exerting over matters is unknown. He was prone to spurts of lucid action and would not take kindly to the royal power that had been his almost from birth being threatened or questioned. It is equally possible and perhaps more likely that he was a puppet, held up by the straps of his armour rather than any strings, to do the bidding of his wife and her followers, whose gravest, all-consuming wish was to see York utterly destroyed.

Whatever the reason, taking the field of battle against God's anointed king was, at best, treason. At worst, it represented the sinful opposition to one appointed by God himself and risked eternal damnation, a fate sorely to be avoided. St Albans had been about saving the king from his enemies. Now Henry led an army that hunted them. York knew that this changed the landscape. He had intended to plead loyalty to his king, but the king was now leading an army against him as though he were a convicted felon. To stand and fight risked everything that he had in this world and beyond, along with the fates of his wife and children. He could be certain too that his men would no longer be so willing to take the field once they saw the royal banner fluttering above the king. It mattered little now whether Henry were truly in command or not; it mattered only that he was there. York's letter may never have reached Henry, as had been the case before St Albans, but that counted for little now as well. York would have to turn tail and run to his earthly ruin or stand and fight, risking ruin in this world and the next.

The Yorkist army withdrew all the way back to Ludlow. This offered York not only time but also the facility to claim that he was simply defending himself, his lands and those dependent upon him. The royal army was hot on their heels, undeterred by York's unwillingness to fight. At Ludford Meadow, just across the River Teme from Ludlow, York set up camp, digging huge earthwork defences and mounting cannon atop them. Late in the evening of 12 October the royal army came into sight, still flying the royal banners, and arranged their own camp within sight of the Yorkist army. The Parliament Rolls of November 1459 record the royalist perspective of the events. Before giving chase to the rebels, the king had given a speech to his men 'in so witty, so knightly, so manly and so cheering a style, with such a princely bearing and assured manner, in which the lords and people took such joy and comfort that their only desire was to hasten the fulfilment of your courageous knightly wish'.

The difficult terrain had slowed them down so that they had not arrived until evening was falling, by which time York and his allies had 'traitorously placed their troops, fortified their chosen ground, set carts with guns in front of their troops, made skirmishes and laid their ambushes there to take your army unawares'. Richard Beauchamp, Bishop of Salisbury, was sent with terms from the king to York. Henry would pardon them all, except a few who would bear the blame for Blore Heath, including Salisbury, if they dispersed immediately. It had been Margaret's force destroyed at Blore Heath and the offer bore a whiff of her desire for revenge. It also made the terms unpalatable to York, who would have to abandon a close ally, and certainly to Salisbury and his son Warwick. York's reply that Queen Margaret could not be trusted is clear evidence that he believed she was in control, while Warwick accused her of attempting to have him killed when he had been in London in November to answer the charges of piracy. Their assertion that battle on the morrow was welcome as the only way to resolve the matter was probably a bluff.

Parliament also recorded that York had put about a rumour that the king was dead, 'causing Mass to be said and attending it, all to make the people less afraid to give battle'. If this is true, it was a signal of desperation in the Yorkist camp, but York may have heard Mass at St Laurence's Church in Ludlow, or in the castle's chapel, on his own account, as he had done at Worcester. Those at Ludford on the duke's side would have reason and cause to explain away their presence at his expense.

As night fell the Yorkist cannon thundered out into the night, barking more in fear than anger. A night bombardment would never be accurate and was aimed more at frightening the enemy or preventing their rest, though those behind the guns can hardly have slept soundly with each crack of the artillery shaking the earth. The Parliament Rolls condemn York for firing 'at your most royal person, as well as at your lords and people then and there with you', though no casualties are recorded as a result of it. Perhaps sensing the desperate situation more keenly than others, or because he did not approve of being instructed to take the field against a king he had served for thirty years, Andrew Trollope led his men of the Calais garrison over the Yorkist earthworks, fleeing into the night and the arms of the king's pardon. When news reached the leadership of the defection of a core force within their army, they knew all was lost. The garrison was gone, but the effect on morale would be another blow, the knockout delivered by Trollope's ability to provide Henry's army with vital intelligence on the Yorkist encampment and their plans.

Around midnight, York, Salisbury, Warwick, March and Rutland left their army in the meadows at Ludford to retire to the castle for some refreshment. When morning broke the men found themselves gathering under banners that still stood but whose noble owners were nowhere to be found. The lords had moved to the castle for an emergency council of war. They had three choices.

Standing and fighting was risky and even winning could bring problems. If the king was defeated in the field, how was he to rule? It remains entirely possible that York still genuinely sought only peace, the removal of men most of the country believed were governing appallingly in the king's name, the decrease in influence of a queen generally mistrusted and disliked and the restoration of law, order, good governance and financial security. This was what he continually made oaths to affirm and tried to assure Henry of. His later actions have caused earlier motives to be questioned, but York had never yet threatened Henry nor challenged his right to rule and, while all of his promises may have been honey to sweeten the bitter pill of rebellion, it is often overlooked that he may have felt genuinely obliged to protect Henry and the country from what he saw as wrongdoers.

Their next option was to submit to the king and hope for mercy, but each man there surely knew what would follow such a decision. Salisbury had already been specifically excluded from the offer of pardon because of his role at Blore Heath. If they believed Henry acted under the control of Margaret, Somerset and others then surrender would be swiftly followed by arrest, the loss of all of their lands and titles and probably their lives too.

The third option was surely equally hard to swallow. The

Parliament Rolls record that Henry's presence 'struck the hearts of the said duke of York and earls from that most presumptuous pride into the most shameful cowardice imaginable'. Packing quickly and travelling light, York and the four earls fled into Wales before sunrise. It was indeed an act of cowardice that would have offended the honour of each man, yet they had little real choice. That they remained unwilling to fight Henry points to the truth of their lingering allegiance to him. That they could not surrender suggests their belief that they would not be delivering themselves into the hands of justice issued by Henry. Fleeing was no better option, but at least it offered a way to prevent bloodshed that day. The men drawn in from the north and the west could be spared the devil's choice of fighting for their lord or their king and each could take the king's pardon. York and the others would live to see another day, free but probably permanently outside the law.

The duke and his second son Edmund rode west and took a ship over to Ireland where York enjoyed a wealth of support. The Pale of Ireland, the small area around Dublin nominally under the control of the English crown was in fact all but independent and the royal writ did not run there. York and Rutland would be safe. Salisbury, Warwick and Edward, Earl of March, turned south, making for the aid of Sir John Denham. Sir John helped them through Devon and at the south coast they purchased a boat that carried them first to Guernsey and then on to Calais, where they dug in behind the stout walls of the town.

Another legend has arisen surrounding York's wife, Cecily Neville. It is certain that when York and the earls fled Ludlow they left behind Cecily, George and Richard. A story grew up that the noble duchess led her young sons out to the market cross to meet the royal army as it poured into the town. As with the story of Margaret at Mucklestone Church, there is no contemporary evidence to corroborate what is essentially a local myth documented much later. Whether the duchess and her boys stood at the market cross or hid behind the castle walls, their experience would have been one of fear as the vast royal host filed into the small town. Cecily and her sons were taken before King Henry, where she implored the king to allow her husband to plead his case. There was little chance of this and Cecily, George and Richard were placed into the care of the Duke of Buckingham, who was married to Cecily's sister Anne. Gregory describes how 'she was kept full straight and many a great rebuke', suggesting that she took the brunt of the ill feeling about her husband's actions in his absence. It is worth considering the effect of this experience upon a seven-year-old boy. Richard was caught up in an affair he could not understand, moved to a war camp, abandoned by his father and his dashing older brothers, left to the mercy of enemies and witness to something terrible.

The town of Ludlow would not escape lightly. Having supported the duke's preparations, supplying men and providing food and lodgings to the rebel force, Henry, or those making his decisions, sanctioned the punishment of the town. The royal army was unleashed upon Ludlow as though it were a defeated French town, sacking the castle too. Gregory records;

> The misrule of the king's gallants at Ludlow, when they had drunk enough of wine that was in taverns and in other places, they full ungodly smote out the heads of the pipes and hogs heads of wine, that men went wet-shod in wine, and then they robbed the town, and bore away bedding, clothe, and other stuff, and defouled many women.

York and his adherents would no longer be tolerated and those who offered them aid would suffer the consequences. The action had more of Margaret or Somerset's fingerprints to it than those of the peace-loving Henry, yet in his unstable state he may have been capable of such vengeance. The lesson was far from over for York, Salisbury, Warwick, March and Rutland, though. Parliament met on 20 November 1459 in Coventry. Writs had been issued summoning attendees on 9 October, before the events of Ludford Bridge, and its purpose was singular and crystal clear. Later dubbed the Parliament of Devils for its savage attack on the Yorkist faction, it roundly condemned a long list of knights and gentry involved with York as traitors.

The Parliament Roll gives great detail of the events building up to Ludford, beginning all the way back in 1450, when it was alleged that Jack Cade had sought to overthrow Henry and place York on the throne. The duke's continuous disruption of government was lamented and berated. St Albans was raked over, as was everything since, right up to Blore Heath and Ludford. An Act of Attainder was passed against Richard, Duke of York; Edward, Earl of March; Richard, Earl of Warwick; Richard, Earl of Salisbury; Edmund, Earl of Rutland, and others. In petitioning the king to enact the attainder, Parliament requested that these men all 'be reputed, taken, declared, adjudged, deemed and attainted of high treason, as false traitors and enemies to your most noble person, high majesty, crown and dignity'. Henry agreed to the enactment of the attainders, which stripped all of the men of every title and every piece of land that they owned. They were all common traitors now.

Those lords deemed to have remained loyal to the crown, which really meant those loyal to the court party headed by Queen Margaret and the Duke of Somerset, were required to each take a formal oath of allegiance to the king in Parliament. Three dukes, five earls and twenty-four other lords, along with both archbishops and sixteen bishops, gave their pledge. In turn, beginning with Lord Stourton, they stood and pledged the same oath, confirming Henry as their 'most dread sovereign lord, and rightfully by succession born to reign over me and all your liege people'. The oath also required them to swear fealty to Queen Margaret and to Prince Edward, 'my most dread lord the prince your first-born son'. This bears the fingerprints of the queen once more, as she fought to ensure that, should her husband's health fail again, it would be her who would rule in her son's name and that never again should the lords turn to York or any other but her.

Thomas, Lord Stanley, was also accused of treason by the Commons, who asked the king to attaint him also. They reminded Henry that although he had sent Stanley a summons from Nottingham, 'Lord Stanley, notwithstanding the said command, did not come to you; but William Stanley his brother, with many of the said lord's servants and tenants, a great number of people, went to the earl of Salisbury, and they were with the same earl at the attack upon your liege people at Blore Heath'. Furthermore, when another summons to arms was sent out in the name of Prince Edward, the Prince of Wales, Stanley 'falsely excused himself, saying that he was not then ready', even though he freely admitted that he had received the king's earlier order to be ready at a day's notice. His absence was cited as 'a major reason for the defeat and discomfiture of your said people at Blore Heath'.

The charge continues to berate Lord Stanley, accusing him of ignoring further orders to appear and of failing to arrive when he promised that he would. Stanley requested permission to lead the vanguard against Salisbury to allay the obvious suspicion that he was held in, but was denied and ordered to bring his men to join the royal army. He failed again to do this and during the battle 'was within six miles of the said heath at the same time, accompanied by 2,000 men, and stayed with the same company for the next three days at Newcastle', which was only six miles away from the queen's base at Eccleshall Castle. After sending a flimsy excuse to the queen the morning after the battle, Stanley simply 'departed for home again'. Furthermore, Stanley was accused of writing a letter of congratulation to Salisbury following the earl's victory 'trusting to God that he should be with the same earl in another place, to stand him in as good stead as he should have done if he had been with them there' and of preventing residents of Wirral and Maxfield from going to the king's army as they had been summoned to do.

Finally, the impeachment states that Stanley's retainers, wearing his livery, were alongside his brother William's men at Blore Heath and several were captured in the forest of Morfe the day after the battle. A cook from Stanley's household was among the wounded left at Drayton and he told the Earl of Shrewsbury's men that 'he had been sent to the said earl of Salisbury, in the name of the said Lord Stanley, with more of his company'. The soldiers captured at Morfe were executed, but not before they had confessed that they had been sent to William Stanley's side by Lord Stanley 'to assist the said earl to carry out his aims'.

With that the Commons requested that Stanley be arrested and imprisoned to face trial as a traitor. Henry's reply was simply that he would consider the matter further. This was an early escape for a man who would make a career of this kind of careful tightrope walking, offering secret support to both sides and open aid to neither. Whether his brother William possessed more conviction or was simply an instrument of Lord Stanley is a matter for debate, but his allegiance certainly seems to have remained more consistent.

The combined effect of all that had gone before and which had reached a head at Blore Heath, Ludford and in Parliament was to tip the two sides beyond the point of no return. Margaret's fear was real, whether its basis was true or imagined, and she would not tolerate the perpetuation of a threat to her husband and her son. York had tried to act within the bounds of his political power but was now left with nothing to lose and nowhere to go. The divide had always previously been between the Yorkists and the court party. It was now, after the events of 1459, that it was to spiral into a dynastic conflict between the House of Lancaster and the House of York. Determining right and wrong and picking a side will always be a matter of perspective, as much now as it was then, depending upon interpretation and preference. Either York was a ruthless, ambitious man who pushed Margaret into a corner so that she, like a lioness, defended her young cub, or else Margaret was the uncompromising aggressor whose paranoia drove York, a man trying only to restore the kingdom he had watched disintegrate in the name of a king he was steadfastly loyal to, into a position he had never intended or wished to occupy. As with so many things, the truth is probably contained within the shades of grey between the black and the white. One thing is for certain: King Henry must shoulder a large portion of the blame for the nation's dissent into anarchy.

8

The Wheel Turns Once More

The attainted lords of the Yorkist faction were not idle in their exile, nor were they afforded any peace as the crown hunted them. A campaign was underway to deprive them of support. One paper that was circulated compared York and his allies to a rotten tooth in England's mouth. 'Is it better to pull him out and so make a gap in my mouth, the which I know well is not good, or else to plaster him to the confusion and undoing of all the other, and at the last he will fall according to his nature.' The vitriolic piece concluded, 'They have been inextirpable, they have been incurable.' Somerset was made Captain of Calais, but first had to root Warwick out of there. For their part, the Yorkists were writing to sympathisers all over England insisting that they had been wronged and intended to return.

Somerset took a large fleet over to Calais to claim the rich captaincy that had once belonged to his father. Trollope's defection from Warwick may have offered hope that the earl could be unseated, but when Somerset arrived and ordered the gates of Calais to be opened they remained tightly sealed, with Warwick, Salisbury and March safely inside. Somerset managed to get into Guisnes Castle, a fortress in the Pale of Calais, but could not force his way into the town proper. When Queen Margaret commissioned Richard Woodville, Lord Rivers, to reinforce Somerset and bolster his attempts to capture Calais, a fleet was amassed at Sandwich. The Paston Letters record Warwick's daring raid on the fleet, led by John Dynham. His men ghosted in under cover of darkness and stole away with the ships. Not only that, but when they found Lord Rivers asleep beside his wife, he was seized along with his son, Anthony Woodville, and both were hauled over to Calais as prisoners.

Richard Woodville was the son of a chamberlain to Henry VI's uncle John, Duke of Bedford. Richard had served as a soldier in France and had a solid reputation. When Bedford died in 1435 it was just a year later that Richard Woodville married the duke's widow, Jacquetta of Luxembourg, Duchess of Bedford. Jacquetta was a daughter of Peter of Luxembourg, Count of Saint-Pol, and the marriage had caused a scandal when it became public knowledge. Richard had received a barony in an attempt to smooth over the gulf in their social standing, but as a firm adherent to the court party who owed his position to the favour of the enemies of the Yorkists, the three earls could not resist the chance to vent their spleens at him and he was hauled before them at Calais. William Paston recorded:

> And there my Lord of Salisbury rated him, calling him a knave's son, that he should be so rude to call him and these other lords traitors, for they all shall be found the king's true liege men, when he should be found a traitor. And my Lord of Warwick rated him, and said that his father was but a squire, and brought up with King Henry the Vth, and sithen himself made by marriage, and also made lord, and that it was not his part to have such language of lords, being of the king's blood. And my Lord of March rated him in like wise. And Sir Anthony was rated for his language of all three lords in like wise.

If this was the first time Richard and Anthony Woodville met Edward, Earl of March, it was not to be the last. Richard was to become Edward's father-in-law in a few years' time, becoming Earl Rivers. Edward's bride was never to lose the taint of what was perceived as her low birth and given Edward's taunting of her father he could have little complaint at that. This episode at Calais must have made family occasions a little awkward for a time, though.

All of this was contained in the uncertain future that lay before

York and his adherents. In March 1460, Warwick managed to get out of Calais and visit York at Waterford in Ireland. It is testament to Warwick's skill and flair that he was able to slip out of a besieged city and slip back in again on his return. It is also a mark of his ascendancy that it was he rather than his father or the duke's son who was chosen to visit York, although perhaps he was the only one foolhardy enough to attempt the voyage.

What was discussed at Waterford is not recorded in any surviving source. It is sensible to conclude that the events that followed had been agreed to be the way forward. Letters into England had been warmly received by men and regions suffering under Henry's weak rule and the chaos that was spreading like a disease throughout the land. In spite of York's part in the opening of these now infected wounds, he seems to have been viewed by many as the only man capable of healing the sickness that afflicted England.

The plan sprang into action on 26 June 1460 when Warwick, apparently from this point onwards accepted by all as the leader of the invasion, landed at Sandwich with around 2,000 men accompanied by Salisbury, March and William Neville, Lord Fauconberg, Salisbury's younger brother. Fauconberg was a towering military figure. A veteran of the wars in France, his reputation was probably in excess of that of his older brother. At St Albans he had fought for the royal army but during York's second Protectorate had been courted by the duke and appointed to the Council. Since then he had grown close to his nephew Warwick, acting as his deputy in Calais and partaking in his piracy in the Channel. Fauconberg's defection to the Yorkist cause, which may seem natural given the ties of blood that existed, was a huge boost to their hopes and a blow to the king's party. Although his reputation today is overshadowed by his nephew's, Fauconberg, in his day, was possibly the best and most highly respected military leader and sailor in the family.

There was some small-scale resistance at Sandwich, but it was quickly overcome and Warwick began to move north toward London. As he moved through Kent, the men of that county, ever ready to rise up and storm the capital, flocked to his side. Warwick seems to have been possessed of a natural magnetism and likeability rivalled only by that developed by Edward, Earl of

March. Men loved him, not least for his exploits on the sea against the French. His reach extended all the way to the heart of the capital. The merchants there found Warwick's control of the seas and even his piratical activities toward the Hanseatic League and Spanish merchant ships benefitted their business. Warwick was a frequent visitor to London before his exile, a rich man who loved to spend his money, a combination that purchased for him the certain love of the City of London and its merchants.

Henry was still in the Midlands and London was in the care of the Lords Scales and Hungerford. Scales, the same man who had held the Tower against Cade's rebellion, doubtless feared witnessing a repeat of the terror a decade earlier, made all the worse by the presence of three earls and a baron at the head of the force approaching out of Kent. Scales and Hungerford ordered the gates to be closed and locked against the oncoming mass of humanity. They were roundly ignored as another of Salisbury's sons, George Neville, Bishop of Exeter, had the gates opened to allow his father, uncle, brother and cousin entry into the capital. Scales and Hungerford withdrew into the Tower and refused to surrender it.

Lord Scales reacted to the second threat he was to face from a mob seizing control of the capital in an extreme manner. He was heading toward his mid-sixties now, having been a soldier and commander for nearly forty years. The reasons for his reaction are hard to fathom. Perhaps he was concerned that his substantial military record was in danger of being overshadowed by failure at home. Cade had held the city and now Warwick, in his early thirties, half Scales' age, was trying to do the same. Experience had taught him that the king would not come to his aid and that he would have to help himself. Perhaps the chaos of a decade earlier had left a deep scar on the old soldier that caused him to panic and lash out in fear.

As the knot of Warwick's soldiers, Kentish men and London residents approached the castle Lord Scales ordered the artillery on the Tower's walls to open fire. Cannon thundered gun stones (an early form of shot) into the crowd, wreaking wild and reckless destruction. Scales went further, though. There existed within the Tower a weapon of almost legendary status. The Byzantine Empire had called it Greek Fire. In England, it was known as Wildfire. A thick substance every bit as dangerous to those using it as to its target, it was notoriously unstable and difficult to handle. It would burst into flames on impact with anything, clinging and burning hotter and hotter. Water made it worse. The Byzantines had used Greek Fire primarily as a naval weapon, coating the surface of the water in a seemingly impossible sheet of flame that could not be extinguished.

Recipes for this toxic chemical weapon are all but lost and probably varied widely based on what was available at the maker's location, but the basis of the substance was probably petroleum mixed with sulphur and other combustible substances to add to the explosive destruction it would cause. The closest modern parallel is napalm, and this was what Lord Scales unleashed upon his own countrymen in July 1460. If the cannon fire had caused fear, the terror was surely amplified as the long metallic tubes that would have been recognisable today as a form of flamethrower spewed the horrifying substance down onto the crowd packed together outside the Tower's walls.

Running was not an option. The wildfire clung on tight, following wherever the victim went, leaping onto anything and anyone the carrier touched. Jumping into the nearby Thames would only make it worse, causing the foul substance to burn hotter still and set the river aflame. Lord Scales succeeded in repelling the horde but he also ensured that he would be despised by his victims, their family and friends for evermore.

The Yorkists laid siege to the Tower of London on 2 July and a few days later Warwick, Fauconberg and March departed north toward the king's base in the Midlands. Several contemporary chronicles credit Warwick with a force of 60,000 men, though others cite 80,000 or even more, marching from London at his back. Robert Bale recorded the huge host leaving London in two parts, one heading towards St Albans and the other to Ware. He believed that this was because the king's army had moved south to Northampton, but that his lords were encouraging him to seek refuge on the easily defensible Isle of Ely. Estimates of the king's force vary wildly from 12,000 to 50,000. The variances make it impossible to pinpoint exact numbers, but all seem to concur that Warwick's army was larger than the king's.

On the morning of 10 July Warwick's forces arrived together outside Northampton, soaked to the bone by heavy summer rains that had turned the ground to thick, sucking mud. *An English Chronicle* records that, upon his arrival, Warwick sent 'certain bishops' to the king to beg an audience for the earl, who wished only to swear his loyalty. Humphrey Stafford, Duke of Buckingham, stood beside the king, his face showing the scars of the injury he had received at St Albans. Buckingham berated the clergymen for coming before the king 'not as bishops to treat for peace, but as men of arms'. When the bishops retorted that the Yorkists had brought so many men only for protection against their enemies around the king, Buckingham sent them away with a flea in their ear, warning, 'The earl of Warwick shall not come to the king's presence, and if he comes he shall die.'

Negotiations to avoid a battle were an accepted part of the politics of chivalry. None should wish for the spilling of Christian blood and so must do all that they could to avoid conflict. At least, they should appear to do so. The veracity of such a parley is always hard to determine and it seems likely that Warwick knew it had to come to a fight. Nevertheless, to his credit, the earl persisted. *An English Chronicle* explains how Warwick next sent a herald of arms to ask Henry to supply hostages for Warwick's safe conduct into and out of his presence, but this messenger was sent away too. In a final effort to avoid fighting, Warwick sent one more message to Henry that 'at two hours after noon, he would speak with him, or else die in the field'.

The royal army had not been idle since its arrival at Northampton. It had taken up a position near Delapre Abbey that put the River Nene at its back. A sound defensive tactic, it also precluded any hope of retreat. As Cade had done at Blackheath and York had done at Ludford, they dug earthwork defences, planted wooden spikes and mounted guns atop their barricades. Unlike those other occasions the effectiveness of these defences was now to be tested. As two o'clock came with no safe passage to the king, Warwick gathered his men to give them two important orders. *An English Chronicle* records his instruction that 'no man was to lay hands upon the king nor on the common people, but only on lords, knight and squires', while the Burgundian Waurin reported that Warwick had told his commanders that any who wore the black ragged staff livery of Lord Grey of Ruthin should not be harmed, 'for it was they who were to give them entry to the park'.

It appears that Edmund Grey, Lord Grey of Ruthin, had made contact with Warwick before hostilities began to offer to switch sides and help them breach the defences. Grey was a great-grandson via his mother of John of Gaunt, Edward III's son from whom the Lancastrian kings were descended, and the reasons for his defection seem to lie deep in a property dispute which he felt might be better resolved if Warwick were to win the day. This kind of score settling was to define the coming war every bit as much as the machinations of the major figures. It was the constant refuge of men of any rank, preserving their own interests against the prevailing winds of fortune by switching side or fuelling greater disputes that would provide a constant stream of fuel to keep the fires of war burning so long.

On the sopping mud, as he surveyed the daunting royal defences with rain lashing his face, Warwick could not have been certain Grey's offer was not a trap. He led the centre of his army himself, facing the Duke of Buckingham at the royal centre. On Warwick's left was his uncle, Fauconberg, and the right flank was commanded by York's heir Edward, Earl of March, who, at eighteen, may well have been chomping at the bit for his first taste of real battle after the debacle at Ludlow. With Grey on the left of the royal army, it was March who would find out whether his offer was genuine or not.

Abbot John Whethamstede, who had described the horror in the streets of St Albans after the battle there, recorded what happened as trumpets sounded and the cluttering mass of Warwick's army marched toward the royal position. March's army reached the barricades and 'as the attacking squadrons came to the ditch before the royalist rampart and wanted to climb over it, which they could not quickly do because of the height ... the lord with his men met them and, seizing them by the hand, hauled them into the embattled field'. March and his men set about butchering their way through the royal army, stunning Buckingham and his comrades. Their plan had relied upon holding the barricade and the man entrusted with control of their left wing was helping the enemy over it.

[handwritten margin note: Wrong! Mowat was on Warwick's left flank Grey. Warwick centre flank Baurlait and Buckingham and Fauconberg on right flank Salisbury.]

Sources variously time the fighting that followed at between half an hour and two hours, and casualty figures run from less than sixty to over 1,200. It is certain that the royal force was utterly crushed and their strong defensive position now turned against them. *An English Chronicle* noted the devastating effect of the damp weather and soaked ground: 'The ordnance of the king's guns availed not, for that day was so great rain, that the guns lay deep in water and so were quiet and may not be shot'. The rain had ruined the gunpowder and kept the cannon silent, but as those who had hoped for safety behind the barricade turned to run, they were faced with the impassable obstacle of the swollen River Nene. *An English Chronicle* laments that 'many were slain, and many were fled, and were drowned in the river'. Caught between a rock and a hard place, some perished at the end of a sword, while others were dragged down into the Nene by their heavy armour.

Among those who fell in the battle was the fifty-seven-year-old Humphrey Stafford, Duke of Buckingham. A great-grandson of Edward III, Humphrey was considered a pillar of chivalry and seems to have tried to heal the rifts between his brother-in-law and his king. In the end, though, he had been unable to forgo the oaths of loyalty that he had made to Henry VI. However ineffectual the king might be, he was still king. God had placed him there and Humphrey had sworn to do all that he could to keep him there. He died keeping his oath.

Also among the fallen were John Talbot, 2nd Earl of Shrewsbury, and the thirty-seven-year-old Thomas Percy, Lord Egremont. A perennial thorn in the Neville family's side, Egremont had led the raid on the Neville wedding party and seen his father slain at St Albans. Warwick must have taken some pleasure in Egremont's demise, both personally, for the trouble Thomas had caused his family, and because it was a body blow to the Percy family, who, aside from being mortal enemies of Warwick's house, were also firmly tied to the royal cause.

Warwick, Fauconberg and March found the king and had him taken to the dry safety of his tent. Here, they each pledged their loyalty to him once more, assuring him that their only quarrel had been with the evil men who had surrounded him. Their actions at least suggest some degree of honesty in their protestations. The three lords had the king alone in his tent. All of the great men who had protected the king were gone. If their plan at this point was to depose Henry then they had the perfect opportunity to have him murdered and found among the dead on the field, accidentally caught up in the fighting. They did not do so, and Henry was escorted back to London.

By the time Warwick returned to London, his father had broken the siege of the Tower. Although Scales had continued to fire cannon into the city, the residents had located and appropriated some ordnance of their own and returned the bombardment. Between the threat of breaching the walls and several days of starvation, Scales and Hungerford petitioned Salisbury for terms of surrender. Both men were given safe conduct out of London in return for handing the Tower over to the earl. Lord Hungerford escaped, but when Lord Scales tried to slip out of the Tower by boat he was spotted by Londoners unable to forgive his cruel treatment of them and their city. His boat was attacked and the old soldier was killed, his body thrown into the Thames to wash up ignominiously downriver a few days later.

Warwick set about taking control of the government, and his already blossoming reputation as a charismatic statesman was further enhanced. A report from England to Milan written in July 1460 that can be found among the state papers of the period describes the situation after Northampton, carrying information about the imminent return of the Duke of York and also reporting Warwick's intention to make York's son March king in Henry's place. The letter focusses heavily on Warwick's leading role in recent events, concluding, 'Thus one may say that today everything is in Warwick's power and the war at an end, and that he has done marvellous things. God grant him grace to keep the country in peace and union!' The earl's continental reputation was flourishing as news of his brave daring spread far and wide. Warwick's two brothers Sir John and Sir Thomas, captured after Blore Heath, were freed, having escaped execution in the intervening time.

Queen Margaret had been at Eccleshall Castle awaiting news from Northampton. When it arrived, it must have horrified her. Her husband was once again the prisoner of her enemies and her cause was in tatters. With her son she fled west toward Wales.

Gregory reports that her journey was fraught and filled with danger. At Malpass Castle, west of Crewe, she was met by one of her servants, a man she had promoted and installed in her son's household, but who, in her hour of need, 'spoiled her and robbed her, and put her so in doubt of her life and her son's life' that she could find no refuge she trusted until she reached the security of her husband's half-brother Jasper Tudor, Earl of Pembroke.

Just as Margaret had seen her enemies driven out of England, she was in her turn a fugitive. Her young son was on the run with her and a Yorkist government was being reinstalled in London. Warwick's brother George, who had opened the gates of London to them, was created Lord Chancellor and given custody of the Privy Seal. The Nevilles had snatched control of king and country, and if Margaret feared that worse was to come she was to be proven right. Parliament was summoned for 7 October and it was a session that would define the very nature of the conflict that was ripping England apart.

9

New Wounds

In a search for the date of the beginning of the Wars of the Roses, 10 October 1460 cannot be overlooked. If the troubles that had blighted England over the last decade can be characterised as a fight for control of the weak king and his ailing government, then on this date it was transformed into the dynastic struggle for the throne that is more recognisable as the Wars of the Roses. Until this date, the opposition of Richard, Duke of York, to the court party was considered and careful, always wrapped in the armour of overtly professed loyalty to Henry. When York arrived at Westminster on this day something had dramatically changed. He strode to the vacant throne and placed a hand on it, clearly signalling his intention to claim the crown of England. There was to be no rapturous response, though. The hall fell silent until the Archbishop of Canterbury uncomfortably asked Richard whether he wished to see the king. All had not gone according to plan.

York had delayed his return from Ireland until the second week in September, two full months after the Battle of Northampton. He had landed in Cheshire and taken a month more to make his way to London, travelling under the arms of England and France now, as a king might, rather than his livery of York. He visited his wife, now freed from her sister's custody along with her other children. It had the air of a casual royal progress but the calmness surely belied great tension and no little uncertainty. Abbot Whethamstede of St Albans describes Richard's momentous change of direction at Westminster, noting that he 'walked straight on until he came to the king's throne, upon the covering or cushion laying his hand, in this very act like a man about to take possession of his right, he held it upon it for a short time'. After lingering a moment, his heart in his throat, he turned to the gathered lords and 'looked eagerly for their applause'. The silence was deafening.

This incident is often viewed as the arrogant fulfilment of York's long-held desire. Certainly Queen Margaret would see it that way, but that is to forget twenty-five years of service, the last ten doing all that was within his power to avoid a situation where Henry was unseated while desperately protecting his own interests. York had been presented with successive opportunities to replace Henry if he had wished. Who was to know if Henry succumbed to his illness in 1453? He could easily have perished from that terrible wound sustained at St Albans. Even after this, Henry was in York's power during a second Protectorate but emerged unscathed.

Henry's kingdom had suffered a decade of radical policy shifts, lurching between polar opposite leaderships and crying out for a strong figurehead who could never hold any rank other than king. Henry was not the man for this job and his continued presence there promised more of the same for decades to come. York must have seen this and finally decided to act conclusively. He might well have been deeply uncertain about this move and his hesitance, as well as giving the lie to the notion that he had wanted this all along, was a part of the problem. He and his allies probably looked to the example of King Henry's grandfather's deposition of Richard II. What they appear to have underestimated was the gulf of difference in the prevailing circumstances.

Richard II had grown deeply unpopular. Mistrusted and despised as a tyrant, the country had been ripe for Bolingbroke's usurpation and his challenge to Richard's throne had been warmly welcomed. Bolingbroke, then Earl of Derby and seeking to claim his inheritance as Duke of Lancaster after his father's death, landed at Ravenspur in Yorkshire and slowly made his way south, his support swelling as he travelled until the tidal wave of popular opinion and noble support saw him lay a hand upon the throne. The Duke of York, seeking to reclaim his own lands and titles from exile, made a similarly leisurely journey through England but failed to attract the same support that had seen Henry IV carried to the throne. The main difference lay in the personality of the kings to be deposed.

Although Henry VI's government was farcical, but for the damage it was doing to the country, there remained a great well of affection for the king's person. Richard II had been feared and hated. He had taken to depriving great lords of lands and inheritance on a whim, and that made anyone with anything to lose very nervous. Henry's government was atrocious, but fault for this could be laid at those around him, either the court party or the Yorkists, depending upon the viewpoint, as well as his lack of will. At the core, he was a nice man who had done nothing to earn the hatred of his subjects. Henry had been king for almost thirty years by this point, since he was a baby. Many had known no other king, and those who had still loved the son for the father. Henry V's ghost loomed over the Lancastrian dynasty and still afforded his incompetent son some protection. York misjudged the situation and, in doing so, embarrassed himself and all of those present within the Painted Chamber.

A few possibilities exist to explain this change in York's policy and direction. The first is simply that he saw no other way to resolve the matter. He had shown himself to be a competent and direct ruler in France, Ireland and during both Protectorates. Following Northampton, his faction had control of the government for the fourth time in a decade. The last three times their ascendancy had been short-lived, and each rise was followed by a fall deeper and darker than the last. Henry could not be relied upon to arbitrate fairly and had gone back on his word more than once in the face of pressure from his favourites. The country was a mess and York perhaps believed that the only way it could be straightened out, for the nation's good and also for his own personal comfort, was with a change at the very top. If this was the case he seriously underestimated the authority and personal affection that still lingered about Henry.

The turning point might also have come at York's meeting with Warwick at Waterford before the earl's landing at Sandwich and subsequent victory at Northampton. Warwick was a daring figure, without a doubt more willing to take a big risk than York had shown himself to be. Warwick may have made his voyage to take a message from Salisbury and March, saying that they believed the only way forward was to press a claim to the throne. He might have felt the need to personally convince the cautious duke that it was the right decision and then offered to seize the initiative on his behalf by defeating the royal forces and capturing the king to clear a path for York. In this scenario, the time the duke took to reach London could have provided an opportunity to think through what was planned and to formulate a legal basis for his challenge. This explanation, however, relies upon Warwick making several false oaths of loyalty and failing to lead any applause when York placed his hand upon the throne. Indeed, the silence within the Painted Chamber raises the question of whether any of York's allies knew what he was planning to do.

Another figure at work during this period was the papal legate Bishop Coppini of Terni. Coppini had been despatched in 1459 by Pope Pius II to encourage Henry VI to support a crusade against the Turks. Coppini's patron was Francesco Sforza, Duke of Milan, who gave his envoy the secondary objective of encouraging an invasion of France that would keep Charles VII's eye out of Italy. Given short shrift by Queen Margaret, Coppini had skulked off to Burgundy to nurse his wounded pride. Warwick, ever the opportunist, had courted Coppini, assuring the bishop that his aid would help to resolve the internal conflict in England and free the way for a Yorkist-controlled government to invade France as his master wished. Flattered by the attention, Coppini took up the Yorkist cause, landing with Warwick at Sandwich. In London he had preached in Warwick's favour to the English bishops and wrote to King Henry advising him to receive the Yorkist lords for an audience and to hear their cause. Coppini was at the Battle of Northampton when Henry was captured and began to overestimate his own importance to the Yorkist effort, his ego inflated by the flattery of Warwick's silver tongue. Coppini might have had an audience with York, either in Ireland when Warwick visited or after the duke's landing in Cheshire and nonchalantly advised the overthrow of the feeble and troublesome King Henry. It was, after all, how things were done in his native Italy and Henry's government would never share Coppini's master's aims.

However York arrived at this course, it was ill advised and

poorly executed. The three months between Northampton and the claim had allowed a perception to settle that all was remaining the same. The heat of the victory had dissipated and York's gesture fell upon a stone-cold room. The slow arrival may have been a symptom of uncertainty on the duke's part, of buying time to formulate his legal arguments or even of a desire not to seem too keen for the main prize. Sadly, the precise point at which Richard, Duke of York, decided to change his policy and the cause of such a radical *volte-face* are lost in myth and opinion, but the fact that it happened speaks volumes of Henry's lack of control over his country, his peers and his people. How much longer could the country continue to see violent upheavals and reversals of power before a final solution had to be imposed from some quarter? Queen Margaret and the Duke of York had evolved into implacable enemies. Neither would tolerate the other and Henry could not impose terms upon them. York was a wounded animal with nothing left to lose and everything to gain. Margaret was a proud mother defending home, hearth and family. Perhaps the only real surprise is that the establishment was so stunned by this development.

Yet the shock was very real. Six days later, on 16 October, York had the Chancellor, George Neville, present his detailed claim to the throne, which meticulously laid out the lineage of Henry and of York from Edward III. The thrust of York's claim lay in descent of right through the female line. Henry was descended from John of Gaunt, Duke of Lancaster, the third surviving son of Edward III. York's male line ancestry fell from Edmund of Langley, Duke of York, Edward III's fourth son. However, Richard could also claim descent from Lionel of Antwerp, Duke of Clarence, whose daughter Philippa had married Roger Mortimer. Their son, another Roger, was York's maternal grandfather and he claimed that at the time Richard II was deposed, Philippa's grandson Edmund Mortimer had been heir apparent. There is some justification for this claim, and Edmund was treated as the heir of the childless Richard II. York's case was therefore based on the descent of the right of Edward III's second son to him, which was senior to the right descended to Henry from Edward's third son. It was tenuous, but not without merit.

It was reported that as York presented his claim to Parliament in the House of Lords a crown that decorated a chandelier in the Commons toppled from its perch with no movement or breeze, clattering to the floor of the chamber. At the same time another crown sitting high upon Dover Castle also fell to the ground. To superstitious onlookers the portents were dark and clear. The signs were deemed to be signals that Henry's kingship had fallen, his dynasty was toppled and a change was coming.

The document presented to Parliament by York is also interesting because it bears the first written instance of the use of the family name of the dynasty in power since Henry II in 1154. York is described as 'Richard Plantagenet, commonly called duke of York' in the description of his ancestry. Never before had this name been used as a surname for the ruling family. The origins of the name are somewhat obscure and appear to relate to the use of a sprig of yellow broom worn as a badge by Henry II's father Geoffrey, Count of Anjou. The French for this piece of plant was *planta genista*, which earned Geoffrey a nickname that eventually became Plantagenet. The name must have born some significance prior to 1460 in order to warrant inclusion in a document designed to magnify York's descent from rightful kings, and it must have carried some currency in the circles of power or it would not have been included, but this use of it appears to be the first official recording of a name now applied to a dynasty that ruled England for 331 years.

A state of panic gripped Parliament. York demanded a swift answer to his claim and the issue became a hot coal none would grasp. The Parliament Rolls chart the nervous chaos that ensued as the issue was passed around. Firstly, 'it was thought and agreed by all the lords that they should all go to the king to announce and explain the said matter to his highness, and to learn what his good grace wished to be done about it'. There was a certain safety in numbers as all of the peers present herded to the king's chamber to ask him whether he wished to oppose a claim that would topple him from his throne. They were surely glad that Queen Margaret was not there to hear them ask. Henry simply asked the lords to search as best they could for anything which might be objected to in the claim of the duke. It was hardly the rousing rebuttal the lords may have hoped for. In return, the lords 'begged the king to search his memory to see if he could find any reasonable matter that might be objected against the said claim and title, because his said highness had seen and understood many different writings and chronicles'.

The lords were in an impossible position. Their duty to the king was to defend his throne, but if York did prevail he was unlikely to take kindly to those who had opposed his attempts to claim his right. Similarly, if they failed to resist York and he was to be removed from authority once more, they would be forced to explain their actions to the king, or even his formidable and less forgiving wife. Either course laid them open to a charge of treason later, so it can hardly be surprising that they wanted Henry to compile his own response to York's petition. The request may also have been a desperate plea to Henry to fight for his rights, as he had never done so with real conviction before. If the king was happy to meekly leave this for others to decide then what kind of a king was he? Most surely knew the answer by now but reached out to him with a final olive branch, hoping to spark something within a man in whom they were desperate to find vindication of their faith.

Two days after York had submitted his claim, on 18 October, the lords summoned the king's justices and ordered them in the king's name to investigate the matter and find any objections that might be offered. A further two days later the justices returned with the hot coal. They refused to offer an opinion 'because the matter was so high, and touched the king's high estate and regality which was above the law and surpassed their learning'. The justices were too afraid to involve themselves in the argument and passed it back to the lords. Next, the king's attorney and his sergeants were summoned. Their reply was simply that 'since the said matter was so high that it surpassed the learning of the justices, it must needs exceed their learning'. The Chancellor refused to relieve the attorney of his duty, for which he was paid his wage. The atmosphere must have been fraught within the walls of the Painted Chamber as none were willing to grasp the matter.

Finally George Neville, as Chancellor, resorted to instructing each of the lords present to go away and find objections to York's claim. They were to return, at liberty to speak freely on the matter, and each was to present at least one objection. Once compiled, the most compelling of these arguments would form the response to be given to the duke. It seems that in spite of their best efforts the lords had been unable to shirk their ultimate responsibility to defend the king's right to his throne. There followed the presentation of the objections that they had arrived at and a few days later York returned with his response to each doubt.

The first objection raised was that the lords felt bound by the oaths that they had frequently made to Henry as their king, most recently in the Parliament at Coventry. The lords did not feel capable of simply ignoring such weighty oaths. To this, York entered a response that 'no man may discharge himself by his own deed or act, promise or oath from this bond and duty of obedience to God's law', reasoning that no duty was higher than that owed to God and that if God's law decreed that Richard was king, then no oath taken by any man could hold against that truth.

Secondly the lords pointed to the numerous Acts of Parliament that had confirmed the House of Lancaster as rightful kings and legitimised the succession of their heirs. These Acts, the lords contended, conferred greater right than any other evidence. In reply to this York contended that there had not been the profusion of Acts referred to by the lords, but only one passed by Henry IV in 1406 which formally settled the crown on Henry, his heirs and the heirs of his four sons. This very Act, York suggested, was evidence of the fault in the title of the first king of the House of Lancaster, for 'if he had obtained and enjoyed the said crowns, etc., by inheritance, descent or succession, he would neither have needed nor have requested and caused them to be granted to him in such a way'. The logic was faultless. If Henry IV had truly been king he would not have needed to pass an Act of Parliament to confirm the fact. The existence of that Act denied Henry's legitimate right.

The lords next pointed out that Richard had always borne the livery and arms of Edmund of Langley and the House of York, never those of Lionel of Antwerp, Duke of Clarence, so his sudden claim that this was his primary line of descent was flawed and simply a convenient reference used to defeat Henry's title. To this York simply replied that he could have borne the arms of Lionel of Antwerp at any time, had he wished, 'but he abstained from bearing the said arms, as he abstained for a time from seeking and pursuing his right and title, etc., for reasons not unknown to the entire realm'. To this he added the dark, thinly veiled but erudite threat that 'although right for a time rests and is silenced, yet it does not rot nor shall it perish'.

To these replies the lords could offer no further objection. Somewhere in the panic stricken corridors of power, someone suddenly hit upon an idea, a compromise solution that offered what everyone wanted. On 25 October 1460, forty-five years after the king's father had stood victorious against a French horde in the knee-deep mud of Agincourt, his son was being presented with a plan that would end their dynasty's rule. The lords had devised a scheme that would 'save the king's honour and estate' while meeting Richard's demands. King Henry would remain upon the throne for the rest of his life, or until he chose to abdicate his responsibility, after which York and his heirs would succeed as kings. In this way, all could preserve their oaths to Henry, including York, and after Henry the crown would pass to those deemed to hold the greater right.

The Chancellor made a request to the House of Lords that, since it would fall to him to take the compromise offer before the king, they should all stand with him no matter how the king took it. To this they all agreed but their fears seem unwarranted. It was reported in the Parliament Rolls that Henry, 'to avoid the shedding of Christian blood, by good and serious deliberation and the advice of all his lords spiritual and temporal, agreed to the settlement'. The compromise was enacted by Parliament, named the Act of Accord, and provided also for an income of 10,000 marks for York and his heirs from royal estates to reflect their positions as heirs to the throne. York, followed by his two oldest sons Edward, Earl of March, and Edmund, Earl of Rutland, took an oath to uphold the agreement and Henry's rights under it.

In the name of God, amen. I, Richard, duke of York, promise and swear by the faith and truth that I owe to Almighty God, that I shall never do, agree, instigate or incite, directly or indirectly, in private or in public, or as far as I can or shall be able, allow to be done, agreed, instigated or incited, anything which may cause or lead to the shortening of the natural life of King Henry VI, or the harm or injury of his reign or royal dignity, by violence or in any other way, against his freedom and liberty: but that if any person or persons would do or presume anything to the contrary, I shall oppose it with all my power and strength, and cause it to be withstood as best I may; so help me God, and these holy gospels.

York also pledged to support the lords against any enemies and in their turn the lords swore that they would treat Richard and his sons as the rightful heirs to the throne. Parliament declared that anyone trying to kill the duke or plot against him would be guilty of treason to reinforce York's position. This was aimed squarely at Margaret, Somerset and the court party. In all of the jubilance unleashed by the finding of a compromise acceptable to and accepted by all parties, the obvious issues with putting the theory into practice appear to have passed everyone by.

If the provision preventing acts and conspiracies against York was designed to offer protection against Margaret and her allies, then this was at least an acknowledgement of the potential for trouble. However meekly Henry had given in to York's argument, or under whatever pressure he had been placed, he had effectively acknowledged that he was not the rightful king. He would retain his crown on the basis that it was constitutionally awkward to take it from him so that he would not really be affected by the change of succession. The real harm was done to Prince Edward, who was to be relegated to the position of Duke of Lancaster, his old family title. Born into royalty, he was now firmly ejected from that birth right.

Prince Edward had just passed his seventh birthday and how much he might understand is a matter for debate, but his mother was under no illusion as to the meaning of the Act of Accord. Her precious son had been disinherited and would not be king. Her own position was no better, for her enemies had permanent control of the government sanctioned by Parliament and the man she hated most in all the world would take the throne she believed belonged to her son. Somerset knew that his comfortable flow of patronage would be at an end and his influence with it. Others such as Northumberland, Exeter and Lord Clifford would be acutely aware that they were now on the outside, where they had so enjoyed seeing York, Salisbury and Warwick languish only months earlier. Far from a final solution, this was simply another revolution in the fortunes of bitter enemies.

It is questionable whether the compromise really suited anyone other than the lords, who had been able to walk a fine tightrope with a fatal fall on either side. The king was nearly thirty-nine years old but York was a decade older, having turned forty-nine just before his return to London. In spite of his breakdowns Henry did not appear likely to succumb to anything fatal in the near future and might well outlive York. If the crown had been York's ambition all along he cannot have been satisfied with a solution that prevented any further action to seize it while failing to guarantee that he would ever sit upon the throne himself, even if his son might.

The only circumstance in which York can have found this arrangement satisfactory was if he had not truly wanted the throne but only control of the government that would allow re-instatement of his lands and titles. Having failed to achieve this through any other means, this arrangement at least allowed him that security. Even in these circumstances, York cannot have held his position permanently secure. He had won power four times and lost it three times. Having upped the ante to the highest possible level, a fall now would be the farthest and hardest yet and it could so easily happen. The two sides remained entrenched in their hatred and opposition to each other. Margaret would not give up on her son's right and York would never again be banished to the wilderness as a common man.

As the duke and his allies tightened their grip on the reins of power in London the queen was equally hard at work. Having taken ship from the security provided by Jasper Tudor, Margaret arrived in Scotland to find a queen in mourning. James II had been killed by an exploding cannon, leaving his wife Mary of Guelders to worry about her nine-year-old son, now James III. Margaret must have felt that she had found a kindred spirit in a woman deprived of her husband and having to concern herself with the succession of a young boy lacking a father's support. Whatever they might have had in common, Margaret's mind was firmly on business. Her forces had been depleted and she was in Scotland to secure support.

Margaret left with what she wanted. Mary sent the Earl of Angus and a large force south to swell the English royal force, but the price of this army was high. Margaret ceded the tactically sensitive town of Berwick-upon-Tweed and betrothed her son to one of Mary's daughters. Most controversially of all, Margaret, as deprived of funds as her Scottish counterpart, had promised that the Scots army at her back could take its wages in plunder from the English towns that had betrayed her husband. Somerset and Northumberland had been busily recruiting in the strongholds of the north and Margaret came down to meet them. As this horde gathered, word could not be kept away from London any longer. York, his second son Edmund, Earl of Rutland, and Salisbury gathered all of the men that they could muster and marched north.

Having collided with Somerset's forces, as they both moved around the national chessboard placing pieces, York arrived at his castle of Sandal near Wakefield in Yorkshire. It had become clear that, although York had arrived with around 5,000 men, the royal force and Margaret's new allies were twice their number. Sandal was a mighty fortress; York was safe behind the walls as he awaited reinforcements from the Marcher heartlands around Wales and the border, which were being raised by his son Edward, Earl of March. The large army huddled within the castle's shelter over the Christmas period, but on 30 December 1460 York led his force out against Margaret's army.

The reason York left the safety of his fortress is unclear and several theories exist. It has been suggested that he underestimated the size of Margaret's army or that he believed only a small portion was nearby, but having had reports of their numbers that led him to take refuge within Sandal Castle it seems unlikely that he would then fail to appreciate that he was outnumbered. A second theory teaches that York's men were attacked while out foraging for supplies, suggesting that the huge numbers could not be easily supported by the castle's supplies for long. Rutland may have been among those outside the walls, and York led a sortie out to save his son. There is believed to have been a Christmas truce in place, which Margaret's men violated by attacking York's men. A further suggestion is that York was taunted to come out from behind his walls by Somerset and Northumberland, who teased him for cowardice. Such rashness does not appear to fit with the man who had been so very cautious for over a decade, but it remains possible that his new position made him over confident.

A more plausible explanation can be found in *An English Chronicle*, corroborated by the Burgundian Jean de Waurin. Although little told, it appears to fill in the unsatisfactory gaps in other theories. The story also provides another layer to the bitter feuding in the far north of England and relates to John, Baron Neville. Salisbury's father, Ralph Neville, Earl of Westmorland, had sired his vast brood between two wives. Salisbury was the oldest child of his second wife, Joan Beaufort, the daughter of John of Gaunt, Duke of Lancaster. Sir John Neville, Ralph's eldest son by his first wife, Margaret Stafford, had predeceased his father, but left three sons. The eldest, another Ralph, was now 2nd Earl of Westmorland and the middle son was John, Baron Neville. This branch of the family was not on the best of terms with those allied to York, but, according to *An English Chronicle*, Baron Neville raced to Sandal Castle and 'went to the said duke of York, desiring a commission of him for to raise an army for to chastise the rebels of the country'.

Waurin describes an odd visit to York by Andrew Trollope, the leader of the Calais garrison who had abandoned the duke at Ludlow, claiming that he was returning to York's cause with hundreds of men. Neville returned with 8,000 men too, reporting to York at Sandal, and it may be that York felt this tipped the odds in his favour. York rode out at the head of his army with his son Edmund and Salisbury beside him. Before the fighting had properly begun, Baron Neville, Trollope and their men turned on those they had feigned allegiance to. Baron Neville had thrown his lot in with Somerset, Northumberland and Margaret against his relatives and the huge force fell upon York in a field outside Wakefield.

Whatever the reason that York left his fortress, he was now in the field against a force vastly superior in numbers. The fighting was brutal and casualties on York's side were high, perhaps as many as 2,000 against only a few hundred on the queen's side. Among those slain was Richard, Duke of York. Some later sources suggest that he was taken and executed after the fighting but it is most likely that he was killed in the press, as reported by *An English Chronicle*, along with Thomas Neville, Salisbury's son.

Edmund was overtaken as he tried to flee the field by Lord Clifford, who relished the opportunity to exact his long-awaited revenge. Clifford's words have been passed down in many forms, all amounting to the same spiteful glee. The Victorian *History of England Volume II* relates the words as, 'The son of York; thy father slew mine; and so will I thee, and all thy kin.' With that, he struck the seventeen-year-old Edmund down, beheading him and fulfilling his vow after St Albans to avenge his father's death. In a brutal act that contravened the rules of war, York's body was mutilated after his death and his head cut off.

The Earl of Salisbury was captured and taken to Pontefract Castle, according to *An English Chronicle*, 'for a great sum of money that he should have paid for grant of his life', but the chronicle reports that 'the common people of the country, which loved him not, took him out of the castle by violence and smote off his head'. It was an ignominious end for the sixty-year-old earl who had risen so high.

The queen, along with Somerset, Northumberland and Lord Clifford, had the heads of York, Rutland and Salisbury set upon spikes above Micklegate Bar, one of York's entrance gates. It was a grisly sight, made more macabre by a paper crown that had been fixed to York's head. The initiative had swung back to Margaret. Her deadliest enemy was dead and England lay at her feet once more. The sons of St Albans had their vengeance and surely enjoyed looking up at the faces of their fathers' murderers gazing out emptily from the city walls. In the short-sighted fog of angry vengeance, those satisfied figures failed to either notice or care that they had, in their turn, opened new wounds as their own healed. The sons of St Albans were revenged but they had unleashed the wrath of the sons of Wakefield. Edward, Earl of March, now 4th Duke of York, and Richard Neville, Earl of Warwick, would want their pound of flesh next.

10

The Wheel Spins Faster

The first son of Wakefield to seek vengeance was Edward, Earl of March. At eighteen, he was head of the family and champion of the opposition to Henry VI's rule. News reached him in the Welsh Marches that his father and brother were dead and that the Battle of Wakefield had been lost. Queen Margaret was heading south with Somerset, Northumberland, Clifford and the Scottish army keen for their booty. Edward had a force of around 5,000 men and was preparing to head to London to rendezvous with Warwick against the closing royal forces.

As Edward prepared to move, reports arrived that a force almost the size of his own was marching out of Wales behind Jasper Tudor, Earl of Pembroke, his father Owen Tudor and James Butler, Earl of Ormond and Wiltshire, son-in-law to Edmund Beaufort, 2nd Duke of Somerset, who had been slain at St Albans. A staunch ally of Queen Margaret, Wiltshire too was marching to reinforce the northern army driving south. Edward was left with a dilemma. He could hurry to join up with Warwick and face the oncoming army of the queen, possibly allowing the Tudors and Wiltshire to reinforce the huge army from the north, or he could move to cut off the Welsh army's route to their allies and stop them ever reaching the queen. If he did this, it still left open the possibility of reaching Warwick before the queen did.

It seems likely that a thirst for swift revenge also drove the young man. News of the death of his father and of a brother so close to his own age must have been an upsetting blow. If his blood was heated and he wanted to vent himself upon his enemies, the Tudors and Wiltshire were in the wrong place at the wrong time. Edward led his men out to block Jasper and Owen's path near Wigmore Castle, one of the Yorkist Marcher properties inherited through their Mortimer heritage. Located in the north of Herefordshire, Wigmore sits on the Welsh border and provided an ideal base from which to bar the royal reinforcements' route to meet the queen.

On 2 February 1461, Edward placed his army to block the royalist forces at the point where they would cross his lands. Accounts of this battle are scarce and offer little detail. One thing that is well noted, though, is a phenomenon that struck fear into the heart of Edward's men. Some sources describe the event taking place on the very morning of the battle, though *An English Chronicle* states that it was some days before. All agree that Edward's men were frightened by the sight of it. At around ten o'clock in the morning, three suns flared in the winter sky. Edward's army was convinced that it was a sign of evil and that they were doomed to lose the coming battle. When superstition still held sway over science, it was a dangerous situation for Edward, whose army could easily evaporate in fear.

What the Yorkists witnessed that morning was a parhelion, also referred to as a sun dog or mock sun. A parhelion occurs when a cirrus cloud contains ice crystals falling in a specific pattern. The effect of this alignment of features is to create a spot of bright light at 22° on either side of the sun, usually glowing more red on the side closest to the sun and moving through the spectrum to blue colours on the edge farthest away. It is possible to see left-hand and right-hand parhelia, but what presented itself to the soldiers on the Welsh border as they awaited their enemies was a full sun dog, three suns blazing in the sky. They did not like the omen and it would take a firm leader to force them to stay and fight.

Edward elected instead to use the sun dog to his own advantage in a stroke of propaganda genius. The young duke, now also legally heir to the throne of England, would not be deprived of the opportunity to quench his thirst for revenge. *An English Chronicle* records Edward's clever reversal of the portent as he addresses his men, telling them, 'Be of good comfort, and dread not; this is a good sign, for these three suns betoken the Father, the Son, and the Holy Ghost, and therefore let us have a good heart, and in the name of Almighty God go we against our enemies.' Convinced and reinvigorated, with the sun dog at their back denoting that God was behind them, the Yorkist army squared up to the king's supporters coming eastward out of Wales.

The fighting that followed was a brutal rout of the forces trying to pass Edward's blockade. *An English Chronicle* numbers the dead at 4,000 Welshmen, which would account for most of the army. *Gregory's Chronicle* records 3,000 dead littering the field of battle, the overwhelming majority from the Lancastrian army. Edward's reversal of the ill omen had served him well. His men fought with passion and belief. Jasper Tudor, Earl of Pembroke, and James Butler, Earl of Wiltshire, escaped the field and fled into hiding. The remnants of the royal reinforcements were chased as far as Hereford, some twenty miles south. One of those overtaken and captured was Owen Tudor, father of Jasper and grandfather to the young Henry Tudor.

Although about sixty years old, Owen Tudor was a robust man and his long life had been eventful, the stuff of romantic legend, even. Owen's father, Maredudd ap Tudur, had been first cousin to Owain Glyndwr and, along with his brothers Rhys and Gwilym, Maredudd had supported Glyndwr's rebellion against Henry IV in 1400. Although Glyndwr evaded capture and slipped into Welsh legend, when the uprising eventually failed, which was by no means certain from the outset, the Tudur brothers were left with nothing. Rhys and Gwilym had been party to the capture of Conwy Castle in 1402 and would not be forgiven. Tudur lands were seized by the crown and the two brothers hunted down. In an attempt to give his young son a new start in life, Maredudd moved to London.

After the rebellions Welsh rights were severely diminished, particularly in England, so the move was a brave and daring one. Maredudd had a proud heritage and counted the twelfth-century Welsh prince Rhys ap Gruffydd among his ancestors. He married the daughter of the Lord of Anglesey and so young Owen was of gentle birth in his native Wales, but that would count for little in London. Owen, the anglicised form of Owain, was given the surname Tudor to aid his absorption into English society. It was not usual for a Welshman to use a surname, designating their family and descent by adding 'ap' and their father's name after their own. Thus Maredudd ap Tudur in its anglicised form was Meredith, son of Tudur. Maredudd's father was Tudur ap Goronwy, and so Owen's appellation would have been Owain ap Maredudd, which could be anglicised to Owen Meredith. Had Maredudd's decision been different, England's most famous dynasty might well have been the Meredith monarchs.

Shortly after the death of Henry V in 1422, Owen took up a post in the household of his widow, the beautiful young French princess Catherine of Valois. The dowager queen's position was awkward, not least for her brothers-in-law John, Duke of Bedford, and Humphrey, Duke of Gloucester, who were to rule in the name of their infant nephew. Catherine was young and, as a daughter of the French king and mother of the English king, she remained a desirable marriage proposition. If she were to make a foreign match it would give an unhealthy influence over the upbringing of England's new king to someone the dukes had no control over, perhaps even one of England's enemies. The only scenario that could be any worse would be a marriage within England to one of Henry VI's subjects. This would give the same unhealthy position, influence and access to patronage to one the dukes would consider well beneath themselves. Neither outcome could be tolerated.

The solution Bedford and Gloucester settled upon was aimed squarely at making Catherine such an unattractive prospect that none would wish to marry her. An Act of Parliament made it illegal for the dowager queen to remarry without the permission of the king, who, as an baby, was many years away from being able to give his mother such consent. By the time he was capable of giving consent, any marriage would not be an issue any longer anyway. The punishment for any breach of this law was the forfeiture of all lands, positions and titles by the man who would marry Catherine. With the attraction of such a union not only negated but reversed to become deeply unpalatable, Catherine was stranded.

Edmund Beaufort, before he had become Duke of Somerset, had been a high-profile figure linked to the queen. It was reported that both wanted a marriage and this law was a reaction to those rumours. Edmund would not lose all that he had for the match and Catherine was trapped, facing a decade or more of loneliness with no hope of love or more children, and could not have been happy with the settlement.

Owen Tudor caught the young Catherine's eye. One story recounts him emerging from a swim as Catherine passed by and the young French princess was captivated by the handsome, well-built Welshman. Another account tells how Owen was dancing furiously at a party in the queen's household when he span out of control, tripping and landing in the dowager queen's lap. As their eyes met, both pairs burned with passion. However they really came together and how much love or lust was involved is not known, but they married in secret. Even the validity of their marriage has been questioned because of its secrecy, though this may have sprung from a later desire to question the legitimacy of their children. One thing is certain; Catherine had defeated the trap set by her brothers-in-law by marrying a man who had no power, possession, land or titles to forfeit.

In 1436 Catherine, still only in her mid-thirties, was ill and dying. She finally revealed the existence of her other children to Henry VI, who suddenly had half-siblings he had not known of. There was scandal and outrage. Catherine died in January 1437 and Owen was thrown into prison from whence he escaped only to be captured again. Finally pardoned, he was freed and delighted that two of his sons, Edmund and Jasper, had been embraced by Henry VI and created earls. It was a meteoric rise through a society in which he had had no place when his father brought him to London.

Owen's six decades had been eventful, and perhaps he would not have changed a thing. He was, though, a prisoner in a vicious war, a conflict that was tearing up the chivalric rules that had controlled conflict for centuries. At Wakefield, prisoners had been murdered on the battlefield and executed after the battle was ended. Owen had fallen into the hands of a young man whose father had been killed and whose younger brother was one of those murdered after his capture. Owen's allies had redefined again what was acceptable. The old Welshman would now pay the price his step-son's forces had set.

The day after the Battle of Mortimer's Cross, Owen was taken out to the market square in Hereford for his execution. As he approached the block set up for the dispensing of revenge thinly disguised as justice, the easy charm and wit that had attracted a queen to him did not desert him. According to *Gregory's Chronicle*, looking down upon the spot where he knew his head would be separated from his body he wistfully quipped 'That head shall lie on the stock that was wont to lie on Queen Katherine's lap'. Perhaps he was content to join Catherine now. With that, he knelt to receive his fate with all of the composure of a born knight. Perhaps reflecting the fate of his own father, brother and uncle's heads in York, Edward had Owen's severed head set atop the market cross in Hereford centre. Gregory reports that a local 'mad woman' spent days caring for the grisly head of the handsome Welshman, during which she combed his hair, washed the dried blood from his face and set candles about him.

Edward had achieved a swift vengeance, but he was not satisfied, nor was he finished. He gathered his men and marched east to join up with the Earl of Warwick to meet those truly responsible for his rage. The young duke was a huge man who was now carving out an unrivalled reputation on the field of battle, and, as he stalked across the country, he surely wanted the fight that was to come. In his wake, as was the mark of this period of bitter civil war, he left another powerful man, Jasper Tudor, Earl of Pembroke, deprived of a father by enemies to whom he would never now be reconciled. For every wound to which a salve was applied, another was opened, ugly, ragged and in need of its own balm.

Warwick, still only thirty-three, had not waited for his young ally before leaving London. With the queen far in the north, he mustered the men of Kent to add to his own men and the Burgundian mercenaries he had acquired. Many of the Burgundians arrived carrying early handguns that fired lead shot, something never before seen in England. The earl reached St Albans when shocking news arrived of just how close the army from the north now was. There was little choice but to set up around St Albans and prepare the town for its second dose of war. Warwick's thirty-year-old brother John was with him and they set up wooden palisades to protect the town and laid caltrops, nets dotted with spikes designed to break up cavalry charges by injuring the horses.

Tension north of London must have reached melting point. The queen's army had descended south, with Scotsmen in tow who had been promised their pay in whatever they could pillage as they passed. Warwick was moving north to meet them. Both sides had scores to settle and folks in every part must have feared for their property and their lives. *Gregory's Chronicle* tells of a butcher who led a band of men in the king's name to a fight at Dunstable, where they encountered a detachment of the Scots, perhaps seeking out their booty. The butcher led the ragtag band of raw recruits onto the field but they were slaughtered, 800 men perishing due to the 'simple guidance' of the butcher. Gregory laments that soon after the fighting, either for shame at his dismal performance or for the loss of all of his goods to the Scots, the butcher hanged himself.

The tide seemed to turn in Warwick's favour as the queen's army approached St Albans the day after the butcher's failure at Dunstable. By then, 17 February 1461, many of the Scots had fled, either growing concerned by the distance between them and their homes or else already so heavily laden with their pay that they saw no further need to fight. Gregory estimates that less than 5,000 men remained in the queen's force. That was still an impressive number. Campaigning in the winter was all but unheard of and it was almost two months into this round of brutal exchanging of blows. All of her army wore the livery of her son the Prince of Wales, bands of black and crimson with an ostrich feather badge. It was clear that she was calling men to her in the name of the dispossessed heir of the House of Lancaster rather than his father.

Andrew Trollope was to play a prominent role in the coming fighting once more. Having left the Yorkist cause at Ludlow and possibly contributed to tricking the Duke of York out of Sandal Castle at Wakefield, he led a lightning strike into the town of St Albans, catching those within the city unawares and driving them away. This allowed him to catch John Neville's large force, set up outside the town, in a pincer movement with the rest of the queen's army. Around 2,500 men died in the intense fighting. In an early blow, a large contingent of Kentish men took up their weapons and walked away from the field. Their leader, a man named Lovelace, had been captured at Wakefield but released upon giving his oath never to take up arms against the queen and her prince again. He and his men deserted Warwick to maintain his honour.

Either in the sudden confusion or because of the cold, damp weather, Warwick's expensive artillery failed. Gregory recounts that there were not only the new fangled handguns, firing either lead shot or unusual double-flighted arrows, but also wildfire, the weapon of terror deployed against London by Lord Scales. All failed to be deployed, some backfiring in the hurry to react, guns blowing up in the faces of their operators and wildfire turning viciously back upon those who would use it. Although Warwick probably had far superior numbers the tactics of the queen's army maximised the advantages of the tight streets of the town and the element of surprise.

Warwick and the other lords fled. King Henry had sat beneath a tree as the battle had raged, singing and laughing, completely oblivious to the carnage about him and the stakes involved in the fighting. Lord Bonville and Sir Thomas Kyriell stayed behind to protect the king when all others fled, passing up their own opportunity to make good their escape. Henry assured them that they would not be harmed while they were with him for the protection and loyalty they showed. Margaret had the men seized and with the encouragement of the Duke of Exeter and the Earl of Devonshire placed them on trial for treason the next day. Their judge and jury was the seven-year-old Prince Edward, who duly pronounced a sentence of death upon the two men for their crimes. William Bonville was nearly seventy years of age and Kyriell was only a few years younger. Both must have been bewildered at the sentence passed by a little boy, doubtless at the instigation of his mother and two lords with land interests in Bonville's homeland in the West Country. Once more, land disputes played a pivotal role in the vicious feuding below the surface of the Wars of the Roses. Bonville had turned to the Yorkist cause at Northampton and may have been responsible for guarding Henry there after his capture, giving Margaret a thin motive for revenge too.

King Henry was reunited with his wife and son. On the battlefield, Henry knighted his young son and then watched on as the boy knighted several others in turn. The first was Andrew Trollope, stalwart of the king, queen and prince's cause. Trollope had been wounded trying to cross the net of caltrops. With his foot painfully pierced he had not been able to move any further.

Gregory reports that Trollope, with a modesty that was probably false, knelt before Prince Edward and told him 'My lord, I have not deserved it for I slew but fifteen men, for I stood still in one place and they came unto me'. Sir Andrew's star was in the ascendant. His service had turned the tide of the struggles more than once in favour of Queen Margaret's party and his rewards were coming.

No party appeared capable of the act of clemency or kindness that might soothe the worst of the fighting. Too many now had personal vendettas to follow, land and money to gain from seeing rivals destroyed and their own fortunes too closely aligned with one party or the other to give an inch. There was no mercy in England now. There was one odd exception to this rule. Warwick's brother John was captured for a second time, yet just as he had after Blore Heath he escaped punishment once more to be inexplicably released. In light of the fates of Bonville and Kyriell, the leniency shown to John Neville, who had led the vanguard of Warwick's army in the fields outside St Albans, defies belief.

The queen's unexpected victory against the previously undefeatable Earl of Warwick, who headed west to meet his cousin Edward, sent London into panic. The city was terrified that Margaret, who had no love for the capital, would exact a cruel price for the city's support of Warwick. She had promised the remaining Scots soldiers payment in loot and London was the main prize. The city officials fell into a frenzy. Margaret sent the Duchess of Buckingham, the widow of the old duke, to negotiate and promise that no harm would come to the city, its inhabitants or their property. Dubiously, the mayor and aldermen wrote to the queen assuring her of their loyalty and good will. When soldiers were seen approaching the gates shortly after, possibly led by the Duke of Somerset, the citizens attacked them, killing many and driving the rest away. The mayor and aldermen panicked even more, gathering food and money in carts to send to supply the queen's army in the hopes of appeasing her. When the citizenry learned of the plan they seized the keys to the gates, locked them tight and divided the carts of provisions among themselves.

In an uncharacteristic act of acquiescence Margaret decided to take her army back northwards. Fear of the Scots would never work for her and those that had already left were pillaging their

1. Victorian engraving of a scene from Shakespeare's *Henry VI, Part 1*, showing lords picking a red or white rose in the garden to show their allegiance. (Author's collection)

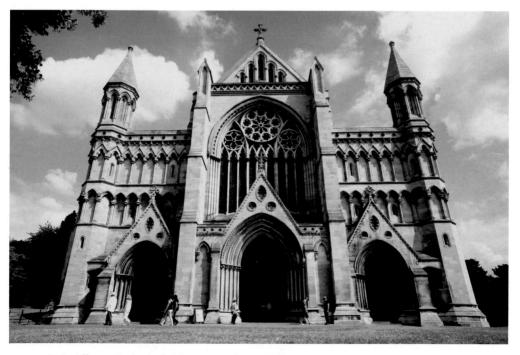

2. St Albans Cathedral. (Courtesy of Dan Wilson)

3. Richard, Duke of York,
in a stained-glass window at
St Laurence's church, Ludlow.
(Author's collection)

4. The church of St Mary and All Saints, Fotheringhay. Founded by Edward, 2nd
Duke of York, as a family mausoleum. The bodies of Richard, Duke of York, and
Edmund, Earl of Rutland, were moved here in 1476. (Courtesy of Robert Stewart)

5. Outer bailey of Ludlow Castle, a Yorkist stronghold and rallying point. (Author's collection)

6. Inner bailey of Ludlow Castle where the Yorkist leaders met in 1459. (Author's collection)

7. Ludlow town, ransacked by the royalist army in 1459. (Author's collection)

8. The Yorkist falcon and fetterlock in a misericord at St Laurence's church, Ludlow. (Author's collection)

9. A parhelion, or sundog, as seen before the Battle of Mortimer's Cross in 1461. (Author's collection)

10. King Edward IV in a stained-glass window at St Laurence's church, Ludlow. (Author's collection)

11. Hornby Castle, the root of a dispute between the Stanley and Harrington families in which Richard, Duke of Gloucester, intervened. (Author's collection)

12. Richard, Duke of Gloucester, leads his men into the Battle of Tewkesbury at the 2014 re-enactment. (Author's collection)

13. King Edward IV orders his men to attack at the Battle of Tewkesbury for the 2014 re-enactment. (Author's collection)

14. Edward of Lancaster, Prince of Wales, at the Battle of Tewkesbury re-enactment in 2014. (Author's collection)

15. Edward, Prince of Wales, is despatched at the Battle of Tewkesbury. The avenging hand at this re-enactment belonged to Edward IV. (Author's collection)

16. Tewkesbury Abbey, near the battlefield, where many Lancastrian men fled into sanctuary. (Author's collection)

17. Interior of
Tewkesbury Abbey.
(Picture used with the
kind permission of
Tewkesbury Abbey)

18. The ceiling of Tewkesbury Abbey, painted with the Sunne in Splendour of
Edward IV to celebrate his victory and atone for removing men from sanctuary.
(Picture used with the kind permission of Tewkesbury Abbey)

19. Sacristy door at Tewkesbury Abbey, lined with armour retrieved from the battlefield by the monks. (Picture used with the kind permission of Tewkesbury Abbey)

20. Tewkesbury Abbey sacristy door, showing arrow holes in the armour. (Picture used with the kind permission of Tewkesbury Abbey)

21. The Tower of London, scene of several sieges, the death of Henry VI and the last place the Princes in the Tower were recorded as seen. (Author's collection)

22. Edward V, son of Edward IV, in a stained-glass window at St Laurence's church, Ludlow. (Author's collection)

23. St Michael's Mount, seized by John de Vere, Earl of Oxford, connected to the mainland at low tide. (Author's collection)

24. St Michael's Mount moated by the sea; it was a fortress that could be held indefinitely. (Author's collection)

Left: 25. Richard III and his wife Anne Neville from the Rous Rolls, a contemporary history of the Earls of Warwick. (Author's collection)

Right: 26. Portrait of King Richard III, a man who divides opinion over 500 years after his death. (Author's collection)

27. Romantic Victorian illustration of the sons of Edward IV, the Princes in the Tower, being separated from their mother, though Edward V was not with her after his father's death. (Author's collection)

28. Archers fire their longbows at the Battle of Bosworth re-enactment weekend 2013. (Author's collection)

29. The armies of Richard III and Henry Tudor on a collision course at the Battle of Bosworth re-enactment in 2013. (Author's collection)

Above: 30. The last cavalry charge of King Richard III at the Battle of Bosworth re-enactment weekend. (Author's collection)

Right: 31. Prince Arthur, oldest son of Henry VII, who moved to Ludlow with his new wife, Catherine of Aragon. (Author's collection)

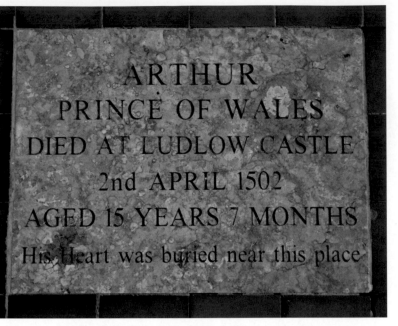

32. When Prince Arthur died in 1502, throwing the new Tudor dynasty into disarray, his heart was buried at St Laurence's church, Ludlow, and his body was placed in a magnificent chantry at Worcester Cathedral. (Author's collection)

33. The statue of King Richard III outside Leicester Cathedral where he has been laid to rest after the discovery of his remains in 2012. (Author's collection)

way back home, taking property, money and even the beasts that worked men's lands, leaving them with nothing. Her heartlands were north too, in the Midlands, and maintaining a siege of London with a dwindling, cold, tired army who just wanted their home and hearth was hardly practical.

The widowed Duchess of York, Cecily Neville, feared that the situation was spiralling out of control and that her family's cause was in mortal danger. She had lost one son and another was set upon a path to war from which he was unlikely to be shaken. Cecily sent her two youngest sons, George and Richard, into a comfortable exile at the court of Philip the Good, Duke of Burgundy, until the dust settled. Clearly Cecily feared the eleven- and nine-year-old boys were no longer safe from the brutal ravages of the conflict that had mutated within England, although they had been well treated following the events at Ludlow, just two years earlier.

Power and the initiative in the spiralling conflict was changing hands faster than ever before, and the two sides were becoming more deeply entrenched in their bitter opposition to each other, both acting as a beacon for anyone with an axe to grind or a score to settle; so many feuds had festered under the unmanaged rule of Henry VI that there was an unhealthy glut of powerful men driven to the battlefield to obtain the justice or vengeance that they wanted. All of the fighting so far had been building toward a climax that could not be avoided for long. What was to come is too often a forgotten instant in English history, but in its time it shook a nation and changed the course of its history.

11

England's Apocalypse

29 March 1461 was Palm Sunday, the Christian celebration of Jesus' triumphal entry into Jerusalem a week before Easter Sunday. It was bitterly cold, and sleety snow was driven by swirling winds. It was also to see a cataclysmic event in English history. Although often overlooked, that bleak day saw the largest and bloodiest battle ever fought on English soil. For over a decade, pressure had built until an explosive release became inevitable.

King Henry, along with his wife, son and allies, withdrew all the way up to York after their victory at St Albans. Perhaps more decisive action in the opposite direction would have served their cause better, but they chose instead not to poke the frightened beast that was London, for fear of its rage. In the north they could regroup, gather more men and refresh the cold, tired soldiers who had done them sterling service at St Albans.

With London left open, Warwick met up with his cousin Edward outside Oxford and the two were welcomed into the capital in triumph. Edward, along with Warwick, set about engineering a repeat of recent history, but the duke stage-managed the affair far better than his father had. Gregory recalled the city's anger toward King Henry, with chants in the street of 'He that had London forsake; Would no more to them take'. In contrast, Edward was being hailed in the same streets. He retired to Baynards Castle and waited patiently. On 1 March, George Neville addressed a large gathering to extol Edward's claim to the throne. It was so warmly received that by 3 March, a council gathered at Baynards to ask Edward to take the throne in Henry's place. The king had violated the Act of Accord by attacking York and his family, an act expressly marked as treason. His unpopularity and ineffectualness had plumbed new depths and there was no end to the conflict in sight under Henry's kingship. A new direction was needed.

On 4 March Edward attended Mass at St Paul's Cathedral where he was publically proclaimed King of England. He would not consent to be crowned, though, as long as Henry was at large with an army at his back. He resolved to break his opponent before even attempting to enjoy his new position. Edward left London just over a week later on 13 March with a large army, swollen by men unhappy with King Henry and keen to see the Duke of York's death avenged. Between London and York, Edward, Warwick and Fauconberg recruited heavily, increasing the horde that followed them.

As news reached the Lancastrian forces of the Yorkist approach they broke several bridges to slow their enemy's progress. The River Aire crossed the Yorkist route and Fauconberg, who was ahead of the remainder of the army, sent his scouts in front to examine the road ahead and to find signs of the enemy. Led by Lord Fitzwater, the scouting party began to repair the bridge for the rest of the approaching army. The use of scouts and outriders was the only way for any force in the field to secure solid information about the strength, position and setup of the enemy. Only with this information could commanders decide upon their own tactics for a forthcoming battle.

As Lord Fitzwater and his men began their repairs, a Lancastrian force, sent out from York to scout the enemy and to harass them if possible, watched on. Lord Clifford, who had taken his own vengeance at Wakefield, led his 500-strong crack cavalry force, known as the Flower of Craven. Dark was falling as they set up camp, their Yorkist counterparts doing the same, the light guard they set suggesting that they were unaware of Clifford's force on the other side of the river. At the crack of dawn, Fitzwater's camp was rudely awoken by Clifford's mounted force thundering over the repaired bridge. Lord Fitzwater emerged from his tent to be struck down by a blow that would later see him dead. His men were caught unawares and slaughtered. As those lucky enough to escape fled back to the safety of their main force, Clifford's squad crossed back over the river, pleased with their morning's work.

When those stragglers reached the Yorkist army the news of the attack caused panic. There is a legend that Warwick took his men to clear the bridge but found that Lord Clifford had set himself up perfectly to defend the narrow bottleneck. Warwick was struck in the leg by an arrow as his assault failed and returned to the main army, trying to quell the growing concerns of the men there by dismounting and promptly killing his horse, swearing that he would fight and live or die beside the rest of them now.

The main body of the Yorkist army now pressed on to the crossing. Clifford still held firm as the huge bulk of men tried to repair the bridge and cross the river. Eventually Lord Fauconberg took a detachment of cavalry to ride down to the next bridge and drive Clifford's men away. The Flower of Craven and their leader saw the threat, fending off the Yorkist army for as long as they could. Dusk was closing in as they began their ride back, with Fauconberg in hot pursuit, toward their base at York. Clifford's men and their horses were tired after almost a full day of fighting. Jean de Waurin claimed that 3,000 of the Yorkist men lay dead in the river and on its banks, so Clifford's 500 had done their work well, buying the Lancastrian forces, led by Henry Beaufort, Duke of Somerset, another twenty-four hours to prepare.

Just south of his target Clifford was ambushed, possibly by a Yorkist scouting force. The delay they caused allowed Fauconberg to catch up and in the fighting Clifford was killed by an arrow to the face after taking off his helmet. The rest of his crack force was crushed and the Flower of Craven were utterly destroyed. It has been suggested that Somerset left Clifford to this fate because he was jealous of a rival's success and close relationship to the king, though it seems more likely that the ambush took place out of sight and beyond earshot of Somerset's position. The trouble that was brewing had claimed its first high-profile victim and Edward had seen his younger brother avenged.

As night fell on the 28 March Edward's army set up camp a few miles away from Somerset's position, near the village of Towton. They must have struggled to get any rest, tired from a long march and the melee at Ferrybridge, exposed to the biting cold and icy winds. They rose early the next morning, Palm Sunday. Polydore Vergil, writing at the beginning of the next century, claimed that Henry tried to do all that he could to avoid any fighting on that day, wishing to spend it in prayer instead. It is not beyond the bounds of possibility for a pious man averse to violence, but Vergil was writing for King Henry VII, who actively sought to have Henry VI beatified so had an interest in presenting his religious devotion. Pleading for a delay in the unavoidable violence that would decide the fate of the crown of England to make room for prayer is, though, a fitting summary of Henry's rule.

Warwick's uncle Lord Fauconberg, by far the most experienced commander on the Yorkist side of the field, and probably on either side, led the main body of Edward's army. The night had been harsh but the dawn showed the benefits of the position they had taken up. The armies lined up opposite each other in the swirling snow, wind whipping their faces, unable to see their enemies clearly. Fauconberg had one huge advantage and he meant to make the most of it. The wind was behind the Yorkist force, extending the range of their huge longbows. They opened fire upon the enemy, causing chaos in the Lancastrian ranks as an arrow storm fell out of the white sky, unseen until it was too late. The Lancastrians returned the barrage but Fauconberg had judged his distances perfectly in the difficult conditions. Their arrows fell short. The Yorkists continued to shoot, wreaking havoc as men screamed and fell in the snow on the other side of the field. When they had spent all of their arrows, Fauconberg had his men step forward, pull up the Lancastrian arrows that had fallen harmlessly into the mud and fire them back at their owners.

Somerset realised that he could not keep this up and ordered his men to advance against the Yorkists. Sir Andrew Trollope led the assault with 7,000 men, joined also by Richard Woodville, Lord Rivers, and his son Anthony, who had received the dressing-down from Edward, Warwick and Salisbury in Calais the previous year. The Duke of Somerset took another 7,000 men, according to Waurin, and together they charged the Yorkist lines. They thundered into the Yorkist cavalry with such force that Edward's mounted men fell back and began to flee. Waurin says that the Lancastrians chased the Yorkists for eleven miles, believing that the battle was won. Henry Percy, 3rd Earl of Northumberland, was meant to charge at the same time. If he had it is likely that the strike would have resulted in a swift victory for the Lancastrians. The delay allowed the battle to become even again.

Fighting persisted for hours; Polydore Virgil later stated that there were ten full hours of slaughter. With the advantage passing to and fro and the outcome impossible to predict, the turning point arrived late in the day, when the Duke of Norfolk arrived to reinforce the Yorkists. Fresh soldiers were too much for the exhausted Lancastrians to face and they began to flee, mercilessly chased and cut down by Edward's army. The white snow was stained red and innumerable corpses littered the field.

Estimates of the numbers on the field that day vary but around 100,000 men probably came together there, with a light advantage in numbers on the Lancastrian side. Edward's heralds, a letter he wrote to his mother and a report sent by George Neville to Bishop Coppini all place the number of dead at around 29,000 men, with more injured who would never recover. Waurin placed the final number at 36,000 dead. With so many dead in wintery conditions it was not feasible to individually bury all of the bodies. Great pits were dug to act as mass graves. These have since been discovered and excavated, some of the skulls exhumed displaying savage wounds. Facial reconstruction has been carried out on one soldier, who was in his late thirties or early forties and displayed healed wounds from previous battles. Obviously a veteran, the man would have borne deep scars when he took to the field at Towton. It was to be the last in his experiences of battles. Gregory lamented that 'many a lady lost her best beloved in that battle'. Waurin coined a phrase that came to sum up the period of bitter fighting in his account of Towton, complaining that 'father did not spare son nor son his father'.

As well as Lord Clifford, the Earl of Northumberland lay among the dead. The sons of St Albans had obtained their revenge but had in turn been slain by the sons of Wakefield. Lord Neville, who had supposedly contributed to the tricking of the Duke of York at Wakefield, perished on the Lancastrian side and Sir Andrew Trollope, perhaps one of the most accomplished soldiers of his day and whose star had risen so high in service to King Henry and

Queen Margaret, had also fallen. Somerset, Henry, Margaret and Prince Edward along with any other nobles able to escape the field rode north and rode hard, heading to Scotland.

Edward tarried in the north a while to try and see the region settled. The Lancastrians were only in Scotland and his departure might be all that was needed to bring them back south into a region traditionally sympathetic to them. There was more to concern the new king now, though. The rest of his kingdom held its breath, and upheaval, though raw and open in the far north, was not restricted to that region alone. Wales was destabilised, with Jasper Tudor resiliently holding on to his castles and showing no sign of leaving nor of bowing to the new king. Edward needed to get back to the capital, arrange his coronation and summon a Parliament that would recognise and legitimise his title.

Finally, on 12 June, Edward could wait no longer and marched south. He was again received in triumph by London. Writs had been issued the previous month summoning Parliament, which opened but was adjourned immediately until November. The first item of business was naturally the declaration of Edward's right to the throne. The change in tone is striking but perhaps not surprising. Gone was the deference to Henry VI and careful laying out of the Yorkist lineage. The Commons requested that Edward take the throne because during the 'usurped reign of your said adversary Henry, late called King Henry VI, extortion, murder, rape, the shedding of innocent blood, riot and unrighteousness were commonly practised in your said realm without punishment'. The right of the House of York to the crown was rehearsed as it had been in 1460, though now Henry IV's seizing of the throne was an illegal act offensive to God for which England had been punished ever since. The House of Lancaster had persecuted the House of York but now Edward had acted decisively to save the country from God's ongoing wrath. Parliament was quite clear that Edward had only resorted to arms after Henry had breached the Act of Accord, thereby excusing Edward from his oaths under its provisions.

Parliament undid many of Henry VI's grants, bringing valuable lands and income back to a crown that had haemorrhaged money for decades. From the outset, though, Edward was clearly utterly realistic about what had gone before. Many had flitted from one side to the other but plenty had remained resolutely loyal to one party or the other throughout. If Edward was to be king of a united England he knew that he would have to deal with the situation that he found and he elected to seek an end to the circular conflicts of the last decade. The new regime welcomed any who would reconcile themselves to Edward now, whatever their previous allegiances. Among those keen to take advantage of the king's offer were Lord Rivers and his son, who had received short shrift at Calais and fought for Henry at Towton. Warkwoth wrote that Edward aimed by the provisions of his Parliament to 'have the more good will and love in his lands'.

Henry, however, was attainted for high treason but treated by the Act as though he had never been king. His treason lay in leading an armed force against King Edward and his punishment was forfeiture of his lands and titles as Duke of Lancaster. The remainder of the royal estate was Edward's now anyway. Parliament had jettisoned the country's king of thirty-nine years as though he had been an imposter all along. Henry had been a weak and ineffectual ruler who had watched as his country had careered headlong into civil war. Residual affection for him, his father's memory and the royal authority that he held had been stretched thinner and thinner until it had become transparent and men could see through it to another option.

Richard, Duke of York, had been a stark contrast to Henry. He was a man experienced and proven in government, who understood what the country wanted and needed. His family was large, his children growing strong. His wife was a model of a medieval noble woman, happy to live in her husband's shadow. Henry had not acquitted himself well as a governor. He had only one son and showed no sign of producing more. His wife had disrupted the political fabric of the country, stretching it further still. At six foot four inches, Edward IV is the tallest king ever to rule England, taller than Edward I, known as Longshanks, and taller even than his grandson Henry VIII, who bore a striking resemblance in looks and personality to Edward. Described universally as incredibly good looking, athletic, a fierce warrior and committed womaniser, he was also prone to laziness and happy to allow others to deal with issues that did not grasp his attention.

The new king took the opportunity now presented to him to reward his closest allies and his family. His remaining brothers George and Richard were retrieved from their exile in Burgundy and created dukes. George was made Duke of Clarence, a title that had belonged to the second sons of Edward III and Henry IV, and Richard was created Duke of Gloucester, a title granted to the youngest sons of Edward III and Henry IV. Warwick's uncle William Neville, Lord Fauconberg, was created Earl of Kent in recognition of his invaluable contribution. Edward's close friend William Hastings became Lord Hastings and William Herbert was given Jasper Tudor's title of Earl of Pembroke, the incentive of winning his lands serving to meet Edward's need to be rid of Henry's half-brother. John Howard was created Lord Howard and Sir Thomas Blount became Lord Mountjoy. Finally the Yorkist party was reaping the rewards of its commitment to the House of York.

Prominent Lancastrian nobles who refused to be reconciled were charged with treason. Notable among their number was John de Vere, 12th Earl of Oxford. In his mid-fifties, he appears to have initially been excused attendance before Parliament in 1461, perhaps on grounds of ill health, but he was arrested in February 1462 along with his oldest son, Aubrey de Vere. John had been slow to declare his hand in the previous troubles, sitting on York's Council during Henry VI's illness but arriving too late to participate in the First Battle of St Albans, meaning it was left unclear which side he might have taken. By 1460 it was clear that he had thrown his lot in with the Lancastrian camp. His son Aubrey married Anne Stafford, daughter of Humphrey, Duke of Buckingham, and the family were now firmly Lancastrian. Tried and convicted before John Tiptoft, Constable of England, Aubrey was executed on 20 February and John followed him to the block at Tower Hill six days later. John's second son and namesake became his heir and in 1464 Edward allowed him to succeed to his father's lands and titles as 13th Earl of Oxford.

Edward was afforded little time to enjoy his new status. Towton had been a crushing victory but it had not eradicated the Lancastrian threat, nor would Margaret rest while another took what belonged to her husband and son. She had visited the widowed queen of the Scots, Mary of Guelders, to ask for more assistance. With the Scottish coffers habitually empty, Mary had no money to offer, but she was not short of men willing to cross the border on a mission to kill Englishmen. Margaret and her allies drove hard into Northumberland and swiftly captured Alnwick Castle, the ancestral seat of the Earls of Northumberland, Bamburgh Castle, Dunstanburgh Castle and Walworth Castle.

Edward sent commissions into the southern and western counties, raising men and money to head back up north. The king laid siege to all of the castles and much of 1462 was spent in renewed conflict. Towton is often understood to be a watershed, an end to the conflict that had divided England, but Towton ended nothing other than Henry's rule. War, faction and fracture continued. As King Edward besieged the castles in which the Lancastrians had embedded themselves, another force from Scotland set off to reinforce Margaret, Somerset, Exeter and their allies. An anonymous report dated December 1462 described the state of the sieges far in the north. Warwick and the lords Cromwell, Grey of Codnor and Wenlock were at Walworth. Fauconberg, now Earl of Kent, was at the siege of Alnwick Castle with the new Lord Scales and 'many other knights and squires'. Dunstanburgh Castle sat under the watchful pressure of the Lords Fitzhugh, Scrope, Greystock and Powis. John Tiptoft, Earl of Worcester, Warwick's brother-in-law, oversaw the siege of Bamburgh Castle aided by Warwick's other brother John, Lord Montague, and Lords Strange, Say, Grey of Wilton, Lumley and Ogle. It was at Bamburgh that Somerset had installed himself. According to the writer, Edward's forces in the north were estimated at between 30,000 and 40,000 'without the King and his host'.

A French knight named Sir Peris le Brasylle was in Scotland at the time, possibly to assist Margaret, though Scotland and France were old allies anyway. Warkworth, in his *Chronicle*, described le Brasylle as 'the best warrior of all that time' and reports that when news of the French legend's approach, heading toward Alnwick and the other castles with a force of 20,000 men, reached Edward's forces 'they removed from the siege and were afraid'. The Scots apparently feared that this was some trick on the part of the king's forces and hung back. Warkworth also believed that the Scottish forces were not keen to venture too close to the stoutly defended castles for fear of being perceived to be attackers rather than a relief force. Those within the castles took the opportunity of the stand-off to slip away, clearly unconvinced that they could prevail in the confusion.

Edward achieved something of a coup at this point. Henry Beaufort, Duke of Somerset, surrendered Bamburgh Castle and went before the king. The two men made their peace, with Edward agreeing to pay Somerset a pension of 1,000 marks per year. Somerset was, without doubt, the military leader of the Lancastrian party, having commanded at the victories of Wakefield and St Albans and overseen the close battle (but ultimately, crushing defeat) at Towton. Somerset had also spearheaded this new Lancastrian drive into northern England, allowing Edward no time in which to enjoy his new throne. To have welcomed the enemy's foremost general into the fold not only continued Edward's efforts to reconcile the country to his rule but was a huge victory against Henry and Margaret, a blow to their frantic efforts without swords even being drawn. Six months later, though, his pension unpaid, finding himself impoverished and outside the halls of power, Somerset fled back into Scotland to be re-united with the Lancastrian royal family. Edward had failed to maintain his upper hand and capitalise on great opportunities and it would not be the last time.

The Battle of Towton was apocalyptic for all involved and for the country. It was a watershed moment in history, yet it changed almost nothing. The balance of power swung to the Yorkists as it had done before. Edward was king, proclaimed, crowned and confirmed by Parliament, yet recent experiences would have left most unconvinced of the finality of his victory while such strong enemies watched from just across the border, their menacing presence like the bright eyes of hungry wolves glinting in the dark forest of an uncertain future. King Edward IV is remembered fondly by history, a jovial giant with an eye for the ladies. That was a man yet to emerge, softer than the visceral, angry youth who had snatched the throne. In one hand he held out an olive branch to those willing to take it. For those who would not, his other hand held the sharp, swift sword of cruel, uncompromising justice. England was still divided but now had a king willing to act against his enemies. Peace was not won yet, and some of Edward's decisive actions merely left him more time to rue them later. Towton did not end the strife; it merely closed one chapter, only for another to follow.

12

Rise High, Fall Far

On Wednesday 17 April 1465 Anthony Woodville, Lord Scales, was returning from hearing Mass in the chapel of Sheen Palace when he was mobbed by women of the court. They surrounded him and fixed a gold collar to his thigh that was encrusted with jewels in an SS shape, representing *souvenance*, or remembrance, with an enamelled forget-me-not hanging from it. Anthony knew immediately what it meant. In his mid-twenties, Lord Scales was the flower of English chivalry, the country's champion. He recognised all too well a tournament trophy. This was to be no ordinary tournament, though. It would be remembered in the annals of chivalry for all time and famed across all of Europe. How Anthony Woodville came to be in a position to take part in this famous event is an adventure in itself.

When Warwick, Salisbury and Edward, now king, had snatched Lord Rivers and his seventeen-year-old son from Sandwich and subjected them to a rude telling-off in Calais, their family was little more than minor gentry. Richard Woodville had been created Lord Rivers in an attempt to draw a veil over the scandal of a mere knight marrying a duchess. Jacquetta of Luxembourg, Dowager Duchess of Bedford and widow of John, Henry VI's uncle, continued to use her lofty title, but their union seems to have been one of genuine love and passion for each other that crossed the social barriers between them. The couple had thirteen children who lived to adulthood. All had been born before Richard took the field at Towton to fight for the beleaguered Henry VI, and Richard was among the first men to throw himself upon the mercy of the new King Edward IV.

Anthony was the couple's second child and oldest son. Eighteen or nineteen years old at Towton, he had remained at his father's side as the family made peace with the new Yorkist regime. In 1462 he married Elizabeth Scales, widow of a son of the Earl of Essex, and acquired her title. He was summoned to Parliament in December of the same year as Baron Scales. Anthony's family, under the steady guidance of his father and politically experienced mother, had weathered the storms ravaging England well enough.

Elizabeth Woodville was the oldest child of Richard and Jacquetta's large family. She had been married to Sir John Grey of Groby, a casualty of the second Battle of St Albans in 1461. She had been left with two young sons and no income with which to provide for them. Her determination to make a personal plea to the king on her sons' behalf was to change the course of England's history once more.

Richard Neville, Earl of Warwick, had reached a zenith of power that was perhaps a just reward for his flamboyant but relentless support of the House of York. A rich and powerful man in his own right, Warwick was now the king's right-hand man, his mentor and the person to whom Edward owed his crown. Warwick the Kingmaker is an epithet that came many years after his death, but he was, in the eyes of many, the maker of this new king and the true power behind the throne. Warwick had cause to be proud and saw no need to show reservation in his celebration of his new position. His uncle William was created Earl of Kent in Edward's first parliament. His brother John, Lord Montagu, was rewarded in 1464 with the title of Earl of Northumberland, wrest from their old enemies the disgraced Percy family and now in Neville hands. In March 1465 George Neville, the Bishop of Exeter and Chancellor to the king, was given the second most powerful role in the Church in England when he was appointed Archbishop of York.

On the surface, all seemed well. Men loyal to Edward were reaping their rewards and those who had been reconciled to his reign were finding life comfortable, but not far beneath the surface the troubles of the Wars of the Roses still bubbled away. By 1463 Edward had control of all England. Harlech Castle in west Wales, which had remained in the hands of Sir Richard Tunstall, was the last stubborn bastion of Lancastrian resistance in Edward's kingdom. The effort to remove the Lancastrians from control of Harlech descended into the longest siege in English history, lasting for seven years until it was finally captured in August 1468. 1463 also saw a terrible frost and biting cold that prevented men from working fields buried beneath snow. The cash-strapped crown had taxes voted through Parliament granting Edward one fifteenth of every man's money and goods. It was a heavy tax and came at a time when the country could ill afford it. Warkworth recorded that at these demands 'the people grouched sore'.

Early in 1464 Edward was close to securing peace with France, Burgundy and Scotland in a manoeuvre that would starve the remaining Lancastrians of support. John Neville, Lord Montagu, not yet belted as Earl of Northumberland, was sent north with a force of 5,000 men to escort the Scottish delegation south for treaty negotiations. The move clearly caused panic among the Lancastrians, who must have foreseen the withdrawal of Scottish support for their cause as a key plank of the treaty Edward hoped to conclude. If France and Burgundy were similarly sworn to refuse them refuge and aid, all would be lost.

Somerset, accompanied by Lords Roos and Hungerford, invaded the north once more, falling upon the Neville force at Hedgeley Moor on 25 April. The vastly experienced John soon crushed the Lancastrian army, though the sides were of equal strength. Roos and Hungerford fled the battlefield, leaving Somerset to make his own escape as their forces scattered. Sir Ralph Percy, a junior member of the dispossessed family, was left to fight to his death among those who did not escape. John Neville continued north to collect his charges while Somerset rallied his men and pressed south to await Montagu's return.

The Lancastrian force set up camp just outside Hexham, Northumberland, and awaited Neville's force. When it arrived on 15 May it appears to have taken the Lancastrians by surprise. Somerset had barely arranged his men near to Linnels Bridge over the Devil's Water when Neville's force charged them from higher ground. Lord Roos turned and fled into Hexham at the mere sight of the enemy and Somerset's force was left hopelessly exposed. Pushed back to the Devil's Water, men fell in and drowned or were crushed on the steep banks. Somerset was captured, as was Lord Roos shortly afterward, and that same evening John Neville had Somerset, Roos and other leading Lancastrians executed in Hexham. Deprived of his staunchest allies, Henry, who had been with the force but who had kept well away from the battlefields, headed back up north. The Lancastrian threat, if not decapitated, had been made impotent and would not trouble Edward again for several years. It is following these successes that John Neville was handed the title of his family's enemies and made Earl of Northumberland at York.

When Somerset had led his incursion Alnwick, Dunstanburgh and Bamburgh Castles had all been seized by the Lancastrians once again. After Hexham, Alnwick and Dunstanburgh were peacefully retaken, but Bamburgh, under the control of Sir Ralph Grey, refused to capitulate. Edward was, according to Warkworth, still at York at the time and sent Warwick, accompanied by his brother John, to resolve the matter. Warwick sent Chester Herald from the king and one of his own heralds to deliver a chilling threat to Grey. If they surrendered the castle immediately, all within but Grey and Sir Humphrey Neville would be spared. It is perhaps unsurprising that Grey refused, sending back the message that 'My Lords assure you, upon their honour, to sustain siege before you these seven years, or else to win you'. Upon this the heralds informed him that King Edward wished to have the castle delivered back to him unscathed because of its proximity to the Scottish border. With ailing finances and a constant threat from north of the border, Edward could ill afford to see fortresses slighted. Warwick's heralds told Grey that

> … if you deliver not this Jewel, the which the king our most dread sovereign Lord hath so greatly in favour, seeing it marcheth so near his ancient enemies of Scotland, he specially desireth to have it, whole, unbroken, with ordinance; if you suffer any great gun laid unto the wall, and be shot and prejudice the wall, it shall cost you the Chieftain's head; and so proceeding for every gun shot, to the least head of any person within the said place.

It was a grisly threat. The first gunstone they were forced to fire would cost Grey his head. The next the head of his second-in-command and so on down the ranks until the lowliest man inside the castle was beheaded. Grey defiantly left the heralds and prepared his defence. Warwick brought up two huge iron guns, the largest named *Newcastle* and its slightly smaller brother christened *London*. These two beasts pummelled the castle so that 'stones of the walls flew into the sea'. A brass gun called Dysyon managed to consistently fire shot into Ralph Grey's own chamber. The siege was brief and successful, though damage had been done to the castle.

In spite of the threats made, the men inside were spared. Sir Ralph was captured and taken before the king at Doncaster. Here, John Tiptoft, Earl of Worcester and Constable of England, oversaw his trial. Tiptoft was in his late thirties and considered a learned man, having studied at Oxford and Padua. As Lord High Constable of England, Worcester headed the Court of Chivalry and was responsible for dispensing the king's justice. Tiptoft would, over the coming years, carve out for himself a fearsome reputation that led to him being dubbed The Butcher of England. Increasingly harsh punishments doubtless warranted the nickname, though Tiptoft may have born it unfairly.

The Constable had the right to try and judge matters of treason based upon evidence that he had seen without a formal trial before a jury, an important power which will rear its head again. Tiptoft told Grey, 'Remember the law! Wilt thou shall proceed to judgement? These matters showeth so evidently against you, that they need not examine you of them.' Sir Ralph was a Knight of the Bath, a sacred order of chivalry second in prestige only to the Order of the Garter. As part of the ceremony of initiation, recruits had to fast in chapel, allowed to look neither up nor down. Having taken their oath they were presented with their sword and a golden angel. As they left the chapel the king's Master Cook stood at the doorway in a white apron with a large cleaver, warning them all as they passed him by:

Gentlemen, you know what a great Oath you have taken, which is to defend the Gospel, succour the widows and fatherless, right the wronged, which if you perform, and keep, it will be to your great honour; but if you break it, I must hack off your spurs from your heels, as unworthy of this dignity, which will be a great dishonour to you, which God forbid.

Tiptoft now reminded Grey of this threat and the king's Master Cook stepped forward, ready to perform his task. The record in *Warkworth's Chronicle* does not specify that it was done, but given that the penalty was recalled and it was noted that the Master Cook stood ready it seems likely that Sir Ralph Grey's spurs were cut through by the cook's knife as close to his heels as possible. It was a piece of ceremonial theatre, but the dishonour conferred upon a knight by losing his spurs was very real. Grey then had his coat of arms torn from his clothing. No longer a knight bannerette, he was not entitled to wear his own arms.

Grey's hopes may have been raised when Tiptoft informed him that 'the King pardons that for thy noble grandfather, the which suffered trouble for the King's most noble predecessors'. Edward had been lenient to plenty of men and Ralph may have thought that a family connection was about to save his life. Ralph's grandfather Sir Thomas Grey had been beheaded alongside Edward's own grandfather Richard, Earl of Cambridge, for his part in Cambridge's attempted coup against Henry V on the eve of the king's departure for France in 1415.

If Ralph dared to believe he might be saved his hope was short-lived. Edward's desire for reconciliation had its limits and Ralph had strayed beyond them. The pardon in this case only excused Ralph from the gruesome ordeal of being hanged, drawn and quartered as the law demanded in cases of treason. It lay within the power of the king to commute this sentence to the more merciful execution of beheading. Usually this prerogative was only exercised in the case of noblemen, but Tiptoft explained that it had been extended to Ralph Grey:

> Then, Sir Ralph Grey, this shall be thy penance; thou shalt go on thy feet unto the town's end, and there thou shalt be laid down and drawn to a scaffold made for thee, and thou shalt have thine head struck off thine body, to be buried in the Friars, thy head where it pleased the King.

The sentence was duly carried out. With all of this done, the Lancastrian threat in the north seemed finally ended. Edward,

Warwick and Northumberland returned south to continue with the business of ruling England.

Warwick was pressing the king to conclude a peace treaty and marriage alliance with France. Louis XI had come into his throne in the same year as Edward, just a few months later. By a strange coincidence, the French king would also die within six months of Edward IV. France had been resurgent when Henry VI had failed to give attention to his lands and war there. Henry V had won those lands because of the bitter internal feuding in France in the early fifteenth century, which had refused to abate. England was in a similar position, and it was possible that Louis might turn his eye across the Channel to an unsettled enemy and spy the same opportunity Henry V had exploited. As France had rediscovered a lost confidence, it had become clear that they were now a force to be reckoned with on the Continent. It was the obvious alliance for the first king of a new dynasty as he sought the room to settle into his realm.

Warwick was despatched to France to negotiate a treaty and to secure a French princess as Edward's bride. Warwick at least was not put off by England's experiences of Margaret of Anjou. The *Chronicon Francaise* records that the earl was received by Louis at Rouen with enormous pomp and celebration. His ego undoubtedly enjoyed the lavish massaging and he spent each of the next twelve days with the King of France. When he left, he bore not only news of a treaty and an agreed marriage but was also heavily laden with extravagant gifts from the French King. Louis XI was to earn himself the nickname The Universal Spider during his reign. A constant weaver of careful, delicate webs of intrigue, he placed great store upon knowing his enemies and understanding their weaknesses. Warwick's vanity was probably easy enough to spot and Louis found him easy to flatter.

Warwick was triumphal when he returned, his mission successfully concluded. When a meeting of the Council in September sought to finalise the arrangements for the treaty and the wedding, Edward was forced to reveal to those gathered that he had already married in secret, probably in May that year. The date remains uncertain, with many pinpointing 4 May, though Warkworth states that it was 1 May. The date was to be of little importance. It was the identity of the king's new wife that was to confound all and cause particular, personal consternation to Warwick.

The traditional tale of Edward's marriage is that Elizabeth Woodville, or Grey as she then was, positioned herself beneath an oak tree which King Edward was due to pass. As she stood with her two young sons the beautiful, golden-haired twenty-seven-year-old widow easily caught the roving eye of the twenty-one-year-old king. Elizabeth presented the king with her two sons, pleading that she had no way to support them because of their father's death in service to King Henry. Whatever he felt about her cause, Edward was struck by her beauty. He sought to woo her, but she refused his advances. Some stories tell how he drew a knife and threatened to kill her unless she gave in to him, to which she replied that she would rather be murdered than forced to surrender her honour. This threat is often dismissed as beyond Edward's character, but it was perhaps not so far beyond the bounds of possibility at this point in his life.

Elizabeth's refusal served only to stoke Edward's burning desire, but she maintained that only after marriage would she give herself to a man. It is this condition that led to the secret ceremony, probably in early May, at which Elizabeth's mother Jacquetta was one of the very few present to act as a witness. The marriage had been kept secret after Edward had shared Elizabeth's bed for the next few nights. It is a series of events shrouded in mystery, one which was to haunt the House of York much later.

Edward's mother, Cecily Neville, Dowager Duchess of York, was apparently outraged by news of the match. At least as upset, if not even more so, was Warwick. Having negotiated a marriage and an accompanying peace treaty as instructed, the earl had returned bursting with news of his success. It would be comical to imagine the stunned, slack-jawed silence in the council chamber as Edward causally announced to his most trusted advisors that he could not see Warwick's promises through because he had already married without informing them. Worse was to come when he revealed that his spouse, the new Queen of England, was a widowed mother of two from a Lancastrian family, whose husband had died fighting against their cause at St Albans. It would be comical but for the seething rage that gripped Warwick. He was embarrassed, both at home and abroad. His honour would be slighted by the king's inability to follow through with what he had negotiated. Perhaps that was the very point.

The Neville family was all powerful by now. Land, titles and money had flowed to them in recognition of their assistance in winning Edward his throne, but it is likely that as Warwick's ego and sense of self-importance swelled the king grew more and more wary. The over-mighty subject was not a new phenomenon and Edward may have been all too aware that in Warwick he had a similar problem. The question was how to knock the preening earl from his perch. A wedding to a woman of whom Warwick would never approve, made in secret at the very time that Warwick was making such a show of leading marriage negotiations in France, was perfect. Edward had made it clear that he was his own man, no puppet of the proud earl, but he had done so at great expense to Warwick and that was an offence the earl could not forget.

The king's roving eye was to work intermittently in his favour and against it, ultimately proving disastrous. It is not inconceivable that Elizabeth Woodville was one of several ladies tricked out of their honour by the young king and that Edward only revealed the union to confound the proud Warwick as he boasted of his triumphs in France. Having done so, though, he was stuck with the match, though it is clear that it was successful and filled with mutual respect and probably no small measure of genuine love. If Edward sought to avoid a repeat of history then his lessons were only part learned. In his efforts to break a pattern of over-mighty subjects the young king was about to repeat another error from recent history.

Richard Woodville was elevated as Earl Rivers, promoted further into the nobility to reflect his new position as father-in-law to the king. Elizabeth's oldest son Thomas Grey was created Marquess of Dorset, leaping over the rank of earl. The large brood of children fathered by Richard Woodville began to corner the market for eligible marriages. Anne married Viscount Bourchier; Mary was wed to William Herbert, Earl of Pembroke; Jacquetta married John, Baron Strange; the twenty-year-old John married the sixty-five-year-old Catherine Neville, Dowager Duchess of Norfolk; Margaret was wed to Thomas Fitzalan, Earl of Arundel; and

Catherine married Henry Stafford, grandson of Humphrey, 1st Duke of Buckingham, now himself the 2nd Duke of Buckingham, his father having predeceased his grandfather. It is not hard to see why they attracted the disapproval and spite of established noble families.

The Woodville family often shoulder the blame for this veracious rise, but it can only have been achieved with Edward's will and consent. It seems that he found in the Woodville clan a family in need of power that reflected their new position and who could act as a perfect counterbalance to the Neville family. The Woodville power base would be utterly dependent upon the patronage of the king, forcing them to toe the line at all times or face ruin. Edward seems to have remained careful never to give his in-laws power independent of himself, thus marking them as his tools in establishing his own authority.

The next year, 1465, was to be a crucial time. Anthony Woodville was accosted by the ladies of Edward's court and his thigh encircled by the golden tournament prize. The challenge laid was between Anthony Woodville, Lord Scales, champion of England and Anthony, Bastard of Burgundy. In his mid-forties, the Bastard of Burgundy, a natural but illegitimate son of Philip the Good, Duke of Burgundy, was a famous soldier and tournament champion. The tournament between the two men, who immediately entered into excited correspondence to arrange it, was to be something akin to a World Cup Final. It would take another two years for the tournament to actually happen, due to unrest in both England and Burgundy.

In September 1465, George Neville was enthroned as Archbishop of York. The celebratory feasts took place at Cawood Castle just outside York and lasted for four days, during which the vast quantities of food and wine consumed can still be found recorded today in *De Nova Villa*. Warwick and the Nevilles were sparing no expense in demonstrating their power over Church and State. An interesting feature of these feasts is the recording of Richard, Duke of Gloucester, the king's brother, who was installed within Warwick's household for his tutelage, sitting at the top table with the earl's younger daughter Anne Neville. The two would be torn in different directions by the tides of fortune, but were destined to be reunited. The nature of their relationship has long been the subject of debate. Although it will never be settled, it is clear that they knew each other from childhood, sharing triumphal celebrations under Warwick's paternal eye.

A dangerous game of brinkmanship was afoot behind all the glamorous display. Warwick stood firm before the king, who sought to disperse power from the hands of his former mentor. To avoid the threat of an over-mighty subject, Edward was forced to take another problematic route: promoting favourites utterly reliant on royal patronage. As Anthony Woodville stood surrounded by the excited women of court who circled his thigh with a golden prize, the game in which he was truly engaged may have escaped the young man. Or perhaps he knew exactly what he was doing.

13

Warwick's Pride

On 20 March 1470, Lord Berkeley of Berkeley Castle took an army into the field against Lord Lisle of Wooton at Nibley Green in Gloucestershire. The two men had been locked in a longstanding dispute over portions of the Berkeley inheritance, to which Lord Lisle believed he was entitled through his mother the Countess of Shrewsbury. It was possibly Lord Lisle who challenged Lord Berkeley to settle the matter in battle, and both men took their forces, probably less than 1,000 men each, and squared up at North Nibley that morning. Lord Berkeley won the field and built the south aisle of St Martin's church in the village in thanks for his victory; many of the men who fell that day are buried in the churchyard. The Battle of Nibley Green was the last private battle fought on English soil, and the willingness of two barons to settle their feuds outside the king's law demonstrated a fatal collapse in the Yorkist government – one which threatened a repeat of the catastrophes that had cost Henry VI his throne.

The second half of the 1460s saw a terminal decline in Edward IV's relationship with his most powerful subject. The king's new wife is frequently blamed for the collapse in their long-standing and successful friendship, but the Crowland Chronicler, a politically astute writer very close to events of the time and believed to have been a member of Edward's Council, laid the blame firmly elsewhere. This informed source claims that Edward's foreign policy 'was really the cause of the dissensions between the king and the earl, and not the one which has been previously mentioned

– the marriage of the king with queen Elizabeth'. On 11 February 1466 Edward and Elizabeth celebrated the birth of their first child, Princess Elizabeth of York. They were a settled couple and although the king's new in-laws were accruing power and prestigious matches, this in itself does not appear to have upset Warwick.

Edward had entered negotiations with France, Burgundy, Brittany and Scotland to sue for peace. He was keen for France to refrain from supporting Margaret of Anjou, now lodged in poverty in that country, and agreed to stay out of disputes between Louis and Burgundy and Brittany in return for Louis' agreement. At the same time Edward had made a secret promise to Philip the Good, Duke of Burgundy, to assist him. The English king was keeping his options open, playing his cards close to his chest so that none were entirely sure of his plans.

At home, things were beginning to look up for Edward. After the Lancastrians had been defeated at Hedgley Moor and Hexham a Lancashire knight named Sir James Harrington had captured Henry VI near Clitheroe. Warkworth records that Harrington escorted Henry south, the deposed king 'on horseback, with his legs bound to the stirrups, and so brought through London to the Tower, where he was kept long time'. It is also suggested that he was quite well cared for and that 'every man was suffered to come and speak with him, by licence of the keepers'. Control of Henry gave Edward a huge boost. Margaret and their son Edward were still at large but were at least installed deep within France, and Edward's diplomatic efforts were concentrated upon depriving them of support.

In 1467 the Bastard of Burgundy was finally able to visit England to compete in the long-anticipated tourney with Anthony Woodville. As the Bastard of Burgundy sailed across the Channel, he was attacked by pirates, who appeared on the surface to be Spaniards but who were believed to really be French. The Burgundians had a large force, prepared for the threat they suspected, and captured and looted two of the pirate ships. The Bastard was welcomed by an official delegation at Gravesend on the Thames estuary, landing on around 29 May, and escorted to London where he was afforded a state welcome. The Bastard was presented to King Edward and enjoyed the court's hospitality until the tournament was opened with great pageantry on 10 June. The next day there was a one-on-one combat on foot between Lord Scales and the Bastard of Burgundy. They fought in shining plate armour, each using a war axe with a dagger sheathed at their waists. Their bout was hailed as a classic match, the king finally naming it a draw and having them parted. It was reported that after the match Lord Scales' armour bore several gashes made by the spiked back end of the Bastard's axe.

There were three further days of contests between the English knights and their Burgundian counterparts. Fabyan reported that the English held the upper hand when the spectacle was cut short by the arrival of news that the Bastard's father, the ailing Duke Philip, had passed away. The Bastard returned to Burgundy immediately for the funeral and to aid his half-brother, the new Duke Charles the Bold. The tournament had been a memorable spectacle but had ended abruptly and, as much as the cause was unavoidable, closed on something of a flat note. The glamour of the tourney had glossed over a deep and widening crack in the political structure of Edward's rule.

Charles of Charolais, the heir to Philip's dukedom, had sent an offer to Edward of marriage to the English king's sister Margaret. Charles had recently been widowed for a second time and both parties saw an opportunity to cement the relationship that they had been building. Warwick was bitterly opposed to the suggestion, actively promoting a French marriage for the king's twenty-one-year-old sister. The well-positioned writer of the *Crowland Chronicle* asserted that the rivalry was personal and that Warwick intensely disliked Charles, closing his explanation by saying that Warwick 'pursued that man with a most deadly hatred'. Crowland insists that it was this difference in foreign policy focus that was the cause of Warwick's growing discontentment, not the fact that Edward had married Elizabeth Woodville.

Toeing the family line, George Neville, Archbishop of York, boycotted the visit of the Bastard of Burgundy. As Edward's Chancellor, the most senior political figure in the government, it was an embarrassing snub to which Edward reacted sharply and decisively. George Neville was removed from his post and the royal seal taken back from him. The post was filled by Robert Stillington,

Bishop of Bath and Wells, a man on a steady rise through the ranks. If Warwick were under any illusion about his position and influence, Edward's cool reception of a French ambassadorial delegation presented by Warwick left him in no further doubt. If the king was trying to make a point, his game was becoming dangerous. Warwick was a proud man and would stomach only so much insult.

Margaret began her grand journey to her new husband on 18 June 1468, when she rode through jubilant crowds to St Pauls, spending that night at Stratford Priory, where Edward and his queen also lodged. On 19 June Margaret journeyed on to Canterbury for more religious ceremony. On Friday 1 July she set sail from Margate with a large and illustrious entourage, led by Anthony Woodville, Lord Scales. Landing at Sluys the next day Margaret was given control of the town and two days later Duke Charles came to her, his new bride presented to him by Lord Scales, and he excitedly kissed her and each of her ladies. The two spent the next few days in each other's company before enjoying the celebrations of their marriage on 10 July 1468, which included a spectacular entrance into Bruges.

Among the rich treasure trove of the Paston Letters lies one missive from John Paston the Younger, who was a witness to the lavish displays that followed.

My Lady Margaret was married on Sunday last past, at a town that is called the Dam, three miles out of Bruges, at five of the clock in the morning; and she was brought the same day to Bruges to her dinner, and there she was received as worshipfully as all the world could devise; as with precession with ladies and lords, best beseen of any people that ever I saw or heard of; many pageants were played in her way in Bruges, to her welcoming; the best that ever I saw.

John Paston goes on to describe the Bastard of Burgundy committing to answer the challenges of twenty-four knights and gentlemen within the next eight days of feasting and jousting. When he had answered each of the twenty-four challengers he joined with those men as a team of twenty-five to take part in more joust against twenty-five more knights the following day. As part of this round of tournaments, Lord Scales entered the lists against a nobleman of Burgundy, but the Bastard himself refused to compete against his namesake Anthony because the two had 'made promise at London that none of them both should never deal with other in arms'. The Bastard escorted Lord Scales onto the field but was then struck by a horse in an accident and left with an injured leg that side-lined him for the remainder of the tournament, a fact lamented by John Paston, who wrote that 'God made never a more worshipful knight'. John goes on to extol the fabulous surroundings of the Burgundian court, writing that 'I heard never of non like to it, save King Arthur's court: and (by my truth) I have no wit not remembrance to write to you half the worship that is here'. The opulent splendour and conspicuous wealth of the Burgundian court was to make a lasting impression on its new allies and influence the English court for years to come.

The spring of 1469 saw the breaking of the fragile peace that had sat upon England. The whole country had held its breath for years, and the length of time taken to build the pressure only meant that the release was all the more devastating. Edward had created, whether deliberately, to remind Warwick who was in charge, or accidentally, an atmosphere almost identical to that which had seen Henry VI faced with rebellion by the Duke of York. Princes of the blood, specifically Edward's brother George, were being excluded from power. It is likely that Warwick counted his own descent from influence among the complaints that those who deserved the ear of the king were being ignored. Those who did not deserve their influence were being drawn further to the centre of power. Under Henry VI it had been the Beauforts; now it was the Woodvilles. Their reliance on royal patronage kept them well tamed, but the wealth, power and influence this accrued for them made them unpopular with those at whose expense they gained.

The events that unravelled in the north of England in May, June and July are not clearly set down in any contemporary source in a consistent way, a symptom of the south's disregard for, perhaps even disliking of, the north. Some sources point to three uprisings, others to two and some to just one, with leadership and purpose confused and uncertain. It is possible that there was an abortive attempt at an uprising in late March or early May, possibly in the name of Robin of Redesdale. More certain is the existence of a serious gathering under the leadership of Robin of Holderness. Legends of Robin Hood were prevalent by this period, and the name was used to hide the true identity of rebel leaders keen to be seen as championing the weak and poor against the oppressive nobility.

Attempts have been made to identify the leader of the May uprising, but he remains elusive due to the lack of evidence. Robert Hillyard is a name often ventured, and one common thread in the various other suggestions is the connection to the Percy affinity. Hillyard was a Percy retainer, and it is possible that the uprising was in protest at the Neville stranglehold in old Percy heartlands since the family's fall. *The Beverley Records* detail a detachment of archers sent 'to ride with the Earl of Northumberland to suppress Robin of Redesdale and other enemies of the kingdom'. The men were away from the town for about nine days, suggesting that John Neville swiftly crushed the uprising. Warwick's brother's decisive involvement adds weight to the notion that the rebellion had Percy sympathies, if not instigators. *The Brief Latin Chronicle* records that Robin of Holderness made a demand 'for the Earldom of Northumberland to be restored to the rightful heir', referring to Henry Percy, the son of the Earl of Northumberland killed at Towton in 1461.

Unrest was not ended. As June moved into July another threat emerged, more definitely rallying behind the figure known as Robin of Redesdale. This rebel's identity also remains a mystery but it has been suggested that he was Sir John Conyers, a notable member of Warwick's large retained force. As Robin of Holderness's rebellion appears to have been initiated in sympathy with the Percy cause, so Robin of Redesdale's uprising seems to have been in favour of the Nevilles. Certainly John Neville, Earl of Northumberland, made no move to prevent this gathering and Neville men were to be found among their numbers. If an earlier attempt to gather men under the name of Robin of Redesdale had faltered in April and May, and then Robin of Holderness had sought to promote the Percy cause, it may have given Warwick an idea. Cade's Rebellion had become associated with the Duke of York's cause and served to both measure support for and to promote his grievances. Whether York had a hand in that uprising remains unclear, but a perception has developed that he did, perhaps in part because Warwick would use the same tactic to air his grievances now.

News reached Edward of the significant uprising while he was in East Anglia. He swiftly gathered a force and marched north to confront the rebels. In his haste, Edward soon discovered that he had underestimated the size of the force gathering behind Robin of Redesdale. Warkworth describes 'a great insurrection in Yorkshire, of diverse knights, squires and commoners' with their numbers swollen to 20,000, and Edward found himself undermanned. Withdrawing to Nottingham Castle, the king called for reinforcements from Wales led by William Herbert, Earl of Pembroke, and from the south-west under the command of Humphrey Stafford, Earl of Devon.

Humphrey was a leading member of a junior branch of the Stafford family that had been earls of Stafford and were now dukes of Buckingham. This line of the Stafford family was powerful in and around Wiltshire and Dorset and had long been supporters of King Edward's cause. Humphrey had fought for Edward at the Battle of Mortimer's Cross and had joined the King's Council shortly before Henry Courtenay had been tried and convicted for treason, earlier in 1469. On 17 May, Humphrey had been created Earl of Devon, a title which had belonged by right to Courtenay. This led Warkworth to suggest that Stafford had orchestrated Courtenay's downfall in order to obtain the earldom, though this perhaps underestimates Edward's own authority and desire to see loyal men in key positions. The ruthless exercise of this project was precisely what had led to the rebellion that now saw the new earl rallying men to his king.

Edward, waiting at Nottingham, must have had an idea of what truly lay behind Robin of Redesdale's actions because from there, on the 9 July, he wrote three letters. One went to Richard Neville, Earl of Warwick, telling him, 'We ne trust that you should be of any such disposition towards us, as the rumour here runneth, considering the trust and affection we bear in you,' and requiring his attendance upon the king. Clearly stories were reaching the king's ear of Neville, involvement in the uprising. A second letter was sent to George Neville, Archbishop of York, requesting him to come to the king at Nottingham. The third letter went to Edward's own brother George, Duke of Clarence, who seems to have been seduced by Warwick's promise of more power, perhaps even dangling the crown before George's avaricious, dissatisfied eyes. Edward called his brother to join him at Nottingham too, assuring him that 'you shall be to us right welcome'. All three ignored the summons and were already heading to Calais.

Warwick had no sons but did have two daughters. He had long harboured a desire to marry the eldest, Isabel, to George, who was Edward's heir apparent until he had a son. The union would join the Nevilles with the royal house and offered the opportunity of Warwick one day being father-in-law to the king and grandfather to a future monarch. Edward had blocked the marriage at every turn on the grounds on consanguinity; George and Isabel were first cousins, once removed. In truth, the refusal was probably simply part of Edward's scheme to exclude Warwick, and the king had no intention of allowing the earl a way back in. In an early sign of his intentions, Warwick had begun proceedings in Rome to acquire the Papal dispensation necessary for the union and once it was granted, Warwick, his brother and cousin took ship to Calais, where George and Isabel were married on 11 July.

From here Warwick issued a letter accompanied by a manifesto, nominally in the name of Robin of Redesdale's rebellion and detailing their grievances but just as likely penned by Warwick himself to communicate his own frustration. Warwick's letter is phrased in deferent terms that must have appeared disingenuous to Edward. The duke, earl and archbishop informed the king that 'true subjects of this his realm of England have delivered to us certain bills of Articles', specifically naming those responsible for causing the kingdom 'to fall in great poverty of misery, disturbing the administration of the laws, only intending to their own promotion and enriching'. The letter names 'Lord Rivers, the Duchess of Bedford, his wife, Sir William Herbert, Earl of Pembroke, Humphrey Stafford, Earl of Devonshire, the Lords Scales and Audley, Sir John Woodville, and his brethren, Sir John Fogge, and others of their mischievous rule'. Warwick was perhaps trying to kick-start a process similar to that the Duke of York had become enwrapped within. Whether York had been an instigator or not, Warwick was clearly driving events down the same road. Certainly those named within the letter – unusually, including a woman – were the very same people now inserted between Warwick and the king.

The manifesto that accompanied the letter opened with a clear and unambiguous threat. It set out to explain the mistakes and poor judgement that had arisen 'in this land in the days of King Edward II, King Richard II and King Henry VI, to the destruction of them, and to the great hurt and impoverishing of this land'. The reference to three kings forcibly removed from the throne in the last century and a half, one by Edward IV himself, was an obvious challenge to the current king by Warwick and laid out the consequences of failing to repair his ways. The first point made by the document was that each of these former kings had 'estranged the great lords of their blood from their secret Counsel'. It goes on to rant against the failure of justice in the country and the financial ruin caused by those named in Warwick's letter, all in spite of Edward holding 'the Crown, Principality of Wales, Duchy of Lancaster, Duchy of Cornwall, Duchy of York, the Earldom of Chester, the Earldom of March, the Lordship of Ireland … beside Tonnage and Poundage of all this land'. Warwick, Clarence and the Archbishop of York had achieved their ends and did not linger in Calais, setting off for the south coast.

William Herbert and Humphrey Stafford met near Banbury on 25 July 1469. Warkworth has Pembroke bringing 43,000 Welshmen, the finest soldiers of that country, with Devon bringing 7,000 archers. These numbers are probably exaggerated, but the two nobles arrived at the town and 'fell into variance for their lodging', as a result of which Pembroke, who appears to have prevailed, spent the night lodged at Banbury while Devon was forced to seek out billeting several miles away. It was to prove a fatal squabble.

Early in the morning of 26 July Robin of Redesdale's force descended upon William Herbert just outside Banbury. The northern men had skirted Nottingham and avoided the king as they swept south to meet up with Warwick. The site of Herbert's Welshmen in their path proved too much of a temptation, which adds further doubt to Warkworth's figures; these would still have made Herbert's force more than twice the size of that of the rebels, even without Devon. The fighting was intense and moved directly to face-to-face fighting in the absence of archers. The Battle of Edgecote Moor remained evenly balanced for some time until Warwick's force appeared to reinforce the rebels, at which point Herbert's men were routed. William and his brother Sir Richard were captured and executed the following day on Warwick's orders. Only a few days later, Warwick caught up with Devon and saw him executed too, only six months after his elevation to the peerage. Shortly after, Richard Woodville, Earl Rivers, and his son Sir John, who had married the aged Dowager Duchess of Norfolk, were captured near Chepstow and hauled before Warwick at Kenilworth, where both were beheaded on 12 August. Warwick was rampantly victorious.

The triumph was made complete when George Neville, Archbishop of York, learned that Edward had been deserted by his men at Nottingham. In a village outside Coventry, the archbishop politely took the king into his custody and escorted him to Warwick Castle, where he was placed under house arrest by his brother Clarence and his cousin Warwick. Warwick claimed to fear for the king's safety, with rumours abounding that men of the south sought revenge upon the king, so had him moved to Warwick's Yorkshire fortress at Middleham Castle.

With Edward under his control, Warwick began to rule in his cousin's name, but found it harder than he had imagined. Men were unwilling to follow his orders when unsure whether they came from the king. Government, as had been the case under Henry VI, relied so entirely on the person of the king that Warwick found it impossible to manage while Edward was a prisoner. The crunch came when Lancastrian forces made an incursion over the Scottish border under the leadership of Sir Humphrey Neville. Warwick was unable to raise a force to repel the threat without the king's personal authority and was forced to relinquish his hold over Edward, who Crowland explains found himself 'released by the express consent of the earl of Warwick'. The king appeared in York on 10 September and was warmly welcomed by the people, allowing an army to be raised to swiftly crush the uprising.

In splendour the king and his disaffected lords returned to London together. A Great Council was summoned at Westminster to thrash the matter out. After long discussions, all parties made a show of being reconciled to create 'peace and entire oblivion of all grievances upon both sides'. The highly informed writer of the *Crowland Chronicle* was under no illusion that it was an act for public consumption, explaining that 'there probably remained, on the one side, deeply seated in his mind, the injuries he had received and the contempt which had been shown to majesty'. Clearly Edward could not forgive the disrespectful treatment meted out to him. On the other part, the writer simply accuses 'a mind too conscious of a daring deed', leaving the reader to insert meaning into this.

Warwick may have been satisfied with his work. He had taken the template of Yorkist opposition to the royal party over the decade of the 1450s and compressed the parts of that process that worked into a matter of weeks. Within six months he had sponsored a popular uprising against government policy, naming certain of the king's advisors as evil influences, issued pledges of fealty from beyond the sea – though Warwick left no room for doubt as to his real meaning – invaded, given battle conspicuously not aimed at unseating the king, taken the person of the monarch into custody and tried to rule in his name. The canny earl seems to have picked the portions of his uncle the Duke of York's experiences that worked and initiated them all at once. It had succeeded. Many of those men named by the rebel manifesto had been rounded up and dealt with swiftly and summarily by Warwick and Clarence. Edward was not Henry VI, though. He was a stronger character and, at least during this period, not averse to severe and cruel retribution.

The false peace could not be long maintained. Edward made one fateful decision now which would haunt him, though it was possibly an extension and continuation of his previous policy of weakening the Neville faction, a strategy that gained increased importance now. Edward oversaw the full rehabilitation of Henry Percy, restoring him to the Earldom of Northumberland as the revolt led by Robin of Holderness had demanded. This course had one major impediment. John Neville was currently Earl of Northumberland. John had swiftly crushed the rebellion from Holderness and does not seem to have taken an active role in the revolution sparked by his two brothers. John had been loyal and was still one of the most experienced, successful and loyal commanders in Edward's England. In compensation for his loss, John, who had been Lord Montagu, was created Marquess Montagu, a promotion from the rank of earl that sat just beneath that of a duke; John himself described it as 'a magpie's nest', meaning that he was given no means to support his new station. He had lost all of the lands, titles and local prestige that accompanied the Earldom of Northumberland and been given an invented title with no land or income. In further compensation, John's son George Neville was created Duke of Bedford and promised a marriage to Edward's daughter Elizabeth. It seems unlikely that Edward ever really intended to squander his first, and at present only, child on a family he was actively demoting from power and influence. John Neville must have felt poorly rewarded for his service.

In February 1470 matters were brought to a head yet again. In Lincolnshire, Edward's Master of the Horse, Sir Thomas de Burgh, was attacked by his neighbour Lord Welles. Welles, with his son Sir Robert and a friend, Sir Thomas Dymoke, rode to de Burgh's manor and drove him out, tearing the house down and stealing his cattle and whatever else they could lay their hands on. Edward cannot have been oblivious to the fact that Lord Welles was second cousin to the Earl of Warwick. He immediately summoned Welles to London to answer for his crimes. After pleading ill health failed to excuse him from the king's order and with the promise of safe conduct, Lord Welles made his way to London. Here, he apologised to the king and made his peace.

Sir Robert Welles had been gathering men since his father's departure. He would later claim that Lord Welles had instructed him to be ready to fall upon the capital in force if his father was mistreated by Edward. In response, Edward gathered a large force and marched north to Lincolnshire. He demanded that Sir Robert Welles disband his force but the young man would not obey. Edward forced Lord Welles to write to his son, instructing him to surrender, but he still refused. In a further demonstration of his brutally ruthless streak Edward lined his men up before the Lincolnshire rebels on 12 March 1470 and had Lord Welles, in his early forties, hauled out before the two armies and beheaded in the field. With that, Edward's men attacked and the ill prepared and poorly drilled men of Lincolnshire turned and fled immediately. So desperate was their flight that many of the men threw their jackets to the ground, either to remove any incriminating trace of livery or to speed their escape. The battle was christened the Battle of Losecoat Field for the lost coats of those attempting to flee, but the panicked tactic did not work, Warkworth noting that 'there was many men slain of Lincolnshire'.

Lord Welles' son Sir Robert and Sir Thomas Dymoke were captured and executed a week after the battle, but not before Robert was interrogated and provided a full confession that must have confirmed Edward's worst fears. *The Crowland Chronicle* explains that Edward was ruthless with the ringleaders, but merciful to the commoners; 'All the leaders of the hostile force fell into his hands; and after inflicting capital punishment on them for their misdeeds, he showed grace and favour to the ignorant and guiltless multitude'. Sir Robert Welles' confession claimed that on Candlemas, 2 February, a chaplain named John Barnby and a priest called John Clare had visited his father from the Duke of Clarence to entreat them to be ready to rise against the king. Robert explained that after his father had departed for London one of Clarence's servants came to him and helped him to organise his men, and that this servant had been present at Losecoat Field aiding the direction of the forces arrayed there. Robert claims that a man of Warwick's household named John Wright had brought a ring from the earl to show his commitment and urged Robert to act. Robert startlingly reported that it was made clear to him by Clarence and Warwick's men that the intention was 'to make the Duke of Clarence king', insisting in spite of its futility that without the incitement of Clarence and Warwick, 'we at this time would not dare have made any commotion or stirring'. Robert's protestations did not avail him and on 19 March, a week after the battle, Welles was beheaded.

If King Edward had harboured any doubts about his brother George and Warwick's connection to this uprising they were swiftly dispelled. Clarence and the earl had made it as far north as Lancashire in search of support but when news arrived of Welles' defeat they turned tail and headed for the south coast. Edward pushed west to try and cut them off but was too slow and pursued them all the way to the coast. Crowland records the frenzied pursuit, recalling that 'being fully conscious of their share in promoting this insurrection, they consulted their safety in flight; upon which, the king followed in pursuit of them, along their route from the county of Lancaster across the intervening counties, until they had arrived at the city of Exeter in the county of Devon'. Warwick made for his flagship, *The Trinity*, but Anthony Woodville, Lord Scales and now Earl Rivers, arrived at the south coast before them, seizing the ships and skirmishing with Warwick's forces, driving them back. Anthony must have been keen for revenge for the murders of his father and brother, but Clarence and Warwick gave him the slip and managed to hire a ship to take them over to Calais.

Orders were sent to Lord Wenlock, Warwick's deputy in Calais, to refuse entry to the earl. Wenlock was a long-standing ally of the earl but chose in this instance to do as the king instructed, blocking the fugitive ship's entry to the town. Denied refuge by Charles, Duke of Burgundy, too, the refugees were forced to land on the coast of Normandy and submit themselves to the mercy of Louis XI, the French king. Louis rubbed his hands as a perfect opportunity to destabilise the English crown fell into his hands. This whole episode rang with an empty, tragic note though. Warwick and Clarence had taken the heavily pregnant Isabel, Warwick's daughter and Clarence's wife, with them on board ship. On the rough seas she went into labour. Denied entry to Calais and the aid that she might have found there, Isabel gave birth on board to a daughter named Anne. The baby would not survive to land on dry earth and the tragedy must have affected all parties. George and Isabel lost their daughter, their first child, and Warwick had been robbed of his first grandchild. All three must have blamed one person for their sorrow. Edward had ordered Calais to deny them entry. Edward had kept them at sea. As the duke and earl were received at the French court, their minds must have been on revenge. The grinding wheels of the bitter conflict were still turning with no end in sight. The Battle of Nibley Green was a minor symptom of a developing contagion.

14

The Returns of the Kings

King Edward was not minded to be merciful any longer. His policy of conciliation for those willing to accept the hand of friendship had always been tinged with a more ruthless reaction to those who would not grasp it. The Earl of Oxford and his son had felt the sharpened edge of Edward's willingness to be hard when necessary, but it seems to have remained the decision of former Lancastrians when deciding which path they would take. Warwick had reopened the infected wounds of 1459–61 with his round of illegal executions, nothing more than murders committed while he had the opportunity to be rid of men he could not defeat in the political arena. Lord Welles had died for his son's recalcitrance, for which Edward had no patience. Clarence and Warwick had escaped, but someone would pay for their crimes.

Anthony Woodville, Earl Rivers, had captured many of Warwick's men at the south coast when he had cut the earl and Clarence off from their ships. They were hauled before the king at Southampton, where he ordered his strong arm of justice, John Tiptoft, Earl of Worcester, to try the ringleaders in his capacity as Constable of England. What followed was an episode that was the stuff of nightmares as the stakes climbed higher and higher. Tiptoft had been serving as Lord Deputy of Ireland after overseeing the execution of his predecessor, the Earl of Desmond. When trouble erupted in England once more, Edward recalled his enforcer. Tiptoft oversaw the trials, though the verdict can never have been in doubt. The sentence, though, would earn Tiptoft eternal condemnation.

Warkworth explains that twenty 'gentlemen and yeomen', probably the highest-ranking men who had been captured, were found guilty and sentenced to the execution prescribed by law for treason. All twenty were hanged, drawn and quartered, a brutal, slow, painful death designed to discourage others from such betrayal. Even this was not enough in this case, though. Tiptoft ordered the beheaded, mutilated corpses to be hung up by their legs and wooden stakes, sharpened at both ends, were driven through each victim's buttocks and into the ground. Upon the sharpened end that remained visible, high in the air, was mounted the head from the body. Tiptoft won no friends for this extreme act of vicious justice. Warkworth wrote that 'the people of the land were greatly displeased; and ever afterward the Earl of Worcester was greatly hated among the people, for the inordinate death that he used, contrary to the law of the land' and John Tiptoft is not remembered as a learned legal mind, nor as a talented Latin scholar. He is, instead, remembered as the Butcher of England, and the wrath of the English people would not stalk his footsteps too much longer before it overtook him. Tiptoft was merely an instrument, though. That he was neither removed nor even censured by the king speaks volumes for the monarch's attitude toward the punishment.

Law and order was beginning to disintegrate as those at the top of society fell into disorder. Edward's reasonably settled rule over the last nine years had restrained those who might have exploited the weaker rule of Henry VI to settle their scores. Lord Berkeley and Lord Lisle took their legal dispute onto the field of battle at Nibley Green in the west of England, and while theirs was the last pitched action between two private armies it was not the only example of a willingness to exploit a breakdown of law and order to private advantage. The swiftness with which these spats erupted all over England demonstrates the fragility of what Edward had fought to secure.

In the east, the Paston Letters reveal another old score dragged out into the daylight. The Pastons had long been associated with a venerable old knight, Sir John Fastolf, a man all too easily overlooked. An adventurer of Arthurian calibre, he is now remembered as the basis for Shakespeare's famous lovable coward Sir John Falstaff, who was initially modelled on, and named for,

Sir John Oldcastle. When Oldcastle's descendants protested against the depiction of their ancestor Shakespeare tactfully renamed the character, thus burying Fastolf under the towering figure of Falstaff. It is not the only time that the Bard would distort the common consciousness to replace historical truths with convenient character flaws. A great number of the Paston Letters relate to Sir John Fastolf and when he died in November 1459 he left the great mansion of Caister Castle to Sir John Paston in his will. Fastolf had grown incredibly wealthy from his exploits in France and managed his money wisely, but left no heir of his body. The Pastons' acquisition of Caister, a jewel upon which Fastolf had lavished time and a considerable amount of money, immediately caused problems. John Mowbray, Duke of Norfolk, laid claim to Caister and began legal proceedings to wrest it from the Pastons, who would not be dislodged. While the mightiest men in the land were occupied, Norfolk had his cannons brought to Caister to blast the Pastons out. Besieged, the Paston Letters reveal that the castle was severely damaged so that gunpowder ran short and supplies within were exhausted. Finally the duke drove the Pastons out, winning, and keeping, Caister Castle.

It was in the north that one of these unexceptional and apparently innocuous spats was to have lasting implications. In an attempt to circumvent the court action that provided slow and uncertain remedy, Hornby Castle became the focus of another example of great men's willingness to exploit the vacuum at the very top of society. This feud was between two great Lancashire families, the Stanleys and the Harringtons. Thomas, Lord Stanley, owned vast swathes of the north-west, his influence also reaching into North Wales. His grandfather Sir John had begun the veracious expansion of their wealth and power and his father, Sir Thomas, had been promoted to the rank of Baron Stanley. The current Lord Stanley, with his younger brother William, was carefully, assiduously but unrelentingly continuing the work of his father. It was this Lord Stanley who had narrowly avoided prosecution for treason in Parliament in 1459 for failing to support the royal forces at Blore Heath, appearing to have a foot in both camps while declaring for neither. It was a tactic that he perfected by long use. He was at the Battle of Northampton, nominally on the royalist side, but it is unclear whether he engaged. By Towton he was to arrive in the Yorkist force but again, his contribution is unclear. His was a watchful game of biding his time.

The Harrington family were the very antithesis of the Stanleys. The current generation's grandfather had born Henry V's standard at Agincourt. The Harringtons had declared early for the Yorkist cause and never wavered from it. It was the Harringtons who had captured King Henry VI and delivered him to Edward in London, so any security Edward enjoyed by virtue of Henry's imprisonment he owed to the Harringtons, and he did reward them with large parcels of land in their native north-west.

The root of this feud lay at the Battle of Wakefield. Stanley had contrived to miss this confrontation too, but Thomas Harrington, the head of the family, and his oldest son John were to fall alongside Edward IV's father, brother and uncle in the setback. Reports from the battle told how Thomas died during the fighting and his son was taken shortly after the battle by wounds that could not be healed. Upon Thomas's death, John came into his inheritance, however briefly. When John succumbed, the inheritance passed to his two daughters, Anne and Elizabeth. Wardship of Anne was granted to another family, and with it the rights to her marriage, upon which her husband would acquire all of the Harrington wealth and possessions. John's brothers James and Robert seized the girls, went to Hornby Castle, the jewel in their crown, and refused to leave.

In 1468 the Harrington brothers were called to answer for their behaviour to the king in the Court of Chancery. Lord Stanley applied for wardship of the girls and Edward granted it, to the outrage of the Harringtons. Lord Stanley swiftly married the girls into his own family, Anne to his own second son Edward, and laid claim to Hornby Castle, a stunning property overlooking the valley of the River Lune. It lay in the way of Stanley expansion and would make a nice addition to Lord Thomas's portfolio. Edward IV, pragmatic to a fault, saw the value in the huge number of men Lord Stanley could bring to the field, if he were so minded. At the very least, it was worth ensuring he was encouraged not to support any opponent, even if positive intervention on Edward's behalf could not be relied upon. James and Robert Harrington, though, returned to Hornby and, like the Pastons at Caister, refused to leave.

When Warwick had been chased from England by Edward IV he had been heading for Stanley's estates, appearing to expect support. Edward's policy seems to have paid off when none was forthcoming and Warwick was forced to turn tail and run for the south coast. Stanley still did not have Hornby Castle, though. In line with others in a similar position, Lord Stanley resolved to use the new instability to achieve his end more swiftly than the courts allowed. He called for a giant cannon named *Mile Ende* to be brought up from Bristol with the express intention of emulating Norfolk's victory at Caister. Something prevented Lord Stanley from launching his shot at the walls of Hornby, and the only explanation is found in a warrant issued by the king's brother Richard, Duke of Gloucester, on 26 March 1470, signed 'at Hornby'. The seventeen-year-old duke had chosen a side in the dispute and he had picked the unswervingly loyal Harringtons over the more fickle, self-interested Stanleys, placing himself in harm's way as a barrier to protect those he championed. The young man cannot have foreseen as a teenager the consequences of his actions as he wrote his warrant from within his friend's castle at Hornby.

In France, Warwick was equally keen to make the most of the shambolic turmoil in England. Philippe de Commynes was a Burgundian writer and diplomat who had served Philip the Good and then his son Charles the Bold before defecting to the court of Louis XI, King of France, in the early 1470s. He never visited England but met Warwick and Edward IV and knew many other key English figures. In his memoirs, he wrote that during this period he continually visited Calais to keep Lord Wenlock honest. Commynes wrote that Charles sent several warnings to Edward that France was building a fleet and that he should prepare himself to repel an invasion, 'but he never heeded it'. Commynes was disparaging of Edward's refusal to heed the warnings. 'King Edward was not a man of any great management or foresight, but he was of an invincible courage, and the handsomest prince my eyes ever beheld.' It seemed that what was coming was obvious to all but Edward. All Warwick needed was men and funds.

Louis XI, the Universal Spider, rubbed his hands together when Warwick fell into his web and began weaving anew. King Edward had openly declared his intention to lead a huge campaign into

France and the possibility of further destabilising Edward and keeping English eyes away from French territories had obvious advantages. Louis counselled Warwick that his only hope was an alliance with his old enemy, Margaret of Anjou. Louis spied an opportunity not only to make life difficult for Edward IV but also to have French influence about the English throne once more, and possibly to be rid of an embarrassing relative living in poverty squirrelled away within his realm. Margaret was summoned to court and reportedly took immense delight in causing her nemesis to kneel before her for over quarter of an hour pledging his allegiance and pleading for an alliance. It seems unlikely that she ever considered turning down the opportunity presented to her, her only hope of restoring herself and her son in almost a decade, but she made the most of having the mighty Richard Neville, Earl of Warwick, maker of kings, on his knee before her. An accord was reached, under which Warwick's younger daughter Anne Neville was married to Edward of Lancaster, Prince of Wales, to unite the two parties in a military affair that would see Warwick and Margaret's grandchild upon the throne. Preparations began swiftly to deny Edward IV time to restore order. Charles the Bold continued to send warnings. Edward continued to ignore them. Further trouble would enter England at the king's own invitation.

Despite Commynes' obvious frustration with Edward's lack of preparation, he does note that Lord Wenlock, who Commynes was convinced intended to betray Edward and return to Warwick's party, let slip during a conversation that one of the Duchess of Clarence's ladies had passed through Calais from England on her way to see her mistress in France. Commyne asserts that this woman carried messages from Edward for his brother the Duke of Clarence extending the hand of forgiveness. As a result of these despatches she caused 'the Duke of Clarence to promise to come over to the king's party as soon as he was in England'. If the conversion occurred this early it is not hard to see why. When they had last been in England, Warwick had sought to place Clarence upon the throne. Now the earl had made an alliance with the chief enemy of Clarence's house and sworn to place those same adversaries on the throne ahead of Edward or George.

Amid all of the intrigue, Warwick took the French fleet and in

August, just a few months after being chased from England, landed at Plymouth. Men swarmed to his cause, swelling his ranks as he marched toward London. Edward was at Lynn in Norfolk when news arrived of the invasion. Lord Hastings gathered 3,000 men to the king's cause and Earl Rivers joined him there also. The king was installed in a large manor house, which, according to what Edward was to later tell him – although he did not know the name of it – Commynes reported was surrounded by a broad moat with only one bridge providing access so that it was easily defensible. Edward also sent a commission to John Neville, Marquess of Montagu, who raised a force of 6,000 men to support the king. Edward sent word to Charles the Bold to prepare his fleet to attack Warwick when he tried to return to France, 'for on land he knew how to deal with him', but Commynes continued that Charles was less than impressed with his brother-in-law's lazy bravado. 'The Duke of Burgundy was not well pleased with these words, for he looked upon it as a greater piece of policy to have hindered the earl from landing, than to be forced to run the hazard of a battle, to drive him out again.' Edward, though, remained confident and wanted a fight with his erstwhile mentor.

Warwick marched north, drawing men to his cause, and Montagu swept south. Within a few miles of Lynn, Montagu's men began to call for King Henry and it was at this point that, according to Warkworth, Montagu gave voice to his complaint that he had been deprived of the earldom of Northumberland and given an empty title with no means of supporting himself. Edward was caught in the jaws of a trap that was about to snap shut on him. Realising that the odds were hopelessly against him, Edward looked to the nearby Norfolk coast. He gave instructions to his soldiery to submit to Warwick in order to save their lives but to remember him and remain loyal to his cause when he returned. With that, he took ship at Lynn on 2 October 1470 into exile. Lord Hastings and Earl Rivers joined him, as did his younger brother Richard, Duke of Gloucester, who rejected both his mentor Warwick and his brother George to begin a voyage into an uncertain exile on his eighteenth birthday.

Edward had lost his kingdom. His contemporaries were under little illusion where the blame for this lay. Commynes wrote that

'His thoughts were wholly employed upon the ladies (and far more than was reasonable), hunting, and adorning his person'. Warkworth complained that 'when King Edward IV reigned, the people looked after all the aforesaid prosperities and peace, but it came not; but one battle after another, and much trouble and great loss of goods among the common people'. When Edward removed Henry VI after a long and singularly disastrous reign the country had wanted a new, bright beginning from the huge young king who wore the badge of the Sunne in Splendour, but Edward had disappointed. He had not ended the warring, nor had he ushered in a new age of glory. He had replaced the country's coinage with a new system aimed solely at creating the illusion of improved finances. England had not got what it wanted in 1461 and now looked back to the old ways.

Warwick is generally viewed as driven hard by his bruised pride in this period. He turned to Margaret of Anjou in desperation as he flailed about for a way to regain what he had been deprived of by Edward's promotion of those Warwick viewed as lesser men. The Nevilles had spent generations of careful marriages and studious management to reach their lofty position, yet others like the Woodvilles, the Herberts and the Hastings were now seeing their stars shooting way beyond that of the earl's, who waned like an old moon in a new season. This view of the events driven by Warwick overlooks the possibility that, alongside an undoubtedly wounded pride, Richard Neville may, as he always retained an uncanny knack of doing, have captured the feeling of the country.

He had risked all to remove Henry's corrupt regime in which the old blood was ignored and those less deserving promoted. He had been pushed from loyalty to Henry VI by ill treatment that he cannot have believed he deserved. Now Edward had pushed him away too, but he had also excluded George and others of noble birth to make room for his wife's family and other men who would rely entirely on his patronage. This was not the world that Warwick had fought for. The same corruption that he had rebelled against was still rife in the country and so he rebelled again. His new alliance would at least offer him control over the weak Henry VI in a way that he could never hope to govern Edward. It remains possible that Warwick was a genuine protagonist in 1469 and

1470. Of course, it is equally likely that he was simply a proud man determined to hold power however it could be grasped.

England now lay in the hands of the Earl of Warwick once more, much as it had done in 1460, before York's return. The earl was now in his early forties and was perhaps the one man in the kingdom capable of deciding who would sit upon the throne. It was Richard Neville, 16th Earl of Warwick, who entered London and visited the Tower to release the imprisoned Henry VI and return him to the throne he had helped take nearly ten years earlier. Warkworth described Henry as 'not worshipfully arrayed as a prince, and not so cleanly kept as should seem such a Prince', suggesting that his five years in prison had not proved as gentle as they might have been. Henry's health had been a root cause of many of his problems before his fall and once deprived of those who were tasked with taking care of his physical appearance it is likely that he emerged, blinking in the bright light of freedom, bemused, bedraggled and unsure what was expected of him now.

Charge was swiftly taken of the king, who was destined to be a puppet under the control of Warwick and Queen Margaret, who still lingered in France with her son awaiting news that it was safe to come. Henry was given a royal makeover, dressed once more like a king and led to the Palace of Westminster, where the crown was placed once more upon his head. A Parliament was summoned in Henry's name which opened with the message 'Revertimini ad me filii revertentes', 'Return to me oh ye rebelling children'. The message was clear. King Henry was the comfortable father figure, his subjects were each a prodigal son who might now be welcomed back into his family of England. Warwick ensured that this familiar cosiness was edged with a promise of new start. Everything would return to how it was, but would be better. Henry was now signing his official documents 'Anno regni Regis Henrici Sexti quadragesimo nono, et readempcionis sue regie potestatis primo', 'Forty-ninth year of the reign of King Henry VI, and the first since his royal readeption'. The deposing of monarchs had happened before in English history, but the restoration of a king once dislodged was a new phenomenon without a name. Those casting about for a term to apply settled upon a seemingly invented term: the readeption of Henry VI. Warwick's deft hand at the helm is clear in the message. Henry was back where he belonged, where he always should have been. It was the forty-ninth year of his rule, offering familiarity and stability, but it was acknowledged as the first year of a new era in which all would be put right under Warwick's careful eye.

On 18 October 1470 there was an act of retribution by the resurgent Lancastrians. John Tiptoft, Earl of Worcester, had found himself unable to flee with other high-ranking members of Edward IV's government and was captured by those for whom Tiptoft's cruelty only months earlier on the south coast was still raw. Worcester was tried for his crimes and executed at the Tower of London, his head and body buried at the Black Friars. Tiptoft would be remembered as the Butcher of England for his ruthless and cruel punishment of the enemies of York during the 1460s, his more academic achievements lost in the blood spilled. He was not attainted for treason, though, allowing his son to succeed to his titles. It would become convenient to allow John Tiptoft to assume all of the blame for the prosecution of a policy at the very least approved of, if not driven by, King Edward.

Elizabeth Woodville had also been left behind in London when her husband fled from Norfolk. Heavily pregnant and unable to make the perilous journey, Elizabeth fled into exile at Westminster Abbey with the three daughters already born to her and the king. The queen had laid down provisions in the Tower of London to hold the city, but when news arrived that her husband had been driven out of England she was left with few options. On 2 November 1470 she gave birth to a son, named for his absent father. It was hardly an illustrious beginning for a boy both parents still intended to see upon the throne of England one day, though that day must have seemed far off as Elizabeth screamed the pain of her agonising labour to the walls of her uncertain sanctuary.

Parliament reversed Edward IV's legitimacy as king along with the attainders against central Lancastrian lords including Edmund Beaufort, 4th Duke of Somerset, able to assume his brother Henry's title officially at last; Henry Holland, Duke of Exeter, Edward's brother-in-law who had proved a stalwart Lancastrian; Jasper Tudor, returned to his Earldom of Pembroke; and John de Vere, Earl of Oxford. In February 1471 these men found the confidence to re-enter England and dare to believe in a bright future as reward for their loyalty to the Lancastrian regime.

Philip de Commynes provides insight into the confused and tumultuous events of the months following Edward's expulsion and Henry's readeption. He asserts that Charles the Bold was pleased to see the Lancastrian party restored, despite his own marriage to Edward's sister. Commynes was sent back to Calais and wrote that he had 'never seen such mutations in the world before'. He felt compelled to apply for a passport to enter English territory, which he had never done before, and took with him a signet ring from Duke Charles as proof of his mission. Charles also promised to ransom Commynes if he should be arrested. When he met Lord Wenlock under the passport issued, he found the man who had denied Warwick entry to Calais and sworn loyalty to Edward wearing a gold badge of the ragged staff, Warwick's emblem. Wenlock told Commynes that within a quarter of an hour of the arrival of news of Warwick's victory the whole town was issued with the earl's livery, those of high rank wearing a gold badge while others had ragged staffs sewn to their clothing. Calais and Wenlock had clearly been waiting for Warwick's victory, or at least were happy to bend freely with the prevailing wind.

When he met Lord Wenlock, Commynes conveyed news that Edward was dead, 'though indeed I well knew to the contrary', and assured the newly triumphant Lancastrians of the Duke of Burgundy's friendship. Charles's incentives to make overtures of peace were clear and pressing. Part of Warwick's agreement with Louis XI was to provide a large force for a planned war against Burgundy, and Duke Charles was keen to avoid Lancastrian support for his enemy. When Edward arrived at Charles's court on 2 January 1471 in Saint Pol it caused the duke a public relations nightmare. Somerset and Exeter were still resident in Burgundy's court and were outraged by Edward's approach to his brother-in-law for aid, Commynes noting that they 'used all their artifice to keep him firm to King Henry's interest' and that Charles 'was in suspense, and knew not which side to favour; he was fearful of disobliging either, because he was engaged in a desperate war at home'. Burgundy was in a quandary. Eventually Charles erred on the side of caution and gave his promise to the Duke of Somerset, who carried it back to England. Charles, though, was careful to add certain precautions to protect himself from his old foe the Earl of Warwick. Margaret and Prince Edward lingered still at the French court.

As soon as Somerset and his Lancastrian allies departed his court Charles turned his attention to his brother-in-law, who Commynes says was 'much dissatisfied to see how unsuccessfully his affairs went on'. Duke Charles now reassured King Edward that he had been deceiving the Lancastrians and that he would offer support to Edward's cause, though he confirmed that he would not be able to provide open assistance for fear of jeopardising his own increasingly precarious position. Charles issued proclamations forbidding his subjects from helping or accompanying King Edward in any attempt to regain his throne, but at the same time he sent Edward 50,000 florins and a cross of St Andrew that held great value. Three or four large ships were fitted out in secret and a further fourteen ships hired and well-armed in readiness for Edward's expedition.

Making the most of the opportunity presented to him, Charles marched an army to Amiens against King Louis just as Edward set sail on 2 March 1471, reasoning that he had created for himself a situation in which he could not lose. Whether Edward or Henry, York or Lancaster, was victorious in England, his alliance was secured and with almost certain war sent over the sea to England there would be no assistance moving the other way to help Louis against Charles. Edward tried to land on the east coast of Norfolk only to find that his ally the Duke of Norfolk was absent from his lands at that time and the Earl of Warwick had placed patrols all along the coast. Edward's small scouting party that landed from the angry swells of the sea advised him not to try to disembark there. Reluctantly he accepted their counsel and his fleet of loaned and hired ships clambered further north along the east coast. The storm scattered the ships and Edward made land at Ravenspur in Yorkshire, the same place Henry IV had landed on his return from exile when he claimed the throne of Richard II. Though accidental, it was a prophetic chance. There were two kings in England now, and only one crown to be worn.

Edward had set sail into a stormy sea and an equally squally future. He left Flanders on 2 March before the weather hit the Continent. Queen Margaret and her seventeen-year-old son Prince Edward took to their ships on 14 March, but delayed their departure until 14 April, when the sea was calmed and the storm abated. Edward's rash plunge into the fight to recover his realm and Margaret's cautious delay in returning to join her husband were to prove decisive; Easter week of 1471 promised both death and rebirth, as the Wars of the Roses reached another cataclysmic pinnacle from which only one side could emerge victorious.

15

The Arrival of King Edward IV

Edward IV's ship deposited him at Ravenspur on the Yorkshire coast on 14 March 1471 with his close friend and Chamberlain, William, Lord Hastings, and around 500 men. The returning king's fleet had been dispersed by the fierce storm and he landed without sight of any of the others. His brother Richard, Duke of Gloucester's ship had been blown four miles along the coast with his 300 soldiers and Anthony Woodville, Earl Rivers, had found land some fourteen miles from his king with another 200 men. Other ships were scattered along the east coast. Edward found safe lodgings for the night and by the next morning the storm had eased and all of his ships had landed safely. The men disembarked and found their way to Edward's location during the course of 15 March, but there remained a huge problem. Yorkshire, ironically, was traditionally a Lancastrian heartland and it was dominated by Henry Percy, Earl of Northumberland, rehabilitated by Edward but from a family deprived by the House of York and by nature Lancastrian, and John Neville, Marquis of Montagu, dispossessed of the Percy earldom and smarting from the financially compromising position inflicted upon him by Edward in spite of good service.

The key source for the description of King Edward's attempts to regain his throne is a contemporary chronicle known as *The Historie of the Arrival of King Edward IV*, an account written by an anonymous man who identifies himself only as 'a servant of the King's, that presently saw in effect a great part of his exploits, and the residue knew by true relation of them that were present'.

The writer offers detailed insight into the campaign that would see two kings of England reduced to only one claimant. It is naturally heavily biased in favour of King Edward's cause but, provided the obvious leaning is taken account of, it is an invaluable insight into the campaign to regain a throne and a nation.

The Arrival makes it clear that Edward did not receive the welcome he hoped for when he had gathered his forces to him after the storms. Few men rushed to join his cause perhaps, as the writer claims, because they had been warned by Warwick's representatives not to provide any aid to Edward wherever he might land, but equally, in hostile territory far from his power base, few had a natural sympathy for the Yorkist king's cause there. This left Edward dangerously exposed with a small force vulnerable to an organised assault by a larger Lancastrian army. *The Arrival*'s writer points to the lingering affection for Edward's father Richard, Duke of York, and claims that many of the people called for Edward to assume his ducal titles only.

This call from the people gave Edward an idea. He began, just as Henry IV had done in 1399, to claim only his inheritance as Duke of York and insisted that he was not seeking the throne. This appears to have pacified those gathered and armed against the threat of invasion, for the threat was not to the realm any longer. Whether any truly believed Edward's claim or simply sought any flimsy excuse to avoid renewed warfare on their own doorstep cannot be known, but few without a strong partisan allegiance can have wished to see a fresh outbreak of the endless rounds of fighting that had lain low for nearly ten years without ever really going away. With his enemies in London, Edward wanted to push south into Lincolnshire where he might be able to gather more sympathetic support. Such a journey would require a crossing of the Humber, however, necessitating the re-boarding of their ships, and Edward did not wish to give an impression of beating a retreat that might cost him support.

The decision was made to move to the City of York instead, with Edward giving the instruction to all of his followers to vocally maintain the lie that he had returned only to reclaim his dukedom. In fact, Edward's sleight of hand was in his insistence that he sought only the inheritance that was his by right of his father, who had been nominated heir to the throne in 1460, so Edward told a kind of truth as he travelled, but the writer of *The Arrival* insists that the deception worked, causing a force of 6,000 or 7,000 men to move aside and allow them to pass. Edward arrived at Kingston-upon-Hull and demanded entry but the town remained closed to him, so he continued on to York. All along the way he received reports from his scouts of large forces, numbering in the thousands, gathered in various places, yet none came within sight of him. Either his deception worked or, as the writer of *The Arrival* surmises, those levied forces were frightened to give battle to the huge king, his fierce martial reputation going before him and the inherent problems of fighting a man who could be king again tomorrow weighing on their minds.

Three miles from York a City Recorder, Thomas Conyers, rode out to Edward's army and told him to turn back, for the city would not welcome him and may attack if he tried to force an entry. Deciding that he had come too far to back down now and having no intention of appearing the coward, Edward pushed on. A mile outside York two more citizens came to meet Edward: Robert Clifford and Richard Burgh. These two men offered Edward better tidings, assuring him the he would be allowed to pass as long as he was in pursuit of his father's inheritance only. Finally, just outside York, Conyers returned to deliver his warning again. Finally, uncertain what to expect, Edward arrived at the gates of York. He was met by Clifford and Burgh who bid him and sixteen or seventeen of his company to enter the city and meet the aldermen to explain their cause. The invitation surely had the scent of a trap about it, but ever willing to put his cause to the hazard, Edward entered and met the city's leaders. When he managed to convince them with his easy, natural charm that he meant to raise no wars, his company were allowed to rest the night within the city walls.

An evening in the comfort of York must have seemed a triumph to Edward and those who travelled with him. They had been repelled from the Norfolk coast, driven ashore by a storm that dispersed their fleet, travelled under constant threat of impending attack from all quarters and been left alternately unsure whether they would be repelled from York or welcomed behind its walls. Those days must have been trying for all concerned. Edward never seems to have lacked confidence and any who met him could not avoid being impressed by his sheer size and presence, and attracted by his unrivalled good looks and hypnotic charm. In spite of this, he must have journeyed in nervous fear that his rash decision to return so swiftly had backfired. He did not have enough men to withstand the forces gathered in the shadows all about him. A comfortable bed in the security of York's city walls must have replenished the hope that had been ebbing away ever since they had reached English soil.

The next morning Edward and his small force moved south towards Wakefield and Sandal Castle, a stronghold of the Duchy of York from which his father had been drawn to his death. It was a move calculated to give the appearance of visiting ducal land and properties while also providing safety. The journey to Sandal, though, required the negotiating of a great hazard. Edward had to pass close by Pontefract Castle on his left hand side as he marched south. This stout northern fortress not only belonged to John Neville, Marquis of Montagu, but Warwick's wronged brother was in residence as Edward approached. John now had a perfect opportunity for revenge. Edward's forces had not been increasing as he travelled and he would be an easy target for the kind of force Montagu was capable of raising. If John held Edward responsible for his current pecuniary difficulties and the embarrassment of losing a prestigious earldom, it is surprising to find *The Arrival* coolly noting that as Edward passed, the marquis 'in no way troubled him, nor any of his fellowship, but suffered him to pass'.

Montagu's inaction may not have been entirely of his own choosing. He himself had complained before Edward's expulsion that he had been given 'a magpie's nest'. Pontefract was surrounded by Percy territory and even if John called them to fight for him, none might come, awaiting instruction instead from their new master, the Earl of Northumberland, who had been restored by Edward. John Neville's allegiance remains as complex as many men's during this politically difficult period. His family had sacrificed much to see the House of York upon the throne. John himself had been prisoner twice, the executioner's axe hovering over his neck. While it was true that he had lost the Northumberland title and lands, he was a marquis now, senior in rank to an earl, and his son George was Duke of Bedford, a royal title that carried with it the promise of a royal marriage to one of Edward's daughters. Of course, this promise was only good if Edward was king.

On the other hand Warwick was undoubtedly Edward's target and John must have felt the pull of quashing a threat to his brother's life. Yet what hope was there of further advancement under a revived Lancastrian regime once Margaret returned with her famous, burning hatred of the Nevilles? John lacked his brother's wealth and power to protect himself in that uncertain breaking dawn. As Edward's small force stomped arrogantly alongside his castle, John may have watched them grim-faced from a tower window, trapped inside by his own uncertainty so that nothing was all that he could do. The painful uncertainty and tangling of ties of allegiance had been carried back into England by Warwick and now Edward. John was going to have to make his choice, and he probably knew it, as Edward's band drifted from view.

The writer of *The Arrival* is keen to point out the new Earl of Northumberland's role in Edward's safe passage too. Henry Percy similarly did nothing. Had Percy decided to call out the men of the county to resist Edward it is unlikely he would have made it any farther south. York may well have permitted Edward's entry either on the earl's instruction or at least in the absence of his order to deny them aid. Henry Percy owed Edward a clear debt, yet his family were staunch Lancastrians, having sacrificed senior members and many of their liegemen to the effort to deny Edward the crown. The Yorkist leader was marching through lands that had been torn to shreds only a decade earlier by the Battle of Towton. He passed through fields and villages that would have lost men that day fighting for King Henry where the memory would still be raw and the blame placed squarely at Edward's feet. Northumberland restrained this latent hatred, or at least refrained from unleashing it, allowing Edward to pass in safety through Wakefield and Doncaster, where only a few men rallied to his cause.

At Nottingham Edward received some reinforcement as friendlier country brought men more freely to his cause. Among those who arrived with several hundred men at his back was Sir James Harrington. In spite of feeling the rough edge of Edward's political realism, Harrington did not sway from the Yorkist cause. The presence of Edward's brother Richard, Duke of Gloucester, who had placed himself between the Harrington family and the military might of the Stanleys, might well have added to Sir James's resolve to call out those men he could and ride to Edward's side. The news was not so good when Edward's scouts reported a force of 4,000 men at nearby Newark led by John de Vere, Earl of Oxford, and Henry Holland, Duke of Exeter, Edward's Lancastrian brother-in-law.

Newark lay only about twenty miles to Edward's north-east and he knew by now that Warwick was marching north, gathering large numbers to his cause as he approached his own Warwickshire heartlands. Edward had been caught between two forces from north and south only six months before as he waited to see how the game would play out. He had learned his lesson well. Edward was always, and would remain, at his best when acting decisively. He had crushed the Welles uprising by falling upon it hard and fast. He had lost his crown while he sat in Norfolk and waited. Although the size of the Yorkist force by this stage is not clear, it is likely that the army at Newark was larger than Edward's own, yet he mustered them and drove toward Newark. His best hope lay in attacking this segment of the Lancastrian force before it could join with Warwick, when they would outnumber him disastrously.

Edward was three miles outside of Newark when scouts reported that the Earl of Oxford, the Duke of Exeter, the other leaders of the force and most of the men had fled the town at two o'clock that morning when news of Edward's march reached them. It seems that the Lancastrians had decided that they could not defeat Edward there, perhaps uncertain of the exact size of his army or having been warned by Warwick not to be drawn into a reckless early engagement. Edward was a fine soldier and general and Warwick was a careful player. Perhaps disheartened by the lack of a fight or buoyed by the willingness of his enemies to run from his coming, Edward arrived next at Leicester, where *The Arrival* claims 3,000 men swarmed to his cause, predominantly from William, Lord Hastings' lands around the Midlands. It must have finally seemed that the Yorkists had been vindicated in their return and that the perilous trek through the hostile northern counties, a quickly forgotten worry, had been worth it.

On 29 March 1471, just fifteen days after his inauspicious landing in Yorkshire, Edward arrived outside the town of Coventry where he had learned that Warwick, a man described by *The Arrival* as Edward's 'great Rebel', was ensconced with around 6,000 to 7,000 men. In spite of the reinforcements received at Leicester *The Arrival* is adamant that Warwick's army outnumbered the Yorkist force. Even so, Edward stood outside the town and demanded that Warwick bring out his army to meet him in open battle. Warwick refused and over the next few days a stalemate ensued, during which Warwick sent a continuous stream of messages to Edward insisting that he did not want to fight and offering a truce, which would lead to the return of Edward's crown, if Warwick were allowed certain posts within the government. Edward refused. He offered Warwick his life, along with those of the men in his army, but nothing more.

Richard Neville was undoubtedly a proud man. He had good reason to be. Edward's offer could never be acceptable to him and both men probably knew it, just as both probably knew that Warwick's terms could not be met. He had openly rebelled against his king and had betrayed a man who considered him a friend, perhaps even a father figure. Edward could no more welcome him back into the inner circles of power than Warwick could accept ruin and a life of poverty and obscurity. Edward had a well-known ruthless streak and may not have been above promising Warwick his life only to execute him once in custody as a man too dangerous to be allowed to live. Commynes offers an insight into Edward's enraged mind during his time in exile, claiming that 'King Edward had resolved, at his departure from Flanders, to call out no more to spare the common soldiers, and kill only the gentlemen, as he had formerly done; for he had conceived a mortal hatred against the commons of England, for having favoured the Earl of Warwick so much'.

Perhaps Warwick was right to be wary of Edward's offer when he was in such a decisive mood, yet it is interesting that this episode was permitted by both sides to stretch into days. It is possible that both sides were wary of pushing for a fight. Edward would have had to storm a town with a smaller force and Warwick knew at first hand Edward's expertise in the field. Although neither man ever appeared to lack confidence in themselves, Warwick had lost key engagements before. Edward had never been beaten. There is another explanation that bears some examination too. As Edward raged, huffing and puffing outside the town, Warwick may have been genuinely attempting an apologetic reconciliation. The earl was struggling to control lords whose Lancastrian loyalties made them inherently wary of him and unwilling to trust him. The royal finances were a mess and Warwick was having to fund much of the function of government from his own pocket. Henry was a weak fool, which made him easy to control, but with Margaret due to return any day Warwick may have feared that he would not long be the one in control. He had been forced into a humiliating treaty with his most bitter enemy and all was not as he might have hoped under the readeption.

The original aim of Warwick's revolt was to flex his muscles against his increasing exclusion and isolation. It had got out of hand when simply taking control of Edward had not worked and he had been forced to release the king. Edward's continued and revitalised drive to exclude the Nevilles only gathered pace, causing the earl to take the ultimate step. He had tried to teach Edward a short, sharp lesson and failed. His distaste for failure and obscurity had caused him to try to administer a harsher lesson. In this he had succeeded, but his heart was not in the Lancastrian cause. He had spent most of his adult life fighting to remove Henry from the throne, and returning him to it as he tried to ingratiate himself with old foes probably held little appeal.

Edward was also a close friend and a cousin. If Edward viewed Warwick as a father-figure it is natural that Warwick would have had paternal feelings toward Edward. They had endured a great deal together and achieved so much side by side. Did either man really wish to end their relationship at the head of opposing armies trying to kill each other? Commynes suggests Edward might have felt that way, but Warwick might have clung to a vain hope of restoring an old relationship to the good times before it had all slipped away, not only for his own financial and political security but for the genuine love of a man he cared for as a friend and a king. History was repeating itself as a mighty but loyal subject had been forced into opposition by policies he viewed as unfair and unjust, embarrassed and pushed into rebellion. A vengeful royal house was now ready to fall upon that rebel, trying to draw him from safety. Edward sought to do to Warwick precisely what Margaret and Somerset had done to his father.

Neither side seems to have been willing to attack. Edward, fearful of remaining still while his enemies were all about him, pushed south to Warwick, a symbolic slap in the face to the earl. Here one of Edward's more subtle manoeuvres paid dividends, though how much the idea or its success owed to Edward personally is uncertain. The lady in waiting whose passage through Calais had been reported to Commynes had found her mistress, the Duchess of Clarence, in France and passed on her messages to the duke. *The Arrival* lists those involved in negotiating George's return to his brother's side, notably failing to mention Edward himself. Their mother, Cecily Neville, Dowager Duchess of York; their sisters Anne, Duchess of Exeter, and Elizabeth, Duchess of Suffolk; along with Thomas Bourchier, Archbishop of Canterbury, Robert Stillington, Bishop of Bath and Wells and the Archbishop's brother Henry Bourchier, Earl of Essex, a venerable figure in his mid-sixties who had been married to Isabel of Cambridge, the sister of Richard, Duke of York. The Bourchier family had close connections to the York dynasty. Edward had created Henry Earl of Essex shortly after Towton, and Henry's eldest son and heir, William, was among those who found themselves married into the Woodville family after Edward's marriage. Another of Henry's sons Edward had died at Wakefield alongside his uncle Richard, Duke of York.

The prime mover in the barrage of correspondence that found its way to Clarence in France was his other sister, Margaret, Duchess of Burgundy. She worked tirelessly to draw George back into the fold, simultaneously depriving Warwick of vital support. Margaret was also in continual contact with Edward as she brokered a mending of the rift that saw her brothers fighting each other for the crown. At some stage after landing in England, Edward had made direct contact with Clarence, who now came to him at Warwick with 4,000 men that he had raised. In a carefully stage-managed piece of theatre Edward and Clarence met between their two forces and discussed a settlement of their quarrel. George then had a conference with his other brother, Richard, Duke of Gloucester, and finally an agreement was reached. Edward rode with George to meet the duke's army and Clarence made it plain to his men that Edward was no longer the enemy.

The incentive to achieve this reconciliation is clear on George's part, though it left him in an impossibly awkward position thereafter. He had thrown in his lot with Warwick when the earl had promised him Edward's throne. George is remembered by history as a vain and fickle man, cruel to his servants and condemned by Shakespeare as 'false, fleeting, perjured Clarence', yet he was an immensely powerful man as a royal duke. At twenty-one years of age he could perhaps plead that he had been seduced by Warwick's honeyed words and grand promises. George had seen the promise of the throne commuted to a position as legal heir to Edward, Prince of Wales if, and only if, he were to die without children. Not only was this an unsatisfactory relegation of his pretentions but it left him secluded within a knot of his family's enemies, who could never trust a man who had abandoned his brother for the promise of a prize he could not now see himself winning. He would face the same trouble returning to his brothers' side, but at least blood ties carried a greater hope of forgiveness than purely political ones. For Edward's part, his vengeance seems to have faltered when it came to severing those ties of blood. Besides being a brother, Clarence was a potent friend. His 4,000 men would now fight for Edward, not for Warwick.

The duke, having been accepted into his brother's favour, immediately began to petition for reconciliation with Warwick, his wife's father. Clarence managed to negotiate more favourable terms for Warwick, including some of the appointments he had sought. A channel of communication was re-opened with the earl but he remained within Coventry and refused to accept even these improved terms. The author of *The Arrival* appears somewhat disappointed by the failure to reach agreement, suggesting that the earl may not have believed Edward's promises or even that he was unable to renege on the oaths that he had taken in France before King Louis to Margaret and her son. Breaking these promises would have damaged his honour and weakened his position, but Warwick was not above sharp political manoeuvre where it suited him.

The most likely answer lies in the arrival at Coventry of vast numbers of men under the leadership of the Earl of Oxford, the Duke of Exeter and Warwick's own brother John, Marquis of Montagu. The effect of this was twofold. With his numbers further increased, even the loss of Clarence to the king's side was no longer devastating and Warwick surely felt that he had the numbers to challenge Edward effectively now. Even if this did not lead to the hardening of his stance, the arrival of Lancastrian magnates and his own dissatisfied brother about him must have restricted his room to negotiate. Although letters arrived from Edward promising rehabilitation and favour, Warwick would have found himself rounded upon by Edward's real enemies, those who wanted him dead, reminding him of his oaths and of his own precarious position in the new establishment. Had Warwick wanted to take the hand of friendship extended to him it is unlikely that he would have been allowed to.

When it became clear that Warwick would not budge from Coventry, Edward was counselled by his brothers George and Richard to head for London, where they could remove Henry from royal authority, the exercise of which was preventing men from joining Edward and causing them to rise against him. This advice may have been derived from the affection both brothers had for the Earl of Warwick. He was George's father-in-law and although George might have felt misled by the earl, he still campaigned for peace and reconciliation with Warwick. Richard had been raised in Warwick's household and both brothers had grown up not only with tales of Warwick's daring exploits and fame but also seeing their family destroyed by the conflicts they had been too young to take part in. They had been left by their brother Edward and by Warwick at Ludlow, yet perhaps neither wished to see the two largest influences upon their lives tearing each other apart. It is telling that even as he agreed to march to London, Edward took his men past Coventry to demand that Warwick take the field one more time. The earl declined and on 5 April Edward pushed on south.

While the Yorkists had been heading southward, distracted for a time by Warwick at Coventry and the need to recruit men in more friendly regions, Queen Margaret was still attempting to cross the Channel with her son Edward, along with Lord Wenlock and Warwick's wife. Edmund Beaufort, 4th Duke of Somerset, his younger brother John Beaufort, created Marquis of Dorset, and John Courtney, Earl of Devon, were gathering at the south-west coast in anticipation of their arrival. Jasper Tudor, Earl of Pembroke, was raising his Welsh lands and heading there too. This course was a mark both of the importance now placed upon Margaret as the driving force behind Lancastrian efforts and of Edward, Prince of Wales, as the hope of his house in the face of Henry's continued ineffectualness. It also marked their inability to trust in Warwick and their unwillingness to be led by him. It was to prove a fateful caution.

On reaching Daventry, along the road to London, Edward stopped at a church to hear Mass. With Easter only a week away, he knelt in the parish church on Palm Sunday, ten years after his great and bloody victory at Towton, and prayed for the success of his cause. Edward's prayers were answered with the revelation of a miracle more clear by far than the parhelion that he had turned to his own advantage before the Battle of Mortimer's Cross ten years earlier. St Anne was the mother of the Virgin Mary, a patron saint of unmarried women, women in labour and grandmothers, as she was the grandmother of Jesus. St Anne was also called upon by sailors, particularly those seeking protection from storms, and the writer of *The Arrival* recalled that Edward had frequently included St Anne in his prayers, no doubt as he tried to cross the storm-tossed seas during his return to England. For his safe deliverance Edward had sworn to make an offering the next time that he saw a statue of St Anne.

Daventry happened to possess such an image and it was within this church that Edward heard Mass and made his offering. It was an alabaster statue attached to a pillar in the church but concealed behind a closed square of boards, as was traditional between Ash Wednesday and Easter Sunday, when all images within a church were to be covered. In spite of being unable to see the image of St Anne, Edward prayed before it and as he did so a loud crack echoed about the church and the boards hiding St Anne's image split open. As all looked on in amazement they drew closed again without anyone being near them and then proceeded to break completely apart, falling to fully reveal the image. Edward made his offerings, as did all of those with him, for they took it to be a good sign, a miracle that promised success for their cause.

Leading his men on to Northampton and pressing toward London, Edward was renewed by the miracle, as were his men. Little did he know that Warwick was rushing letters ahead of the Yorkist army with instructions for his brother George Neville, Archbishop of York, who was then in London. Resistance to their arrival was being organised and Warwick knew that he could not allow Edward into London unopposed without losing everything, not least the person of King Henry VI, which he had already lost once at the Second Battle of St Albans. Another decisive confrontation was becoming utterly unavoidable.

16

An End of the Wars of the Roses

The period of the Wars of the Roses remains a shifting set of beginnings and endings, some more complete and meaningful than others. One definitive ending occurred on 4 May 1471, but much was to happen on the road to Tewkesbury. There were other endings to be reached before this one, and for one side, nothing would go according to plan.

On 9 April 1471, as instructed by his brother Richard, Earl of Warwick, George Neville summoned all of those lords and gentlemen within London loyal to King Henry VI to a gathering at St Paul's Cathedral. They came in their armour, bringing as many armed men with them as they could find, including their servants. King Henry himself appeared before the gathered force, which numbered around 6,000 men. He rode a fine steed from St Pauls, through Cheapside and in a circuit of the City traditionally used for royal progresses. It was designed to whip the populace into a frenzy of support for their king that would see the City repel Edward's advance. It failed dismally. The sight of Henry's sorry figure, confused by his own presence atop a horse riding through the streets, sowed a seed of doubt in the minds of those that might otherwise have supported him. Some began to speak of welcoming King Edward back into the capital.

George Neville saw the way the wind was blowing. Men feared the retribution that would follow if London tried to resist Edward's army and lost. More than this, Commynes points to three reasons that he was given for the warmth the capital felt toward Edward.

Firstly, his wife and children were still in sanctuary at Westminster. His son and heir had been born there and had not yet met his father. There was strong sympathy for the lonely queen, her scared young daughters and a baby separated from his father's protection. Secondly, Edward owed fortunes to merchants all over London, a symptom of his love of high living. If Edward were kept at bay these men would never see their bills paid and might be ruined, and if he was resisted, why then would he repay those men who had abandoned him? The final reason, another symptom of Edward's famous appetites, was the desire of the female population for a return to his bed and the wealth and influence that came with such intimate encounters. These ladies compelled their husbands and other relations to come out for Edward's cause to win their space at his side. His carnal reputation would serve him well now, though it would not always be so.

The Archbishop of York sent secret letters to Edward asking for grace and promising him London in return for a pardon. It was a proposition too good to refuse. The writer of *The Arrival* insists that the weight of the clergy's feeling was behind Edward and this no doubt influenced the archbishop, yet he may well have seen the futility of resistance and simply made the best of a bad situation. On 10 April the Tower of London was seized in the name of King Edward IV, and on the following morning, Thursday 11 April, Edward entered the city in triumph, welcomed in every quarter with all of the enthusiasm Warwick had intended them to display in resisting his coming. Riding to St Paul's he gave thanks there before moving to the Bishop of London's palace, where King Henry was in residence. George Neville greeted King Edward with the vacant King Henry in hand and several other leading Lancastrians were taken into custody.

This done, Edward rode to Westminster where he gave thanks to God, St Peter and St George before being reunited with his wife and children, meeting his baby son and namesake for the first time. The king took his wife and family to Baynards Castle, his mother's London residence, where more services of thanksgiving were heard. The next day, Good Friday, Edward heard Mass again before gathering his friends to discuss the trouble from which they had not yet extricated themselves. Warwick chose this moment to ride out of Coventry at the head of a large army to drive toward London, hoping either that London had kept its gates closed and a trap could be snapped shut about Edward or that, even if he had taken London, he would be observing the Easter feasts and could be caught unawares. On both counts the earl misjudged his foe.

Hearing of Warwick's approach, Edward gathered his men and rode out to meet the earl on Saturday 13 April. As evening fell the two sides were closing in on each other near to Barnet just north of London. Edward's scouts had encountered the earl's outriders at Barnet and driven them away. Conscious of the problems encountered at both battles of St Albans by forces caught within the confines of the town, Edward ordered his men to make camp in the fields outside Barnet and would not allow any to seek more comfortable lodgings within the town. Darkness fell as the two sides set camp, unaware of quite how close they were to each other. Warwick had his ordnance set up and fired his cannons throughout the night. Every shot flew beyond Edward's camp as the distance was misjudged, thudding harmlessly into the earth behind them. King Edward ordered his cannon to remain silent and his men to make no noise throughout the night to ensure that Warwick's men could not realise their mistake and adjust their aim.

As dawn approached on Easter Sunday, 14 April 1471, both armies were greeted by a thick fog that meant they could not see each other. The only signal of their proximity was the noise of each camp rising and preparing for battle. *The Arrival* recounts that King Edward 'committed his cause and quarrel to Almighty God, advanced banners, did blow up trumpets, and set upon them, first with shot, and, then and soon, they joined and came to hand-strokes'. Beginning at four o'clock, the fighting was brutal and close, *The Arrival* conceding that Edward's enemies 'manly and courageously received them, as well in shot as in hand-stroke' and Warkworth reports that the fighting lasted until ten o'clock that morning.

The battle was made more complex in the confusion created by the thick fog that refused to abate. In the poor conditions the two armies had lined up off centre. Estimates place Edward's force at around 10,000 men while Warwick is credited with a larger army of 15,000. Each stood with their right flank overreaching the enemy's left allowing the possibility of a flanking manoeuvre.

Once engaged, John de Vere, Earl of Oxford, leading Warwick's right flank, quickly spotted the opportunity and routed Edward's left, under the command of Lord Hastings. Oxford's men gave chase, cutting down retreating Yorkists and falling to plundering, assuming the day was won, and some of Hastings' men made their way back to London where they reported King Edward's defeat.

With the trouble at his left obscured by the fog, Edward was unaware of the failing of his flank and his men were not discouraged. Had Oxford's force remained more disciplined and continued to flank the Yorkist army it may have been over quickly. As it was, neither side knew what was happening in any other part of the field. Edward's right, led by his brother Richard, Duke of Gloucester, who was taking the field for the first time at eighteen years of age, found scant resistance at their side where the Duke of Exeter commanded Warwick's force, and eventually began to push across to flank Warwick's centre. John Neville called his brother down from his horse to fight on foot beside his men to increase their courage. Warwick was wont to fight from horseback, allowing him the option to lead a charge when the battle turned in his favour, or to beat a hasty retreat should it go against him. Montagu, a respected soldier, advised his older brother to get down and fight beside his men now. Warwick obliged, sending his horse away to prove that he meant not to flee the field.

At this point, confusion tore the heart from Warwick's force. Warkworth asserts that Montagu had come to an arrangement with Edward to oppose his own brother, and at this moment, the marquis pulled on the Yorkist king's livery. At this, one of Warwick's men turned on John and killed him. As this perceived treachery played out, Oxford returned with 800 of his men, all that he had managed to drag from their victorious plundering. As he approached the flank of Warwick's force the earl's banner and livery of a star and streamers was mistaken in the mist for Edward's sun and streamers. Warwick's men fired their bows at Oxford's force and charged them, supposing them to be the enemy. Oxford's force, assuming that Warwick or Montagu had switched sides and betrayed them, fled the field amid cries of treason, a call swiftly taken up among Warwick's force in the uncertainty of the lingering mist.

Seeing that all was lost, Warwick frantically sought out a horse to make his escape. Warkworth reports that he made it as far as a wood outside Barnet before some of Edward's men caught up with him and killed him, raising his visor as he lay on the ground to deliver the coup de grâce, driving a dagger through his open helm to ensure that he was well and truly dead. He was then stripped of his valuable armour and anything else that he carried and left naked on the ground. When the fighting was over an estimated 1,000 of Warwick's force lay dead compared to 500 of Edward's smaller army, though these numbers vary across the sources with Warkworth reporting 4,000 dead on both sides.

Among those lying in the mud was Henry Holland, Duke of Exeter, stripped of his finery and left for dead. Although badly wounded, Exeter was still alive. He lay there from seven o'clock in the morning until four o'clock in the afternoon, when those clearing the battlefield discovered him alive. He was taken to the home of a man loyal to him, where his wounds were treated before he went into sanctuary at Westminster. The Earl of Oxford managed to escape north with some of Warwick's fleeing men, finally making it over the border into Scotland.

Casualties on Edward's side included Lord Cromwell, son and heir of the Earl of Essex, Lord Say and Lord Mountjoy's son and heir, but the victory was a huge boost to the Yorkist cause. On the morning after the battle Edward had Warwick and Montagu's corpses displayed at St Paul's Cathedral for several days, so that all might view the bodies and know that they were dead, putting an end to the Neville threat to Edward's rule. In an act of clemency, he spared the bodies any further mutilation and allowed them both to be buried in the family's mausoleum at Bisham Priory.

The job remained only partly completed though. On the same day as the Battle of Barnet Queen Margaret had finally landed at Weymouth with her son and was greeted by a horde of Lancastrian loyalists. She was disturbed by news of Warwick's defeat at Barnet when it reached her, though Edmund Beaufort, Duke of Somerset, insisted that they were better off without Warwick's interference and distracting presence.

Word was sent out for all loyal men to meet Margaret and Prince Edward at Exeter and the Lancastrians raised a large number of men from Cornwall, Devon, Somerset and Dorset. They gathered at Exeter and Margaret marched from that city at the head of a large force. She made a feint to march directly on London but turned north, intending to cross the Severn and meet up with Jasper Tudor, who was bringing his own force out of Wales to meet her. News of Queen Margaret's landing reached Edward in London and he immediately raised a fresh army to hunt the last remnants of the Lancastrians. His scouts were not fooled by Margaret's false move toward London and Edward set out west to cut them off before they could join up with Jasper.

What followed was a desperate game of cat and mouse. Edward wanted to engage the Lancastrian force quickly, before it could be further reinforced. Margaret knew that she needed Jasper Tudor's men and that time offered her best hope to raise more men. As news of Edward's approach reached Margaret she took refuge behind the strong walls of Bristol, a town friendly to the Lancastrian cause. From there she sent word to Edward that they would give battle the following morning, 1 May, at a place called Sudbury Hill ten miles east of Bristol. On that morning Edward arrived at the appointed spot with his army arrayed for battle. The Lancastrians marched out of Bristol toward Sudbury, their outriders encountering Edward's scouts, but it was a trick and Margaret quickly turned her army north and marched up the Severn.

Edward knew that they would have to seek out a crossing, meaning that they had to head for Gloucester or Tewkesbury. Edward sent word to Richard Beauchamp, who he had put in control of Gloucester town and castle, to prevent the Lancastrians from crossing. Richard, son of Lord Beauchamp, welcomed Edward's messengers and closed the town as instructed, denying Margaret entry. Some within were sympathetic to the Lancastrian cause and Margaret considered trying to take the town and force her way through, but the delay would have allowed Edward time to catch them up and attack them from behind as the town blocked their front. Tewkesbury was now their only hope. The Lancastrian force pushed on, covering some thirty-six miles, marching day and night through rough, unforgiving terrain with no refreshment or break. They arrived at Tewkesbury exhausted and all too aware that Edward was hard on their heels as night fell on 3 May.

The Lancastrians camped, *The Arrival* records, 'in a field, in a close even at the town's end; the town and the abbey at their backs'. They were surrounded there by 'foul lanes and deep dykes, and many hedges, with hills, and valleys, a right evil place to approach', making a perfect defensive position at the edge of Tewkesbury in fields called The Gastons. Edward's own army had been urged on, marching thirty miles, always five or six miles behind the Lancastrians, on what the writer of *The Arrival* recalled as 'right-an-hot day'. They too were lacking food and water, only managing to refresh their horses a little at a brook almost ruined by the passage of carriages. They arrived at Cheltenham, where they were fed and refreshed, before moving to within three miles of the Lancastrian camp. Here they pitched their tents, knowing that with the dawn a crucial confrontation was coming. *The Crowland Chronicle* recalls that 'both armies had now become so extremely fatigued with the labour of marching and thirst that they could proceed no further, they joined battle near the town of Tewkesbury'. The conditions for both sides were hardly ideal.

When the armies faced each other Margaret took the difficult decision to allow her seventeen-year-old son to take the field with his army. Although not yet at the age of majority, he would not have been considered too young to fight. Edmund, Earl of Rutland, had been the same age at Wakefield. Prince Edward represented the entire hopes of his cause. His opponent was a veteran military leader, and if Prince Edward were to succeed his father and revitalise the Lancastrian line he would have to prove himself the match for the Yorkist leader. The white rose stood proud in the garden of England. The last blossom of the red rose had to shine brighter still. The experienced Lord Wenlock led the centre, where Prince Edward also stood, though he lacked the experience to lead the army. Edmund Beaufort took command of the right wing, the vanguard, and John Courtney, Earl of Devon, the left, which acted as a rear guard.

Edward's Yorkist army was arrayed with his brother Richard, Duke of Gloucester, leading the vanguard, Edward himself in command of the centre and Lord Hastings in control of the rear guard. They opened fire with cannon and arrow, which they had in more plentiful supply than the Lancastrians, who returned fire as best they could. Somerset, realising that he could not withstand the barrage within his nest of ditches and bushes, saw the Duke of Gloucester advancing on his position and moved his men through hidden paths that they had discovered the previous day and worked his way around to the side of King Edward's centre where he fell upon them, taking them by surprise.

The king had not been tactically inactive either. Spying a wood at his side, he had placed a small force of 200 footmen at the edge of the wood to watch for ambushes, giving them instructions to use their position as best they could if no offensive came that way. When Somerset attacked the king he found himself in a bitter struggle as Edward pushed him back. The detachment guarding the wood saw the peril their king was in and, perceiving no danger from the woods, attacked Somerset's flank. Driven back toward the Duke of Gloucester's vanguard, Somerset's men panicked and began to flee, some drowning in the water nearby, others running through the town and some seeking safety within the abbey.

The battle was a close-fought affair for some time, Crowland recording that 'After the result had long remained doubtful, king Edward at last gained a glorious victory'. Leaving the pursuit of these routed men to Gloucester, Edward turned his attention to the Lancastrian centre, mercilessly crushing them, with Lancastrian casualties estimated at around 2,000. The sacristy door of Tewkesbury Abbey is still lined today on the inside with pieces of horse armour recovered by the monks from the field. The metal is punctured with arrow holes in a gruesome reminder of its provenance.

Edward ordered that those survivors who had taken sanctuary within the abbey be removed. They were placed on trial before a court of chivalry convened under Richard, Duke of Gloucester, as the new Constable of England and executed in the town centre on 6 May. Edmund Beaufort was among those condemned. His brother John had died in the fighting and with their death the legitimate male line of the Beaufort family ended. Several had held the apparently cursed rank of Duke of Somerset, each falling in the defence of their cousin's crown. The House of Somerset that today holds the Duchy of Beaufort are descendants of the illegitimate son of Henry Beaufort, Charles Somerset, and represent the

Plantagenet's last line of male descent still in existence. With the removal of the Dukes of Somerset, York had rid itself of a bitter, implacable enemy.

The young Prince of Wales also did not survive the battle. His death has become shrouded in the same rumour and myth that obscures much of the latter period of the Wars of the Roses. In Shakespeare's Richard III the then Duke of Gloucester plots the murder of the seventeen-year-old, revelling in his evil plans. *Holinshed's Chronicle*, first published in 1577, states that Richard struck the first blow against the Prince of Wales. Earlier than this, Henry VII's official historian Polydore Virgil wrote in his *Anglica Historia* in the early sixteenth century that William, Lord Hastings, George, Duke of Clarence, and Richard, Duke of Gloucester, together surrounded and killed the youth. The Yorkist author of *The Arrival*, an eye witness to the battle, simply states that Prince Edward was 'slain in the field' while Warkworth's contemporary chronicle, which leans toward the Lancastrian side, describes the Prince crying out to his brother-in-law the Duke of Clarence for mercy.

The closest to an impartial account derives from *The Crowland Chronicle*, though the writer is sympathetic to King Edward IV. Crowland intriguingly notes that 'there were slain on the queen's side, either in the field or after the battle, by the avenging hands of certain persons, prince Edward, the only son of king Henry' before listing other notable dead. Clearly Crowland was aware that more than one specific person was known to be responsible for the death of the Prince. What of the 'avenging hands'? Edward was the same age as Edmund, Earl of Rutland, had been at the Battle of Wakefield when Lord Clifford had captured and executed him. All three of Edmund's brothers were in the field at Tewkesbury, two having been driven to exile and one having lost his crown. The finger pointed by Crowland can be levelled directly at the three brothers of York.

Shakespeare's attribution of the cold-blooded deed to his brilliant anti-hero is surely no more than poetic licence, laying a foundation for what was to come. *The Arrival* clearly states that Richard had been tasked with chasing Somerset's vanguard away as it fled while Edward pushed on to deal with the Lancastrian centre, where

Prince Edward was located. Whoever was finally involved in the death of Prince Edward, it was a death upon the battlefield, no more remarkable than many others over the preceding decades. It has become the cruel murder of an innocent to suit later eyes looking back, and the blame for it has been conveniently laid at the door of a man who became one of history's great villains. George, Duke of Clarence, was perhaps the most likely to seek revenge upon the boy who had replaced him as heir to the throne. If Henry remained king, Clarence would succeed if Prince Edward died without issue, as determined by statute. With the boy dead, Clarence was one step closer to the throne again, whichever side won, and all was not yet settled.

Even if Prince Edward had been captured his ultimate fate could hardly have been any different. King Edward's primary aim in hunting down the Lancastrian army was to rid himself of the threat posed by Prince Edward. In an act of conciliation which may hint at a guilty conscience at the prince's death, a reminder of his own brother's fate, or for the forced removal of men from sanctuary, King Edward allowed the dead to be respectfully buried at the abbey, or wherever their servants wished to take them, without further dismemberment of the bodies. He also had the prince buried with honour in Tewkesbury Abbey, where a later plaque still marks his grave today, reading:

> Here lies Edward, Prince of Wales, cruelly slain whilst but a youth, Anno Domine 1471, May fourth. Alas the savagery of men. Thou art the soul light of thy Mother, and the last hope of thy race.

Edward also had Tewkesbury Abbey decorated both to celebrate his victory and compensate the monks for the disturbance that he had caused. The ceiling still bears the bright, colourful Sunne in Splendour badges that Edward commissioned there.

As the dust settled in the aftermath of Tewkesbury following the executions of the leading Lancastrians, King Edward set out for Worcester, where news both good and ill reached him. Queen Margaret had been captured at a small monastery not far from Worcester, where she had retreated to await news of the battle.

King Edward now had custody of Henry and his wife and certain knowledge that their only child was dead. His victory was all but assured. However, as he reached Worcester more news arrived that an uprising was breaking out in the north, large enough to cause concern. Edward marched to Coventry, arriving on 11 May. Here he could block the road south and also raise fresh recruits to lead an assault on the rebels. The often lethargic king had the bit well and truly between his teeth now and was determined to rid himself once and for all of any trace of Lancastrian opposition. When news spread north that the rampant Edward was preparing to crush them, the terrified rebels vanished into the northern mists. Lacking a Neville lord to order them and knowing that Henry Percy was firmly allied to King Edward they saw the futility of trying to withstand a king who had already won two battles and seemed hungry for more. The Earl of Northumberland himself rode to Coventry to inform the king that the mere threat of his coming had been enough to end any talk of revolt.

With the king's eyes turned north, a new threat erupted behind him, reaping the ever-ripe harvest of Kentish desires to terrorise London. Thomas Neville was the illegitimate son of William Neville, Earl of Kent, and Lord Fauconberg, who had been instrumental in the Yorkist victories of 1459–61. William had been a great soldier and leader, dying in peace in 1463. His illegitimate son, known as the Bastard of Fauconberg, was in his early forties now and had long been a well-respected sailor, serving alongside his father to see Edward IV win the throne. A first cousin to the Earl of Warwick, Thomas had sided with his family when the Nevilles rebelled against Edward. He had commanded Warwick's ships while the earl was in exile in France, attacking and robbing English shipping. When Warwick returned and drove Edward out of the country Thomas was given control of all of Warwick's fleet and tasked with patrolling the Channel to prevent Edward's return. The storms had allowed Edward to slip past the patrols, but now Thomas landed on the south coast to receive news of Warwick's defeat.

The Bastard of Fauconberg marched north toward London with around 17,000 men at his back, swollen by Kentish men ready to try once again to seize the capital. By the time he arrived at London

Bridge on 12 May, Thomas had 20,000 men at his command. His fleet skirted the coast and weighed anchor in the Thames, not far from the bridge. Thomas had been left instructions by Warwick that if all went ill he should move to London and secure the person of King Henry. Thomas sent word ahead that he wished to pass through London to continue north to offer battle to the king, perhaps relying on his cousin's huge personal popularity within the City. Thomas himself had been given the Freedom of London in 1454 for his work in ridding the Channel of pirates, though it would not aid him now. The City firmly closed its gates on the orders of the mayor and aldermen, though both Warkworth and *The Arrival* insist that there were plenty within the City keen to allow Thomas entry, if only to join in the looting his men were accused of intending.

Anthony Woodville, Earl Rivers, had command of the Tower – an ominous sign given that his other title was Lord Scales – and his sister the queen and her children were within the Tower's walls. Rivers backed the mayor and insisted that Thomas be denied entry. Word was sent to Coventry of the trouble and Edward began gathering his men again. He sent a force of 1,500 ahead to reinforce the city and to protect his family on 14 May, leaving himself just two days later. *The Arrival* laments that even though Edward was now in command of a larger force than at any time since his landing, he was still heavily outnumbered by the Bastard and would be in far more danger than he had been at Barnet or Tewkesbury if it came to blows.

Thomas was enraged by London's refusal to grant him entry. He had his cannons brought up from his ships and lined up along the bank of the Thames at either side of London Bridge. When the City would not relent he opened fire, pounding the walls but causing little damage. The Londoners drew up their own ordnance and returned fire, wreaking havoc among the unsuspecting, easy targets along the riverside. The Bastard's men were forced to fall back, abandoning their guns in their desperate flight from danger. In his fury, Thomas ordered the firing of London Bridge. Then a crowded street of precarious buildings, houses and shops with only a narrow thoroughfare; he planned to clear space on the bridge to allow a full frontal attack by his men. Houses were set alight and the bridge blazed, destroying homes and livelihoods in an act that only served to harden the residents' resolve against the attackers. At the same time, Thomas ordered two parties of 1,500 men to use their ships to cross the Thames and attack Bishops Gate and Aldgate which had both been sealed against them. Slipping over the water, they set fire to these gates too as they fired cannon and arrows into the City wreaking havoc.

As the bridge burned the citizens arranged their cannons to block its entire width. When the smoke cleared and Thomas prepared to cross, he was greeted by the fierce array of guns and knew that there was no hope of assaulting the City that way without a devastating loss of life. Meanwhile, Henry Bourchier, Earl of Essex, arrived in the City with a small force and began to organise the resistance that was already performing so well. Bishops Gate and Aldgate were by now aflame and likely to fall open at any moment. Earl Rivers assembled 500 men from the Tower and slipped out of a hidden postern door to reinforce efforts at the gates. Aldgate was the most threatened and Essex and Rivers, along with the mayor and aldermen, took the brave decision to open the gates and attack out of the City before they could fall and allow the rebels to enter the tight, confusing warren of streets and alleys within. The daring action worked and Thomas's men were slaughtered, forced back into their ships and back to the south bank of the Thames.

Dismayed, Thomas ordered his force to march west where he intended to cross the river at Kingston Bridge ten miles away. Once across the Thames he would pass London and head north to give battle to Edward. Rivers, Essex and the others within the City who had seen the size of the Bastard's army knew that Edward would be sore pressed if forced to confront them. Anthony Woodville sent messages to Thomas and others in his party pleading with them to return home and that they would not be harmed. Whether Thomas's nerve failed at this point or whether news of the complete collapse of the Lancastrian cause robbed him of the will to proceed is unclear, but he turned his vast force around and headed back to Blackheath, south of London. Here they rested for three days until 18 May, when news arrived that Edward was pushing south with a vast host. Rivers' assurances had bought vital time in which the king had not been idle. The reported size of Edward's army frightened them and most took to the ships and fled back across the Channel. Thomas fell back to Sandwich and captured the town, the remainder of his ships having been left anchored in the harbour there.

Edward entered London to a triumphal reception at the head of around 30,000 men. The mayor, recorder and several of the aldermen were knighted for their stout resistance and good service. On the same night that King Edward returned to London, 21 May 1471, Henry VI met his end in the Tower of London. Like the death of his son this is a moment surrounded by myth and rumour. *The Arrival*'s explanation that Henry died 'of pure displeasure and melancholy' is almost certainly a whitewashing of the murder of a king. Regicide would have been an incredibly delicate business. The person of a king was sacred, even an unsuccessful king like Henry, and if Edward overtly permitted the murder or execution of a king he was opening a door that could later prove troublesome to him. Edward II and Richard II had been deposed and had, at least according to official accounts, died shortly after attempts to free them. Edward II was almost certainly not killed by having a red hot poker inserted through his rectum and Richard II was probably starved to death so that no-one actually had to kill him. History taught that a deposed king could not be permitted to live.

Henry had survived this long because his son was at large. In Henry, the House of Lancaster had an incompetent and unpopular figurehead. Had Henry met his end before his son the line would have been revitalised in the person of the young Prince Edward. With that threat extinguished Edward was forced to look at Henry in a new light. He was a threat that no longer had to be tolerated. There were still those within the country who favoured Henry's cause and he would remain a focus for discontent and rebellion as long as he lived. He was nearly fifty now and, though not a well man, he might live for many more years if left to his own devices. Edward had proven himself to be in a decisive frame of mind and he could not afford for it to end now without condemning himself to more rounds of fighting to keep his throne.

Warkworth wrote that Henry was put to death within the Tower of London between 11 o'clock and midnight on 21 May, 'being then in the Tower the Duke of Gloucester, brother to King Edward, and many other'. The chronicler in Leland agreed with Warkworth about the timing and similarly noted 'the Duke of Gloucester and diverse other being there that night'. Commynes reported to his master that '(if what was told me is true) ... the Duke of Gloucester (who was King Edward's brother and afterwards called himself King Richard) slew this poor King Henry with his own hand, or caused him to be carried into some private place, and stood by while he was killed'. The well-informed writer of the *Crowland Chronicle* only noted that Henry died while Edward was absent in Kent, though as will be seen Richard accompanied his brother on this journey. It is not impossible, though, that he did so after ensuring Henry's death.

Fabyan would later write that 'the most common fame went, that he was stuck with a dagger by the hands of the Duke of Gloucester' and Polydore Virgil reported that 'the continual report is, that Richard duke of Gloucester killed him with a sword, whereby his brother might be delivered from all fear of hostility', though he admits that this version of events is not certain. Richard, Duke of Gloucester, was almost certainly present in the Tower when Henry died and is the most likely person to have organised, but not ordered, the death. As Constable of England it was his responsibility, as it had been after Tewkesbury, to dispense royal justice. Edward was not above using his Constable to do his dirty work and to take the blame for it if necessary, as John Tiptoft had discovered. If Richard did organise the execution of King Henry it cannot have been without Edward's knowledge or permission and was most likely on the king's instruction. The rumour that he committed the killing by his own hand may also be plausible. Killing a king is not a task to be delegated to just any person as it would set a precedent Edward could not tolerate; a state-sanctioned king slayer at large in the country who might tell his story or feel permitted to repeat the act. If it had to be done, and it probably did, who better than the king's brother, the one he knew he could trust? Richard almost definitely sanctioned the killing of Henry VI in his role as Constable and may have done the dreadful deed by his own hand. Either or both could only have been done at Edward's behest.

The next day, Henry's body was taken to St Paul's Cathedral and placed on display, his face uncovered. Warkworth claims that

Henry's body bled on the stones below where it was laid and that when the Black Friars were summoned to remove the body it bled afresh, suggesting some foul play. Warkworth is careful to only say that Henry's face was uncovered, hinting that the sight of the rest of his body was not for public consumption, perhaps because of those same wound that continued to release his blood onto the floor. Henry's body was taken by boat to Chertsey Abbey, where he was laid to rest with quiet respect in the Lady Chapel. Although Henry VI must be acknowledged as ranking highly among the worst monarchs in England's history, it is difficult to blame him for his shortcomings. A nice man who struggled with his demons, he was not made to be a king but had no choice in the matter. His reign saw the country slide slowly into a civil war that might have been prevented at any point with the slightest will. Henry V would always have been a hard man to follow, but his son never had any hope.

Thomas Neville was still at large in Sandwich and with little delay Edward left London and moved into Kent where he was pleased to find little sign of a will to oppose him any longer. As Edward approached Thomas sent letters promising that he would swear allegiance in the plainest terms the king would set if he might be pardoned. He also offered all of the ships still lying at Sandwich to the king to further sweeten the offer. Edward stopped at Canterbury, the mayor of that town being among those who had marched with Thomas, and sent his brother Richard to receive Thomas's surrender and his oath. This duly done, Thomas was taken into custody and sent north to Middleham Castle where Richard would oversee his execution six months later. The mayor of Canterbury Nicholas Faunt was hanged, drawn and quartered for his part in the rebellion. Once more, it is hard to believe that Richard executed Thomas Neville, in spite of his promise of a pardon, without Edward's authority or instruction, especially as it was part of wider recriminations that saw many of those captured at London executed too.

Within the space of eleven weeks King Edward IV had returned from exile, taken back his crown and his country and rid himself of anyone who dared to stand against him. It was a crushing tidal wave that ended Lancastrian resistance to his rule. With Henry and his only son Prince Edward dead, the Lancastrian male line was ended and could never again threaten the Yorkist king. If Edward believed this, he was sorely mistaken. Jasper Tudor had slipped out of Wales and landed in Brittany with his fourteen-year-old nephew Henry Tudor. John de Vere was in Scotland licking his wounds. There still remained men who would never and could never be reconciled to Yorkist rule. All they needed was an opportunity. They would be patient but their time would come.

17

The Pirate Earl

The first of the irreconcilable Lancastrians to break ranks was John de Vere, Earl of Oxford. Not quite twenty when his father and eldest brother had been executed by John Tiptoft, making him head of the family, John had initially been attainted but Edward IV later relented, allowing him to take possession of the earldom in 1464. In 1465 he officiated at Elizabeth Woodville's coronation, acting as her chamberlain. In spite of this, it is likely that Oxford's loyalty was always suspected and when trouble began in 1468 he was swiftly arrested and imprisoned within the Tower. Released in early 1469, by the middle of the year he had joined Warwick and Clarence in their efforts to remove Edward, perhaps reminded of the treatment that the king had meted out to his father and brother.

The readeption of Henry VI saw Oxford carrying the Sword of State for Henry's re-coronation on 13 October 1470. Appointed Constable of England in place of John Tiptoft, Oxford oversaw the trial and execution of the man who had condemned his father and brother. When Edward IV attempted to return it was Oxford's men, led by his brother Thomas, who prevented the Yorkists from landing in Norfolk. Unlike many staunch Lancastrians, Oxford did not baulk at following Warwick and his flank performed extremely well at Barnet, routing his opposite number but then losing discipline as they celebrated their victory prematurely. When Oxford returned to the battlefield it was to chaos as his men were mistaken for Yorkist forces and attacked. Amid cries of treason, he finally fled the battlefield and rode north.

Remaining in Scotland for only a short period, Oxford sailed for France, by which time Margaret had left and her cause lay broken in a field outside Tewkesbury. Edward IV was fully restored and all of Oxford's allies, Lancastrian and Neville, were gone. Although remembered as the archetypal Lancastrian, John de Vere's alliances were less clear during the period surrounding the readeption. John had married Margaret Neville, sister of Richard, Earl of Warwick, and his early involvement in Warwick and Clarence's plans to unseat Edward in favour of his younger brother suggests that not only was he fixated upon a Lancastrian restoration, but the removal of Edward was his primary concern.

In the aftermath of his recapture of the kingdom Edward IV had much to deal with. A Lancastrian state had undone some of his work over the previous decade, and law and order had to be restored to a country that had become too used to the lawlessness of civil war that presented opportunities for advantage to the unscrupulous. Edward had suffered dethronement at least in part because he had not been able to end once and for all the trouble within his kingdom. He was determined not to make the same mistakes again. Edward's second rule was a much more assured, mature and confident affair, but it was not without its problems.

In October 1472 Edward summoned Parliament. With so much business to deal with, it was to sit for a total of forty-four weeks over the next two and a half years. The length of this Parliament's sitting was a record that would not be broken until Henry VIII's Reformation Parliament. The immense Warwick patrimony preoccupied much of the early sessions. Richard Neville had been in possession of the vast wealth and lands of the Neville family, but he also held the Beauchamp and Despenser inheritances that had been his wife's. From these, he had taken the Warwick title by which he is remembered. In the time between Warwick's death and Parliament convening, the king's youngest brother, Richard, Duke of Gloucester, had married Anne Neville, the younger daughter of Warwick and widow of Edward, Prince of Wales, next to whom he had sat at George Neville's investiture feast. With Edward's other brother, George, already married to Warwick's older daughter, Isabel, the real issue was how the lands would be divided between them.

Richard had, since 1471, been in effective possession of the huge tracts of Neville lands in the north, and it seems clear that Edward intended it to stay that way. His marriage to Anne simply made the grant more acceptable and brought him the loyalty of the Neville affinity there. This would leave the western Midlands and south-western properties to George. There was bitter disagreement between the brothers as to the precise settlement of the lands, but throughout they remained united in one thing. Both men wished to have the title to their land *in jure uxoris*, in right of their wives, rather than by a fresh royal grant. The advantages of this were instantly clear for George and Richard. If they obtained their titles by grant of the king, Edward could just as easily take them away again. If they were held by inheritance then the rights of them and their wives were protected by law, offering a greater measure of independence from the king. It was a thin slither of accord, but Edward seized upon it, though it presented problems of its own with the creation of mighty men within his kingdom again. It must have seemed unavoidable.

The first issue was that Warwick could not be attainted, since this punishment would mean the confiscation of his lands and titles. If Warwick could not be punished, neither could his confederates. Warwick's widow was still alive and so her lands were not yet free to be passed to her daughters. If she remarried, a new husband would gain legal control of her estates. The final issue was that the Neville inheritance was legally bound to the male line, so Isabel and Anne were not, in fact, their father's heirs. The entire vast inheritance legally belonged to George Neville, Duke of Bedford, son of John, Marquis of Montagu. Edward's solution managed to be unsatisfactory, inequitable, shabby and a seed that would grow to contribute to the undoing of his house.

Warwick's widow Anne Beauchamp, Dowager Countess of Warwick, was dispossessed, declared by Parliament to be dead in legal terms so that her daughters could take their inheritance as though she had died. George Neville was then also disinherited. The details of the dissection of Warwick's estates were completed in February 1473 and Richard's grant was made by Parliament on 23 February, with George's sealed the following day. To the very end of both grants Edward attached a condition to their title limiting their independent enjoyment of their new acquisitions.

Also it is ordained by the said authority that if the said male issue begotten or coming of the body of the said John Neville, knight, die without male issue coming of their bodies while the said duke is alive, that the said duke shall then have and enjoy all the things stated for term of his life.

Edward tied his brothers' titles to the male issue of John Neville so that they would only hold their lands and titles for as long as a Neville male heir existed. This meant that if George Neville or his line were to fail both dukes would only retain a life interest in their properties, which would pass to the crown when they died and not to their children. None of this was ideal for any party. Edward may have believed that he was solving a problem but instead he had stored up trouble for later.

As part of the post-Lancastrian restructure, King Edward also granted his loyal youngest brother the lands of the Earl of Oxford. The earl's lands were forfeit without attainder, but his mother held a substantial portion of the lands in her own right. Now about sixty years of age, the Dowager Countess was living in a nunnery at Stratford le Bow. She had tied up her lands, perhaps fearful of the constant uncertainty that prevailed and the poor condition of her family under Yorkist rule, placing them in the hands of feoffees, who enjoyed the freehold of the land but paid the countess a fee while she retained the right to control who the lands passed to. This meant that she could leave her property to whomever she wished after her death rather than it passing immediately to her oldest son. With four surviving sons and three daughters she may have meant to provide for her other children, since John had already acquired the main Oxford inheritance. Perhaps she even intended to endow the nunnery that currently provided care for her.

In December 1472 Richard paid the dowager countess a visit, but it was not a friendly one. He instructed her to sign over her lands to him immediately, removing her from the nunnery to his own household, then at Stepney. The countess was moved again shortly afterwards to Walbroke and finally agreed to sign the papers. She told one of her feoffees that Richard had threatened to move her to Middleham Castle in Yorkshire if she did not, explaining that she feared the journey and the freezing northern winter would be the death of her. Richard secured the lands, the papers finally signed in January 1473, but he had bullied an elderly lady to get them.

John de Vere had been engaged in piracy in the English Channel since shortly after his arrival in France. He spent almost two years raiding Calais, harassing English shipping and stealing from merchants. The earl appears to have made a good living for himself as a pirate, while simultaneously causing trouble for his enemy Edward IV. In May 1473 he radically altered his tactics, and it is likely that his mother's rough treatment contributed to his decision to act more directly.

George Neville, Archbishop of York, was to find himself another victim of Edward's determination to sweep his kingdom clean. The archbishop did not possess the military might to threaten Edward but he was a wealthy and influential man. He had made peace with Edward, handing the capital and King Henry over in 1471, but a little while later Warkworth recorded that he became a focus of Edward's efforts to ensure his own security. In 1472 George was at Windsor with the king enjoying the hunting, high in the favour of the restored king and bucking the fate of his brothers. Edward told the archbishop that he would honour him by visiting his manor at Moore to sample the hunting there and George, overcome with excitement, hurried home to make preparations. He called for all of his plate and goods that he had placed in hiding after Barnet and Tewkesbury and borrowed heavily to make ready to receive the king. He purchased enough food and drink for his visitors to stay for several days and awaited the king's arrival on the appointed day in April.

The day before Edward was due to arrive a messenger brought a summons for George to go instead to the king at Windsor immediately. The archbishop obliged and on his arrival found himself arrested for high treason, charged with aiding John de Vere, Earl of Oxford. Sending George across the Channel to Hammes Castle at Calais, an unlikely destination for one genuinely suspected of assisting a pirate rebel at large in the Channel and frequently attacking Calais, Edward despatched several of his men to Moore where they seized all of the archbishop's neatly gathered treasure. His properties were transferred to Edward, his mitre was broken and the jewels used to make a new crown for Edward. Much of the wealth was passed to the infant Prince Edward, the king's son and heir. What George Neville had so carefully built over decades was lost in a single day. Although he was released in 1475, George died in poverty and disgrace the following year.

Oxford attempted to land an invasion force on the Essex coast near St Osyth in May 1473 but was repelled. Sailing west along the coast, he eventually arrived at St Michael's Mount, just off the southern tip of Cornwall. Set atop a tidal island, St Michael's Mount is the English counterpart of the French Mont Saint-Michel. At low tide there is a beach connecting the fortress perched atop the rocky mount to the mainland, but at high tide it becomes an island with no bridge connecting it. John, along with eighty other men, including two of his brothers, seized the monastery and dug themselves in. Precisely what John hoped to achieve is worth considering, with Lancastrian hope long gone. It is feasible that he was seeking to resurrect a previous alliance with George, Duke of Clarence, whom he believed could still be tempted to topple Edward, having come into possession of his own large Warwick portion.

In September, word reached Edward that Oxford was moving about Cornwall and was receiving a warm welcome. The king sent orders to Sir Henry Bodrugan, chief landowner in the area, to lay siege to St Michael's Mount and deal with Oxford. Bodrugan duly did as he was instructed, but each day at low tide the Earl of Oxford's men would come out of St Michael's Mount under a flag of truce to parlay with Bodrugan before returning to the security of the fortress, which Warkworth claimed could be defended by twenty men against all the world for as long as their provisions lasted. Eventually, on one of his forays out of St Michael's Mount, Oxford complained that his provisions were running low. At this, Bodrugan had fresh supplies brought to the earl and the mount was restocked.

When Edward heard of Bodrugan's mismanagement of the siege, he was furious, and sent one of his squires of the body to replace Sir Henry. When Richard Fortescu arrived at the end of December he met angry resistance from Bodrugan but laid siege to the mount. Almost every day the two sides fought, Fortescu losing men and occasional truces being called for a day or two. During the truces Oxford's men were offered pardons and grants of land if they would abandon the earl so that finally less than a dozen were willing to stay with Oxford. On 15 February 1474 Oxford was forced to surrender St Michael's Mount. When Fortescu entered he found enough provisions to have lasted many more months. Warkworth believed that Oxford's willingness to speak to the less friendly Fortescu was his undoing, quoting an old saying that 'a castle that speaks and a woman that will hear, they will be gotten both'.

Oxford was taken into custody and sent to Hammes Castle at Calais to be imprisoned indefinitely. John de Vere's part in the story of the Wars of the Roses was far from over but he would be removed from action for a decade now.

With the removal of this threat, Edward spent most of the remainder of 1474 planning an invasion of France. His alliance with Burgundy remained in place despite Duke Charles's tentative game playing in 1471. Louis had masterminded the unification of Warwick and the Lancastrian cause and Edward now felt secure enough to turn his attention to the pursuit of revenge. The campaign would also serve to galvanise England behind Edward and allow any latent Lancastrian sympathies to trickle away. Nothing brought England together quite like an invasion of France. Henry V had firmly established the Lancastrian right to rule after his father's tumultuous reign by his famous victories on the Continent. Edward now hoped to do the same for the Yorkist regime.

In the pursuit of this aim Edward was excitedly led by the Duke of Burgundy, who promised to begin waging war against the French at the beginning of the campaigning season, allowing Edward to arrive three months later and exploit the tired, bedraggled French. King Edward mustered what is believed to have been the largest force ever to have left England for France. Duke Charles sent 500 scuts, low, broad Dutch ships ideal for transporting horses and men, but it still took Edward three weeks to transfer his army across to Calais. The King of England arrived to find no war. His brother-in-law Charles was far to the east laying siege to the town of Neuss, where he had already lost some 4,000 of his finest men. Charles had sworn to meet Edward with thousands of men, but arrived with only a small escort. This was not what Edward had planned for.

Ever alert to an opportunity, the Spider King, Louis XI, sent word to Edward that he was willing to negotiate peace. He knew, he told Edward, that the Duke of Burgundy had lured Edward into France with false promises to his own ends and warned him that he would get little support from those he considered allies once they had seen their own objectives met. Louis had the measure of his opposite number. Commynes, who had by now transferred his services from Charles the Bold to Louis XI, was present at the discussion in the French court and at Picquigny were a peace was concluded. He noted that Edward had changed a great deal since they had met during the king's exile in Burgundy, having put on weight and grown less handsome. Edward was fond of the easy life and Louis exploited that fully, offering him a huge sum of money to take his army out of France, a large annual pension and a marriage between his oldest daughter Elizabeth and Louis's son Charles when both came of age. Edward's councillors were also offered substantial pensions to ensure their compliance.

Richard, Duke of Gloucester, did not agree with the peace. He refused to attend the negotiations and the signing of the Treaty of Picquigny. The duke clearly believed that Edward had a large enough force to press his cause on the battlefield and Commynes' amazement at the sheer numbers of the English force, however disorganised he believed they were, suggests that this might have been true. Richard was in the minority, though, and on 29 August 1475 the treaty was signed, the two kings meeting on a bridge divided by a screen with holes in to swear their oaths to uphold the treaty, with Edward's other brother George among those at his side. Louis flattered Edward, even offering to entertain him in Paris and provide an amenable confessor who would absolve Edward of whatever carnal sins he may wish to commit while he was there.

After the conclusion of the negotiations Louis arranged a private audience with Richard, then just twenty-two and clearly spoiling for a fight and the glory that would accompany it. Louis gave Richard gifts of plate and horses, which the duke accepted, but Louis, the master of knowing his enemy, was surely taking the measure of the King of England's ferocious brother. He probably found Richard a straight, intractable man, not someone who could be persuaded from his course as easily as his brother, and Louis no doubt took note of the young duke.

On the voyage home there was an important casualty, whose death has ever since been surrounded by rumour and controversy. During the short journey from Calais to Dover, the troublesome Lancastrian Henry Holland, Duke of Exeter, fell overboard and drowned. Henry's marriage to Edward's sister Anne had ended in a divorce in 1472 while the duke was imprisoned. In 1475 he volunteered to take part in Edward's expedition to France to prove his rehabilitation was complete. Exeter had been a thorn in Edward's father's side before jabbing himself into the king's. Edward was a great-grandson on his mother's side of Edward III's youngest son, Thomas of Woodstock, Duke of Gloucester. He possessed some Lancastrian royal blood too, being a great-grandson of John of Gaunt, Duke of Lancaster, Edward III's third son, on his father's side, though this descent was also through a female line. His death has been surrounded by rumour that King Edward had ordered him to be pushed overboard to finally rid himself of another long-standing problem.

The last serious incident of unrest in this second period of Edward IV's rule came two years after the return from France in 1477. On 22 December 1476 Isabel Neville, Duchess of Clarence, passed away aged twenty-five, just two months after giving birth to a baby boy named Richard who would not survive his mother by very long. Her husband George flew into a rage possibly fuelled by grief but with dire consequences, not only for himself. George became convinced that one of Isabel's ladies-in-waiting, Ankarette Twynyho, had poisoned her at the time she gave birth, causing two months of degeneration and pain until she died. It is more likely that Isabel was taken by consumption, the name then given to tuberculosis, though it may have been an infection caught during childbirth. The duke, though, would not be calmed.

On 12 April 1477 eighty of George's men barged into Ankarette's manor at Keyford in Somerset in the early afternoon. She was arrested and immediately removed to Bath. The following day she was transported to Cirencester and by the third day she was in Warwick, arriving in the evening after travelling some seventy miles in three days. She was thrown into a prison cell for the night and her daughter and son-in-law, who had followed her, were ordered out of Warwick by the duke, spending the night several miles away at Stratford-upon-Avon. At nine o'clock the next morning she was hauled before George, who accused her of murdering his wife. A jury, who would later insist that they were threatened by the duke, found her guilty with little semblance of due process. Before midday arrived Ankarette had been tried, found guilty and sentenced to death. The sheriff had her drawn through Warwick to the gallows at Myton where she was hanged.

The affair was ugly and sordid, but it was also dangerous for George's brother the king. Clarence had exercised royal authority in a manner only permitted to the Constable of England. Edward had forgiven Clarence his many previous indiscretions and betrayals, but a resurfacing of his lack of respect for Edward's position was something the king could not tolerate indefinitely. An astronomer named John Stacy, referred to indignantly by the *Crowland Chronicle* as a 'great sorcerer', was arrested for, among other things, using his black art to try to bring about the death of Richard, Lord Beauchamp, at the behest of his unfaithful wife. During questioning, which was undoubtedly conducted using torture, Stacy named another man, Thomas Burdet, as an accomplice. Stacy and Burdet were condemned to death and hanged at Tyburn. Upon the gallows they were permitted a final speech, used by both to protest their innocence.

The following day Clarence burst into the council chamber at Westminster, provocatively bringing with him Dr William Goddard, a staunch Lancastrian, and ordering him to read the final words of Stacy and Burdet to the Council. It was rich of Clarence to denounce royal justice in this way, but it was perhaps his own innocence in the affair that he hoped to convey, or else it was a hypocritical open attack upon the king. Edward, then at Windsor, summoned his brother immediately when he heard news of the outburst, having George arrested and placed in the Tower on arrival. When Parliament met at the beginning of 1478 Edward himself presented the case for high treason against his brother. The Parliament Rolls record that 'a conspiracy against him, the queen, their son and heir and a great part of the nobility of the land has recently come to his knowledge, which treason is more heinous and unnatural than any previous one because it originates from the king's brother the duke of Clarence, whom the king had always loved and generously rewarded'.

George's involvement in previous rebellions was restated and it was claimed that he had used Stacy and Burdet's death to try to turn the people against their king. Furthermore, Clarence 'also said that the king was a bastard, not fit to reign, and made men take oaths of allegiance to him without excepting their loyalty to the king'. This charge was not entirely new and seems to have originated as a joke at King Louis's court, where it was insinuated that Edward was the son of a huge English archer named Bleybourne, with whom his mother Cecily had engaged in an affair. It is likely that Warwick heard the story while on one of his many visits to France, where he was well liked, and used it to his own advantage. The story appeared once more to condemn George. Crowland recalled men being called to speak before the Parliamentary trial, but found it impossible to distinguish between prosecution and defence witnesses. George denied all charges, but Edward insisted that he intended to bring war once more to England and that George had kept 'an exemplification under the great seal of an agreement made between him and Queen Margaret promising him the crown if Henry VI's line failed'. There was to be no way out for Clarence this time. Whatever he had truly done, Edward wanted an end to it. The Act of Attainder was passed. George was found guilty. On 18 February 1478 George, Duke of Clarence, was privately executed, as was the right of his rank, within the Tower of London, aged twenty-eight. A rumour grew up and stuck that he had been permitted to choose the method of his own execution and in a final act of defiance he asked to be drowned in a vat of Edward's finest, beloved malmsey wine. This story has been given credence by reports that his daughter Margaret always wore a tiny wine cask as a charm, a trinket that can be seen in a contemporary portrait of her.

Crowland reflects that Edward ordered his brother's death only reluctantly and regretted having to do it. He writes of a whispering campaign moving backwards and forwards between the duke and the king, each hearing the other's every word reported and possibly exaggerated. The queen's Woodville family have been accused of at least contributing to George's downfall, if not masterminding it. There is no proof of this, though later speculation claimed that Richard, Duke of Gloucester, blamed the queen and her family for his brother's death. Dominic Mancini, an Italian present in London for the tumultuous spring of 1483 would write that Richard 'was so overcome with grief for his brother ... that he was overheard to say he would one day avenge his brother's death'. This may have been the result of the application of a degree of hindsight, but it is clear that few, least of all Edward, were pleased by the outcome. Precisely what Queen Elizabeth might have had to gain would soon become clear.

The same Parliament that condemned George, Duke of Clarence, also deprived George, Duke of Bedford, of his livelihood and title. George Neville was approaching seventeen years of age, and although Edward had intended to 'have given the said George adequate livelihood to support the same dignity', the king had not delivered. Whether for lack of funds or fear of facilitating the rebuilding of a strong Neville affinity who would not be sympathetic to him, Edward set about another purge of threats. The Parliament Rolls insisted that a lack of adequate livelihood 'often causes resort to great extortion, corruption and maintenance, to the great trouble of all the areas where such a figure happens to live'. So, outrageously painted as being in the best interests of both the duke himself and all who lived near him, 'all the dignities given to the said George or to the said John Neville, his father, shall henceforth be void and of no effect', so that 'George and his heirs shall not be dukes or marquesses, earls or barons'. George Neville was left with absolutely nothing.

A few months after Clarence's execution John de Vere, the pirate Earl of Oxford, scaled the walls of Hammes Castle and jumped from the top into the moat. The water was only shoulder depth and John was swiftly recaptured. It remains unclear whether this was an attempt to escape or to end his own life. John had been a natural Lancastrian but was also Warwick's brother-in-law and had supported the earl's attempts to place George upon the throne before the readeption. An implacable enemy to Edward as much as a supporter of any other particular cause, all of his hopes appeared finally lost. It may have been an attempt to gain his freedom but the timing makes a resigned bid to end his life possible too.

18

The King Is Dead, Long Live the King

In 1483 Richard, Duke of Gloucester, finally saw the chance he had waited for. He killed his nephews, seized the throne and lost it again because he was so unpopular. Thus the story ends, according to many. The difficulty with this portion of the Wars of the Roses is that it contains a never-ending cycle of questions and few answers, making it so complex and unclear that presenting a conclusion without too much examination, most often of the long-accepted Shakespearean model, is the approved way to conclude the Wars of the Roses. Those unanswerable questions, though, are crucial to an understanding of a man and a period of history lost to myth, legend and one of the best pieces of theatre ever composed.

Before the discovery of the bones of King Richard III in 2012 under a car park in Leicester, the picture most had of him was that bequeathed to the popular consciousness by Shakespeare. For many, that image is unshaken and unshakeable. To others he remains a wronged hero, a good man lost under the waves of Tudor victory and propaganda. The fight for his image as sinner or saint is bitter and unlikely to end, but somewhere in between these extremes, in the grey area occupied by all of our personalities, lies a very real man living in very difficult times. Those facts that are known and the questions left by the gaps are vital to unravelling the self-destruction of the House of York, the ending of 331 years of Plantagenet rule and the violent birth of the Tudor era.

In early April 1483 King Edward IV, aged forty, lay dying. He had contracted an illness that refused to release its grip, perhaps a chill caught while fishing. Whatever the cause, he was not going to recover. His son Edward, Prince of Wales, was twelve and had been in Ludlow for many years, where he had his own court and was being trained to rule after his father. The peace that Edward had slowly, painstakingly built over the last twenty-two years should have protected his son until he came of age. All of his enemies had been destroyed. Only two irreconcilable Lancastrians remained beyond his grasp. Jasper Tudor, Earl of Pembroke, and his nephew Henry, Earl of Richmond, had been in Brittany for over a decade. Henry's mother Margaret Beaufort, now married to Thomas, Lord Stanley, had been negotiating for the return of her twenty-six-year-old son and Edward had been warm to the idea, even proffering a marriage to one of his daughters. Edward, though, had a long reputation of not being true to his word and of seeing his rivals eliminated. The Tudors may have been wary in their exile.

Grafton's Chronicle, completed in the mid-sixteenth century, reports a deathbed plea from King Edward to those about him. Although the words are certainly invented, the sentiment is corroborated by contemporary sources. Edward tells his friends of his fears after his death:

> Such a pestilent Serpent is ambition, and desire of vain glory and sovereignty, Ambition, which among states where once entered, creepeth so far forth, till with division and variance he turneth all to mischief. First longing to be next to the best: Afterward equal with the best, and at the last chief and above the best.

Edward pleaded with the gathered men that 'from this time forward, all grief forgotten, each of you love other, which I verily trust you will'. When he could speak no more, Grafton tells how he 'laid down on his right side, his face toward them: and none was there present that could refrain from weeping. But the Lords comforting him with as good words as they could ... each forgave other and joined their hands together, when (as it after appeared by their deeds) their hearts were far asunder.'

Was the cause of King Edward's fear his ambitious brother Richard, Duke of Gloucester? It was not. His closest friend Lord Hastings, with whom he had shared exile, good times and bad, wine and women, was locked in a bitter feud with the king's stepson Thomas, Marquis of Dorset, Elizabeth Woodville's eldest son from her first marriage. According to Grafton Edward insisted that they must think of his sons, for ' it sufficeth not that you love them, if each of you hate other'. It was these two men that the king forced to shake hands over his deathbed in a desperate bid to ensure his son's safety. They took each other by the hand, swore to be friends and wept for the departing king, but Edward was not blind, nor was he naive. This situation required a different solution.

Knowing that a power struggle would erupt after his death and fearing the impact that it would have upon his son, Edward arrived at the conclusion that neither party could be trusted with power without using it against the other. When Henry VI had become king as a baby his care had been divided into three, separating the government of the realm, the care of his person and responsibility for his education between three trusted men. King Edward now entrusted all three of these aspects to just one man. In a late codicil to his will the king appointed his brother Richard, Duke of Gloucester, to act as Protector of the Realm during Prince Edward's minority. To believe that Richard created an atmosphere of tension and uncertainty in London when he arrived is to ignore the fact that such an atmosphere already pervaded the capital. Indeed, that very problem was the reason that Richard was summoned from his northern estates. Edward's intensely likeable personality and easy charm had held those about him together. With the glue gone, the whole construction of Yorkist government might fall. This was already a very real possibility even before Richard arrived. The simmering rivalries and conflicting intentions of the parties must be remembered in any evaluation of Richard's subsequent actions.

On 9 April 1483 King Edward IV died. His fears were almost immediately realised. His step-son Dorset and widow Elizabeth Woodville led efforts to take control of the government. Dorset boasted in Council that his family were so powerful they could rule without Richard. There must have been fears that this was true, because Lord Hastings wrote to Richard in Yorkshire to urge him to make all haste to take control of the new King Edward V and stop the Woodvilles, who were already planning an early coronation to end Richard's Protectorate before it could begin against the wishes of the dead king.

In York, Richard heard Mass for his brother and led the oaths of allegiance to the new king, which he caused all those gathered to take. If he really wanted the throne from the outset, making men swear holy oaths to another king was a poor start to his campaign. Edward V's household at Ludlow was under the control of his uncle Anthony Woodville, Earl Rivers, and they delayed leaving Ludlow until 24 April to allow them to celebrate St George's Day the day before. Richard made contact with Anthony and they arranged to meet at Northampton. Richard also wrote to a man who had lounged on the outskirts of power and influence up to this point. Henry Stafford, Duke of Buckingham, was the grandson of Humphrey Stafford, the loyal Lancastrian who had fallen at the Battle of Northampton.

At twenty-seven Henry had never been fully included in government, though he was not particularly excluded. He had been appointed Steward of England temporarily in order to pass sentence on George, Duke of Clarence, and had taken part in Edward's French campaign, though for unknown reasons he appears to have left when peace seemed the likely outcome. It is perhaps this shared view and experience, along with Richard's time in the care of Henry's grandfather after the Battle of Ludford Bridge, that caused him to seek out this enigmatic figure now. Henry had become a ward of Queen Elizabeth and had been married to one of her sisters, a match it was widely believed infuriated him as being below him. He could therefore be counted on as an ally against the machinations of the Woodvilles. Buckingham's recruitment suggests that Richard knew he would need help once he arrived in London, whether his aim was to see his brother's wishes fulfilled or to snatch the throne for himself. It also seems a little desperate and was to prove the manifestation of a fatal lack of judgement.

When Richard arrived at Northampton he was joined by Buckingham, but the king was not there. Earl Rivers and Sir Richard Grey, the younger son of Elizabeth Woodville from her first marriage, joined the two dukes along with a few others of the king's party. They passed a genial night eating and talking together before retiring. The king had carried on beyond Northampton to Stony Stratford (a geographical fact that Shakespeare twists to allow Richard to ambush Edward at Stony Stratford on the way to Northampton). Significantly, Stony Stratford was a Woodville manor and when Richard rose the next morning he accompanied Rivers and the others to meet his nephew. Shortly before they reached Stony Stratford Richard ordered the arrest of Rivers, Grey and Sir Thomas Vaughan, Edward V's Chamberlain. At the Woodville manor he took the new king into his custody. The prisoners were sent north to Richard's estates and he escorted Edward V on to London.

Lord Hastings was in London awaiting the arrival of the new king and his Protector. When news arrived of the coup at Stony Stratford, Elizabeth Woodville took her children into sanctuary at Westminster once again. This included Thomas Grey, Marquis of Dorset – her second son with Edward IV – Richard, Duke of York, and her five surviving daughters. Polydore Virgil would write at the beginning of the sixteenth century that Hastings 'bore privy hatred to the marquis and others of the queen's side' and that this was why he had made urgent contact with Richard advising him to hurry to London and to take charge of the new king as soon as possible. Hastings might well have been expected to have been pleased by the flight into sanctuary of the Woodvilles, an act that bears the hallmarks of both dread fear and a guilty conscience but whose true motives are still a matter for debate.

Virgil, however, goes on to state that Hastings in fact called a meeting of all of those men of power and importance in London at that time at St Paul's Cathedral. The Tudor's official historian wrote that the meeting was called because Hastings was shocked and concerned by what had happened and feared for the safety of the young king. Some of those gathered, 'offended with this late fact of Richard, Duke of Gloucester', argued for the immediate removal of Edward from his uncle's care, believing him 'utterly oppressed and wronged by force and violence'. The motion was defeated when the majority 'thought that there was no need to use war or weapon at all, as men who little suspected that the matter would have any horrible and cruel end'. This episode is perhaps recounted to show that Hastings and others already feared and suspected Richard's motives, bestowing upon them some precognition of what would fall out. If it really took place, the meeting shows that not only did the majority see no need to fear Richard but also that Hastings was playing his own dangerous game. Having written to Richard imploring him to seize the king and warning him of a Woodville plot, his response to Richard's seizure of Edward and arrest of his nephew's uncle and half-brother was to summon men of power and ferment outrage at Richard's actions and opposition to the Protector before he had even arrived.

On 4 May 1483 King Edward V rode into London to an opulent outpouring of public appreciation. The mayor, aldermen and richly dressed citizens greeted their new king, who wore blue velvet and was flanked by his uncle Richard and Henry, Duke of Buckingham, both in black. As they moved through the streets the ringing bells competed with the cheering crowds for the ear of the new young king. The date of his arrival was not without significance. The Woodvilles had obtained the Council's agreement to set 4 May as the date for the coronation, an unseemly rush that allowed little time for preparation and risked poor attendance, but suited the Woodville party's desire to do away with a Protectorate that risked their own position. Richard had broken their plans and most seemed soothed by his firm hand and the gentle slowing down of such important affairs. For many, though, the avoidance of a coronation for his nephew was Richard's only concern.

Edward was installed at the Bishop of London's Palace and Richard immediately called all of the Lord Spiritual and Temporal, the mayor and the city's aldermen to swear an oath of fealty to King Edward V. Crowland records that this was done 'with the greatest pleasure and delight' and was considered by all to be a positive sign. Richard had caused men to take public, solemn, religiously binding oaths of loyalty to his nephew in York and now in London. At a Council meeting, the coronation date was settled upon as 22 June and Richard was formerly confirmed as Protector of the Realm, with, Crowland noted, 'power to order and forbid in every matter, just like another king, and according as the necessity of the case should demand'. The Crowland chronicler also wrote that Lord Hastings was falling over himself to aid the two dukes, delighted with the result of their arrival and its effect upon his Woodville enemies, and frequently

was in the habit of saying that hitherto nothing whatever had been done except the transferring of the government of the kingdom from two of the queen's blood to two more powerful persons of the king's; and this, too, effected without any slaughter, or indeed causing as much blood to be shed as would be produced by the cut of a finger.

Council felt at ease enough to gently rebuke Richard for his treatment of the queen and her family, formerly requesting that they be given due care and respect.

London had held its breath, but seemed at last to be able to exhale contentedly. The violent eruption that had been feared had not materialised. Lord Hastings and the Woodville family were well known in London, both to members of the court and the wider citizenry. What, then, did they know about their new Protector, descending from the wild north in a moment of national tension? What might they be expecting from him as he placed a firm hand upon the tiller of government? Richard, Duke of Gloucester's contribution to the Wars of the Roses to date had been immaculately loyal. He had served his brother as soon as he was old enough, shared his exile when he might have faltered, fought bravely in the campaign to win back the throne, carved out for himself a prestigious powerbase in the north, becoming an increasingly infrequent visitor to London. He was more of a stranger to the population of London than the other two points of the triangle of power.

As early as 1472, in Edward IV's first parliament after his restoration, there is a hint at Richard's style and intention. Medieval feudal society had been based upon the notion of service to a lord, who offered protection to those under his authority and in return they were required to provide military service when the lord was called upon by the king. Over the years this principle had crumbled slightly as money was accepted from lords in lieu of providing men and service. This system, known as bastard feudalism, caused the corruption of the practise of livery and maintenance, under which lords provided men with their livery, the badge of their house to identify their allegiance, in return for maintaining the causes of those under their care. This practice led to abuses of the law as powerful lords flexed their muscles to prevent the prosecution of those within their affinity while corrupt men were drawn to powerful ones who would cause the law to turn a blind eye to their worst practices.

A petition was brought before Parliament in 1472 by Katherine Williamson, a resident of Howden near York, whose husband had been murdered by three brothers. The father of this murderous fraternity, Thomas Farnell, had, according to the petition, 'knowing that all his said sons had committed the aforesaid felonies, murders and robberies', provided shelter to them 'on the same day and on several later occasions'. Thomas Farnell sought to enter himself and his sons into the service of 'the most high and mighty prince and most honourable lord Richard, duke of Gloucester' in order that they might be 'supported in their horrible felony'. The plan initially worked and the four men were taken into the duke's household until he was informed of their crimes. The accepted system would see Richard protect his maintained men while they wore his livery. Instead, the twenty-year-old duke immediately 'commanded that the said Thomas should be brought to the gaol at York to remain there until he was lawfully acquitted or attainted'. Katherine requested the prosecution of Thomas and his three sons and Parliament granted her petition.

Why did Richard defy accepted social principles? Perhaps he appreciated his own powerful position and simply did not need these men. In 1472 this was perhaps premature. Only a year earlier he had been driven from the country. Turning maintained men over to the law so freely would discourage some from seeking out his livery and weaken his position in the longer term. That he acted from a position of weakness, turning them away out of fear, also seems unlikely. A weak noble would be all the more likely to accept such men to swell his ranks and draw near less scrupulous allies to progress his own cause. The only explanation that makes sense of this unusual action is that Richard's personal sense of equity and justice overrode the opaque rules of maintaining his affinity. He did not want murderers under his roof and would see them punished by the law as they deserved.

Eight years later, in 1480, John Randson appealed to Richard for aid against Sir Robert Claxton of Horden. Claxton, a leading member of the local gentry, was apparently preventing Randson from working his own land. Caxton had a son and a son-in-law in the duke's service. If social standing were not enough to see Caxton's case championed, the matter of affinity should have. However,

Richard found in Randson's favour, firmly warning Caxton in a letter 'so to demean you that we have no cause to provide his legal remedy in this behalf'. The message was clear: don't make me come down there and sort this out. These were dangerous precedents that bucked the social and political structure within which the duke operated and must not have gone unnoticed by his peers.

During his time in the north Richard had carved out a reputation as a champion of the region, using his influence over his brother to obtain tax breaks, improve trade and deal with contentious issues such as fish garths, dams that raised fish in the water to make them easier to catch but which impacted both fishing downriver and navigation of vital waterways. The north, a region long ignored and looked down upon by the south, finally had a vigorous and powerful defender. Vitally, Richard oversaw the successful protection of the lawless Scottish border region, which had been scarred by conflict and raiding for longer than anyone could remember. In 1481 relations with Scotland floundered after the expiry of a tensely observed truce. It became clear that France was defaulting on the terms of the Treaty of Picquigny and encouraging their friends in Scotland to invade England. Edward IV prepared for war but by now lacked the drive, and perhaps the physical conditioning, to see his plans through. In 1482 Edward handed command of the operation to Richard, who led an army north in July and swiftly recaptured Berwick, leaving the siege of the citadel that was the only resistance to Lord Stanley as he pushed on into Scotland.

The traditional tactics from each side were for the Scots to retreat into the wilderness, taking any livestock and other potential food sources with them, and for the English to harry towns and villages, setting fires to try to provoke a conflict. When their food ran out and none could be sourced, the English would skulk back over the border and the Scots would drift down from their hiding places. This time, though, Richard did not turn back. He fired buildings to no avail but marched on toward Edinburgh. If anything would provoke the Scots it was surely an attack on their capital city. Richard and his army, though, entered Edinburgh unopposed. The Scots sued for peace and Richard insisted upon the return of Berwick, ceded by Margaret of Anjou in return for Scottish support and a base for raids into England ever since, and when the Scots asked for the agreed marriage between their king's heir and Edward's daughter Cecily to go ahead Richard demanded the return of the dowry paid for Cecily and told the Scots that his brother would decide whether he wished the marriage to proceed. By mid-August Richard was back at Berwick, where the citadel fell. Berwick-upon-Tweed has been in English hands from that day to this.

All was not quite as it seemed, though. Hailed as an immense victory, without the loss of a single English soldier under the duke's command, the lack of resistance owed more to Scottish politics than fear of Richard or the English. Just before the duke arrived in Edinburgh King James III had been snatched by his own dissatisfied nobles and seen many of his favourites executed. When the English approached, the Scottish court had moved fifteen miles east of the capital to remain out of the way. From there, they bargained to see the English gone so that they might resolve their own issues. The Crowland chronicler, writing in hindsight but never a fan of Richard, wrote off the whole campaign as a waste of time, effort and money, scathingly recording that

> this trifling, I really know not whether to call it "gain" or "loss," (for the safe keeping of Berwick each year swallows up ten thousand marks), at this period diminished the resources of king and kingdom by more than a hundred thousand pounds. King Edward was vexed at this frivolous outlay of so much money, although the recovery of Berwick above-mentioned in some degree alleviated his sorrow. These were the results of the duke's expeditions into Scotland in the summer of the year of our Lord, 1482.

It was not, perhaps, the consummate demonstration of military leadership that it appeared on the surface.

The campaign had, however, achieved the aims set for it by the king. The Scottish threat was gone and Berwick was returned. When Edward wrote to Pope Sixtus IV of his brother's exploits there was no sign of the vexation Crowland points to.

> Thank God, the giver all good gifts, for the support received from our most loving brother, whose success is so proven that he

alone would suffice to chastise the whole kingdom of Scotland. This year we appointed our very dear brother Richard Duke of Gloucester to command the same army which we ourselves intended to have led last year, had not adverse turmoil hindered us. ... The noble band of victors, however, spared the supplicant and prostrate citizens, the churches, and not only the widows, orphans, and minors, but all persons found there unarmed.

International propaganda aside, Edward was heaping praise upon his brother's achievements and handing the entire credit for the success of the campaign to Richard personally. The control exerted by the duke over an army doubtless chomping at the bit to loot the unguarded pickings of the Scottish capital was also praised.

The duke's relationship with the Woodville family has been characterised as tense and difficult, with the queen's family suspicious of his motives and nervous of his power and Richard blaming them for the death of his brother George. There is no real contemporary evidence of any rift between the king's wife and his brother. In fact, just a month before Edward IV had died, Anthony Woodville had submitted a land dispute in East Anglia to Richard for his judgement, suggesting not only a lack of even underlying hostility but even open trust and co-operation.

When Richard, Duke of Gloucester, arrived in London plenty was known of him, even if he was not a frequent presence at court. The bitter rivalry between Lord Hastings and the Woodvilles was an open wound that invited infection. Richard was a balm from the north, beholden to neither party, seemingly on good terms with both. If anyone could resolve the tension and see Edward V safely installed and guided toward adulthood it was surely his uncle Richard. It must have seemed that the dying king had made the right choice to save his son and his kingdom. The mighty warrior king, undefeated on the field of battle, the tallest man ever to rule England or Britain, would soon be turning in his grave in St George's Chapel, Windsor, as his life's work unravelled in days.

19

Usurper

When the Council met on 13 June 1483 in the Tower of London it would be a watershed moment. The clues were there for those attending. While the larger part of the Council met elsewhere to discuss arrangements for the coronation Richard, Duke of Gloucester and Protector of the Realm; Henry Stafford, Duke of Buckingham; William, Lord Hastings; Thomas, Lord Stanley; John Morton, Bishop of Ely; and Thomas Rotherham, Bishop of Rochester, met at the Tower in a separate gathering. What was to follow has been universally accepted as an immovable stain upon the character of Richard in an outburst of drama befitting the finest fiction.

According to accounts of the meeting, the most famous penned by Sir Thomas More during Henry VIII's reign, the Protector was late arriving. More's account of Richard III's life and reign has long been regarded as definitive and a precursor to Shakespeare's play. Even the obvious flaws and inaccuracies woven through the account cannot diminish its veracity for some. A closer examination, though, offers a different view of these murky days. When Richard entered the room his mood was light and he asked John Morton for some of his famous strawberries from his garden to provide refreshment during the meeting. A little later, Richard excused himself for a while. When he returned his mood had changed. He was clearly on edge, unnerved and fighting to restrain his temper. When the thin thread snapped Richard demanded of Hastings 'What punishment do they deserve who had plotted his death, who was so near in blood to the king, and by office the protector of the king's person and realm?' The confused Hastings, still high on the success the duke had brought with him, replied that death was the fitting punishment, no doubt looking around the other faces at the table to discern who had betrayed the Protector.

More, who had been a member of Bishop Morton's household in the 1490s, then recounts Richard's rounding on Lord Hastings, condemning him as a traitor. The Tudor chronicler Grafton has Richard telling Hastings, 'By Saint Paul, I will not dine 'til I see thy head off,' while *Fabyan's Chronicle* records that the Protector had Hastings dragged outside and 'there without judgement, or long time of confession or repentance, upon an end of a long and great timber log, which there lay with other for the repairing of the said Tower, caused his head to be smitten off'. Lord Stanley, Bishop Morton and Bishop Rotherham were placed under arrest. The question that can never now be answered, but which must be asked, is how Hastings fell so far, so fast, and why Richard ordered the summary execution of an ally.

One interpretation of the events of Friday 13 June 1483 is that Richard used an invented plot to rid himself of men who stood between him and the throne as loyal adherents of Edward IV and his son. Lord Hastings had been Edward IV's closest friend. He owed his wealth, position and influence to Edward and feared the Woodvilles precisely because he envisaged the ending of his power. To maintain his position he needed an independent Edward V on the throne who might look to him for experience and guidance. If Richard wanted the throne he may have concluded that Hastings would never agree to the unseating of his friend's son and so resolved to remove the opposition he would present. Lord Stanley was a militarily powerful man and held great influence. A regular attendee at court, he was close to Edward's family and thus a potential threat. John Morton was an experienced politician and was renowned for his gift of oratory. Such a man, in Edward IV's service for over a decade, might whip up armed resistance to Richard's plans all too easily. Thomas Rotherham had been Lord Chancellor and was close to the queen, so would obviously side with her to keep Edward V on the throne. In one fell swoop Richard could clear his path to the throne.

The other side of this same coin offers a very different perspective. Lord Hastings, according to Tudor chroniclers keen to darken Richard's name, had, in fact, been plotting against the Protector even before he had arrived in London by calling a meeting at St Paul's to stir up already jangling nerves. Anthony Woodville, the senior face of the other side of the political power struggle, was under arrest, so it perhaps made sense to deal with Hastings in the same way. Lord Stanley had a rivalry with Richard that went back to Hornby Castle in 1470, though they had worked together on the Scottish campaign a year earlier. He was notorious for bending carefully with prevailing winds to ensure that he obtained the best outcome for himself. Such a man could be a force for unrest at a time when Richard had to enforce calm and certainty.

Bishop Morton was a wily old fox. He had been a staunch Lancastrian until the readeption failed and Henry VI was killed. With no Lancastrian cause left to follow he had transferred his allegiance to Edward but might conceivably seek to unsettle the Yorkist regime given the opportunity now presented. Bishop Rotherham had been Edward IV's Lord Chancellor, but Richard had stripped him of the post as a result of Rotherham's siding with the queen in Council to prevent the Protectorate and then delivering the Great Seal to her in sanctuary at Westminster when he was not entitled to do so. Although Rotherham had subsequently recovered the seal and passed it to Thomas Bourchier, Archbishop of Canterbury, he had shown his true colours. He was a Woodville adherent and therefore partisan in the precarious situation Richard tried to impose unity upon.

In addition to the considerations noted, Grafton wrote that Hastings and Stanley had been involved in an odd episode the very night before the meeting. Stanley had apparently sent a messenger urgently requesting that Lord Hastings come to his house and leave London with him. Stanley had endured a nightmare so terrifying that he wanted to flee the capital in the dead of night. He had seen a crazed boar chasing him about before goring him with its tusks. He was convinced that it meant Richard, whose emblem was the boar, was out to get him. Hastings sent the messenger back, teasing that Stanley should know better than to be scared of his dreams and pointed out that Richard was more likely to be suspicious of them if they fled, chiding that they courted Stanley's fears by running and that they would be in more certain peril 'if we were caught and brought back, (as friends fail flyers) for then had the Boar a cause likely to raise us with his tusks, as folks that tied for some falsehood'.

The illegality of Lord Hastings' execution has long haunted Richard's reputation, even for those keen to see it re-examined, yet even this is not without issue and the blame may well lie at the reposed feet of King Edward IV. Richard was still Constable of England, a post that he had held since 1471. Now he was also Protector with powers Crowland equated to those of a king. Part of the prerogative of the Constable was to try and pass sentence in cases of treason himself based on evidence that he had seen. Richard was legally entitled to summarily try, sentence and execute Hastings if he had seen evidence of treason on Hastings' part. The exercise of the power does not necessarily mark Hastings as actually guilty, but it was legal. Richard claimed that he had seen evidence during his absence from the Council meeting that Hastings was plotting against him to his own ends. In the confused snake pit of a capital city in upheaval it is not unreasonable that Richard might believe in such a plot, and it is his belief in it rather than its genuine existence that matters for the purposes of this act.

It is possible to read too much into the fact that London did not rise in uproar at the murder of the popular, faithful Lord Hastings, who was a true liegeman of the new king. Richard reportedly had evidence of Hastings' treason publicised and this put minds at rest. The unerring speed with which these documents emerged could suggest that it was an orchestrated ploy to discredit Hastings and excuse Richard of his murder, or simply that the evidence did actually exist, that Richard had been presented with it and acted upon it as he was entitled, if not required, to do. Edward IV had used John Tiptoft to dispense his harsh, summary justice before 1470, leaving the Earl of Worcester to languish for eternity under the epithet 'The Butcher of England'. Richard's first year in the role had seen him deliver that same summary justice after the Battle of Tewkesbury to men Edward had dragged out of sanctuary and probably given the unenviable task of overseeing the death of Henry VI. This is what Richard had been taught by his brother to

threat and use the powers he held to snuff it out. That was
ld those powers. Hastings was a threat. Richard snuffed
out.

the perils of delving into these troubled weeks that
each man had a compelling reason to be selected to attend that
meeting, whether its purpose was to plough a furrow to the throne
or to eradicate threats to Edward V's security. During this period
proclamations were being issued by Richard in the name of Edward
V, coin was being minted with the boy's image and Parliament had
been summoned in his name for shortly after the coronation. Either
Richard maintained an unnecessarily conspicuous deception as to
his intention to crown his nephew or he really meant to see it done
until something finally changed his mind.

Another of Edward IV's less well thought-out policies now reared
its head to further complicate matters in an already dizzyingly
complex London. News had at some point arrived from the north
that George Neville, the disinherited son of John Neville, Marquis
of Montagu, had died after a short illness on 4 May. At any other
time these tidings would have been disastrous for Richard, but
added to the present turmoil it was a recipe for disaster. Richard's
Neville inheritance, which made up the vast majority of his power
base and drew to him the loyalty of the old Neville affinity in the
north, was still tied to the male line of John Neville by statute.
With George's death, unmarried and childless in his early twenties,
Richard's power was broken. His titles reverted to life interests
only. He had nothing of them to leave to his son and his firm
foundation in the north was cracked. At the very moment that he
needed to be at his most powerful Richard was fatally weakened.
Even if those circling the unfolding events could not smell the blood
in the water, Richard knew he was haemorrhaging and that he
would have to bind the wound quickly.

On 10 June, Richard had written to the City of York asking
them to send as many fighting men south to him as they could
muster quickly 'to aid and assist us against the Queen, her blood
adherents and affinity,' because Richard feared they sought to
destroy him and all those of the 'old royal blood of this realm'.
These men would not arrive until the beginning of July, so the
suggestion that Richard was imposing his will upon the city and

the body politic by force seems unlikely, yet no-one openly opposed Richard's moves, accepting the evidence that he presented. On 15 June Edward IV's favourite mistress, Jane Shore, was forced to do public penance for harlotry, walking through London's streets in just her underskirt carrying a lighted taper before being thrown into prison. The following day the Council agreed that Edward V's brother, Richard, Duke of York should be removed from sanctuary to join his brother. Elizabeth Woodville reluctantly handed him into the care of the Archbishop of Canterbury with his promise that the boy would not be harmed. The next day, 17 June, orders were sent north for the executions of Anthony Woodville, Richard Grey and Thomas Vaughan. The three men were beheaded at Pontefract Castle on 25 June.

One man may well have been at work in these days who passes almost unnoticed until he emerges from the mist of uncertainty just weeks later. If news reached Richard's ear that powerful men conspired against him then someone was carrying this news. If the story of Stanley's panicked midnight missive to Hastings is true then it was someone close to one of them. If the evidence was so well collated and presented that it seemed unnaturally so, then there was a professional behind its compilation. William Catesby could be that man and his contribution to this defining period of English history may have been overlooked.

Around the time of this fateful Council meeting it is alleged by Philip de Commynes that Robert Stillington, Bishop of Bath and Wells, visited Richard to break some startling, seismic news. Stillington informed the Protector that Edward IV had been pre-contracted to marry Lady Eleanor Butler at the time that he married Elizabeth Woodville. A pre-contract was created when a couple agreed to marry by expression the intention to wed. 'I will marry you' was the legal equivalent of saying 'I do' before an altar if there were two witnesses and a member of the clergy present. If Edward's marriage to Elizabeth was bigamous then all of the children of that union were illegitimate and legally incapable of inheriting. It would mean that Edward V could not become king.

Edward IV's reputation for womanising is well attested to. Is it believable that in his younger days he would undergo a clandestine ceremony of marriage in order to lure a maiden to his bed with the promise of a dream match with the king? Absolutely. That is, after all, precisely how he came to be married to Elizabeth Woodville. If other women were wooed in the same way then Edward may well have been married several times over before he met Elizabeth Woodville. A woman might remain silent, having found herself tricked and discarded, to save embarrassment, to preserve her future marriage prospects and not least to avoid incurring the wrath of the king. Edward had married Elizabeth in secret, with limited witnesses, including her mother, and the match had been kept secret for months, even from Edward's closest friend, the Earl of Warwick. Whether the union was Edward's one and only, whether he played his game once too often with one who was the match of him, whether he really fell in love or just wanted to spite Warwick as he arrogantly pressed a French princess upon the king is no longer known for certain. Whatever the truth, the story was not alien to the capital city. Commynes had commented on the desire of the city's wives for a return to Edward's bed in 1471 as a contributing factor to the regaining of his throne. His carnal reputation served him well then, but would doom his son now, at least making these allegations plausible.

Robert Stillington supposedly now claimed to have been a witness to the pre-contract between King Edward and Eleanor Butler. A sermon was preached by Dr Ralph Shaa, half-brother of the Mayor of London, on 22 June, the date that had been set in stone for the coronation, entitled 'Bastard Slips Shall Not Take Deep Root'. Dr Shaa revealed that King Edward had been married bigamously and that all of the children of his marriage were therefore illegitimate, including Edward V. There was also some allusion made to Edward IV's own legitimacy, resurrecting the old charge of Warwick and Clarence. Ill received, this charge was swiftly dropped, whether for lack of truth, popular will to accept two decades of loyalty to an illegitimate king, or to limit embarrassment of Richard's mother Cecily.

Stillington had produced evidence, which was presented to a Parliamentary Committee made up of those summoned to the Parliament later that month and already in London. They accepted the evidence and declared Edward V illegitimate and incapable of claiming the throne. This evidence, as with all of the other paperwork that might offer support to Richard's charges during these days, are lost, possibly not by accident, but it was circulated, believed and accepted at the time.

Although doubtless orchestrated by Richard and Buckingham, it is to be remembered that Richard did not seize the throne of England. Emulating his brother's diplomatic approach, Richard went to his mother's London home, Baynards Castle where, on 25 June, he was petitioned by the mayor and aldermen of London and those members of Parliament in the city to take the throne for himself as the only lawful heir of his father and the rightful king of England. Richard accepted and preparations began for his coronation. Although the document presented to Richard is lost, its contents can be found in a copy of *Titulus Regius*, the detailing of Richard's title enrolled in his only parliament. It was later ordered by Henry VII that every copy of the document should be destroyed and he believed it done, yet one managed to survive.

The charge of convenience in the emergence of the story of Edward IV's pre-contract and Edward V's illegitimacy is constantly levelled at Richard to demonstrate that it was simply an artifice by which he might appear to legally get what he really wanted. This may well be true. Eleanor Butler was dead, as was Edward IV, the only two people who might be able to approve or deny the story. George, Duke of Clarence, had a son, the eight-year-old Edward, but his father had been attainted by Parliament, stripped of title and his heirs prevented from inheriting so that little Edward could also not be king. That left only Richard, appearing very convenient indeed. The revelation appears a little too perfect in its timing, effectively insisting that Richard was king. If he invented the story, it worked like a charm.

This coin can also be turned over for a different view. By some measures the revelation was anything but convenient. If Richard had been planning for the smooth succession of his nephew, removing potential threats to the clean transition and then hoping to use his influence over his nephew to see his titles corrected, the news made a mockery of his oaths, of the oaths that he had caused others to swear and of all of his efforts over the last two months. Why had the story only emerged now? Perhaps because Edward IV's death was a pre-requisite to its revelation. During the king's lifetime none would dare to bring such a charge into the light. Warwick and Clarence had made similar claims and both had died as traitors for it. Anyone seeking to unveil the secret would be required to run the gauntlet of angry retribution not only from the king but from the queen and her family, threatened with the loss of all that they had gained.

The circumstances surrounding the unsettled life and controversial execution of George, Duke of Clarence, return to the centre of events unfurling five years after his death. George had been accused of plotting not only against the king but also the queen and their son. Was he threatening to make public the charge now finally hauled into the light? It becomes noteworthy that Robert Stillington, the bishop credited with delivering the tale to Richard, was, by 1478, so close an associate of George that he was imprisoned in the Tower for unspecified offences at the same time Clarence was arrested. Stillington's own career offers tantalising, suggestive hints while denying any actual evidence that he knew something valuable.

Edward IV married Elizabeth Woodville in 1464, when Stillington was an archdeacon and Keeper of the Privy Seal, a position that offered him access to and the trust of the king. In 1465 he became Bishop of Bath and Wells and in June 1467 was appointed Lord Chancellor, a position that he held until the readeption, being re-appointed after the recovery and holding the post until 1473. After his dismissal Stillington gravitated toward the powerful and enigmatic Duke of Clarence, becoming tangled in the net that closed about George in 1478. This may be nothing more than the steady career progression of an ambitious man, yet Stillington was already forty-five when he became a bishop so must have come to his desire to rise late in life.

Alternatively, Stillington was a man Edward used to perform the clandestine marriage ceremonies that tricked ladies into his bed. After the Woodville marriage became public Stillington's silence was bought with position and power. When this dried up, perhaps because Edward characteristically lost interest and saw no need to pander to the bishop any longer, he found his way into the company of one who would eagerly devour his tales for his own ends. Did Stillington tell Clarence that the duke was the rightful heir and that the Woodvilles were stealing his position for a bastard son? His crimes in 1478 may have remained unspecified because their definition would have ruined Edward. Perhaps Stillington's conscience weighed heavy as he watched preparations to crown a boy he knew had no right. A king without right risked God's wrath and the country's security. Perhaps the bishop, by now in his mid-sixties, had believed he would be spared the moral dilemma, certain that Edward IV would outlive him. Certainly that would appear to make sense of events from 1464 to 1483 and of Richard's sudden about-face in mid-June. Frustratingly, though, it is no more than a theory based upon rumour and coincidence.

Another figure lurks in the margins of this story who would later reap the rewards of Richard's accession to the throne and there is another connection that adds to the disjointed heap of circumstantial evidence. Eleanor Butler, the lady at the centre of the pre-contract problem, was a Talbot by birth, the daughter of John Talbot, 1st Earl of Shrewsbury, the famed soldier of the Hundred Years War who had worked alongside Richard, Duke of York, in France. Eleanor's cousin Alice Talbot married Sir Thomas Barre of Burford and the couple's daughter Jane became the second wife of Sir William Catesby Snr. To emphasis the direct connection, in 1468 Eleanor had gifted a manor at Fenny Compton to her sister and Catesby Snr had been a witness to the document. The Catesby family were traditionally Lancastrian in their sympathies. Sir William Snr had probably fought at Towton for Henry VI, his uncle Robert certainly dying there. Gravitating toward the Earl of Warwick, Catesby Snr veraciously built a grand property portfolio until, at the readeption, the combination of Warwick and Lancaster sang out to him. Appointed Sheriff of Northamptonshire, he was later pardoned by Edward IV and remained as sheriff until his death.

William Catesby Jnr, related to the Talbots via his step-mother, was a lawyer in the service of Lord Hastings in 1483 as the Protector arrived and his master panicked, relaxed and then fell. Thomas More asserts that it was Catesby who brought Richard news of Hastings' treachery, perhaps even of the midnight visit of Stanley's messenger pleading that they should flee London together. If this is true then Catesby oversaw the fall of his master and transferred his allegiance smoothly to Richard. If the shrewd lawyer was pulling one set of strings his other hand was perhaps equally busy. Catesby's connection to Eleanor Butler may have given him privileged access to Talbot family secrets. Perhaps Eleanor had taken legal advice from Catesby's father on her position and the story had been stored away in the family vault until it might be of some use.

Whether in search of self-promotion or as part of an early piece of mischief driven by latent Lancastrian bitterness, Catesby could have tracked down Stillington and directed him to tell the Protector what he knew. The complexity of these hot summer days in June 1483 is only made harder to unravel with these new layers. Catesby may have known the story, believed it true and called a known witness to testify to it. He may have invented the tale and used an old family connection to add a touch of credence. Fabricating evidence would have come easily to a trained lawyer. This would leave the question of Richard's position even less clear too. Could he have known the story was a lie and been complicit in Catesby and Stillington's invention to win the throne for himself by a legal lie? Perhaps, but he might also have been the victim of a trick. He may have believed in the evidence presented to him. Certainly the Parliamentary Committee accepted it. If Catesby was behind all of this, what else might he do to win the favour of his new master? One of England's greatest, most enduring mysteries was about to grip the nation and there may have been a shadowy figure lurking backstage who has escaped the attention of a gripped audience.

As the summer faded into autumn it also became clear that opposition was never far away from Richard, offering the tantalising prospect that this puppet master was having his own strings carefully manipulated as part of a much bigger plot. This version of events carries as much proof and indeed likelihood as the view that Richard waited patiently for over a decade, with no opportunity and no outward demonstration of intention, to seize the throne that he had always coveted. It might explain the oaths of allegiance, the execution of Hastings and many things that followed.

On 6 July 1483 Richard was crowned King Richard III in a shared ceremony with his wife Anne, only the fourth joint coronation and the first for 175 years. The crowning of a settled, mature couple with a son and heir must have held appeal for some against the uncertainty of a minority with factions vying for control. Precisely who drove events and who was a pawn remains unclear, but there are plenty of alternatives to the accepted view that Richard III was no more than an evil usurper. Even if he had aimed for the throne from the outset it is to be remembered that precisely four men died to win it, compared to the thousands sacrificed to see Edward IV crowned, Henry VI readepted and Edward restored. It seems odd that Richard is remembered as a bloodthirsty murderer when his tally can be totalled exactly at four. Even if he were guilty of the murders of his nephews, that came after he had his throne. Yet the four executed men might have been removed even if Richard had been genuinely aiming to crown his nephew at that stage. Richard was summoned to London because of the irreconcilable differences between Hastings and the Woodvilles. If Richard cut the heads from these two dangerous snakes it was perhaps the best solution available. Would Edward IV object to the death of his friend and brother-in-law if it would secure his son's throne? Perhaps not. To some, Richard will always be an evil, murdering usurper. To others he remains a good man trying to do his duty in difficult circumstances. The truth probably lies somewhere in between these two extremes. However he had gained the crown, it would not sit easily upon his head for long.

20

Buckingham and Rebellions

Before Richard had been king for five months he faced the first serious rebellion against his rule. Remembered as Buckingham's Rebellion, this misnomer may be covering up the deeper currents buffeting the House of York. Ever since Henry IV had unseated Richard II in 1399, successions had been dogged by trouble. The first Lancastrian king would endure unrest for the remainder of his days either from Richard's supporters, Percy antagonists or a Welsh nation looking to exploit a distracted, fractured England. Henry V had been forced to execute prominent men as he departed for France in 1415 when a plot to replace him as king was exposed. Even the accession of the baby Henry VI had seen a Mortimer execution and careful positioning of those looking for power. The crown had passed from Lancaster to York, back once more and finally rested in Edward IV's lap, but he was never really without threat, perhaps until the suspicious death of Henry Holland, Duke of Exeter. Edward V's succession had not gone well and now there was another new king. For some, a new king meant new opportunities, and not to ingratiate themselves, but to try their own luck.

Henry Stafford, Duke of Buckingham, was another of the period's kingmakers. He had played a pivotal role in placing Richard on the throne with unwavering support throughout the summer. The turning of his coat was as devastating to Richard's fragile new rule as it was utterly unexpected. Although the revolt is now a mere footnote in the period, its side-lining belies the size, complexity and very real threat that it posed at the time. Buckingham had long sought the return of the large Bohun inheritance that he considered his right. Edward IV had withheld it, as he had done to other powerful men including John Howard, now given the title of Duke of Norfolk by Richard. The new king was in the process of handing this huge haul to Buckingham, waiting only on the formality of Parliamentary approval to ratify it. Perhaps even this was too slow for Buckingham who feared that he would go the way of Warwick before too long.

The fate of the two sons of Edward IV, the Princes in the Tower, might also have played a part, though precisely what contribution this mystery, to which we will return later, made is another unanswerable question. Buckingham may have been appalled to learn that Richard had done away with the boys and been driven into rebellion by his revulsion. It is just as likely that the reverse is true; that Buckingham had the boys killed and Richard was enraged when he found out. Perhaps they simply quarrelled over the consequences of such an act and those of failing to commit that act and could not agree, whichever side each man took.

What is probable is that two figures, who would become an unstoppable force, were both at work in Buckingham's disaffection from Richard III. The Tudor antiquary Edward Hall wrote that as Buckingham returned to his lands in Wales he crossed the River Severn at Bridgnorth where he was met by Lady Margaret Stanley, nee Beaufort, a distant cousin. She reportedly pleaded with Buckingham to intervene with Richard to gain approval for the return to England of her son Henry Tudor and his marriage to one of Edward IV's daughters, a resurrection of the plan that had neared completion before Edward IV's death. If this conversation took place Margaret may have sown the seed of doubt in Buckingham's mind that Richard was not delivering what had been expected. Perhaps he would deliver nothing at all. Of little consequence to Buckingham, except that he still wanted those promised Bohun lands. That Margaret would still be seeking to marry her treasured only son to a daughter of Edward IV is telling too. All of Edward's children were bastards now. Why, then, would she be so keen to see her only son, who would be restored to the earldom of Richmond, married to an illegitimate bride? It was a hint at the union of

Lancaster and York that could overthrow Richard. Margaret was a recalcitrant Lancastrian and Buckingham's own family had lost much defending Henry VI. Perhaps he licked his lips at the prospect, particularly if he could be convinced that his star was already fading in Richard's eyes. With his own royal blood stirred, Buckingham might have discerned an opportunity for himself to make a play for the crown in the chaos that might ensue.

If the seed was sown at Bridgnorth it was carefully cultivated and tended by John Morton, Bishop of Ely, at Brecon Castle. Following his arrest at the fateful Council meeting of 13 June, Morton had been released into Buckingham's care under gentle house arrest at the duke's castle. Morton was a persuasive man and may have worked carefully on the vain, haughty duke, tugging at Lancastrian sympathy buried but not forgotten or even tending to Buckingham's idea that he might become king himself. Once fertilised, the ideas took root and grew as Morton worked on his keeper until he was ready for the reaping.

Margaret Beaufort's lifelong dream of placing her son upon the throne, driven by religious fervour, is almost certainly an invention. What she was presented with in 1483 was an opportunity to get her son back that was too good to miss, because as the plan unfolded she came to see that the shifting sands that underpinned the succession of a new king presented a chance to win all if only she would take the gamble. Before playing her hand and risking her only beloved child she would have to tip the odds firmly in her favour. It is well known that Margaret Beaufort opened a channel of communication to Elizabeth Woodville in her Westminster sanctuary. Margaret's personal physician, Dr Lewis Caerleon, became Elizabeth's physician too, relaying messages between the two desperate mothers. Through Dr Caerleon an accord was reached. Elizabeth would call on her husband's loyal men to place Margaret's son on the throne if he would marry her oldest daughter, Elizabeth, and make her queen.

The agreement of this course marks a momentous point in 1483. Elizabeth Woodville accepted that her sons' cause was dead and probably, however painfully and reluctantly, conceded that they were dead too. She must have been certain of this to offer support to another claimant to her son's throne. With their true fate remaining a mystery to this day, Elizabeth Woodville must have been privy to knowledge now lost. The most likely source of her information is surely Dr Caerleon, passing on sad news from Margaret that her boys were lost, murdered by their uncle. Margaret may well have been as uncertain of their true status as the rest of London and the country, but she might also have lied to Elizabeth Woodville, desperate for news in the political vacuum of sanctuary. How better to garner support for her son Henry than to recruit a distraught mother frantic for revenge? It is entirely likely that Margaret lied to Elizabeth to secure her support, even if she had no true knowledge of what had become of the boys.

Plans were laid for a rebellion on the Feast of St Luke, 18 October. Kent was to rise first and attack London from the south-east, drawing Richard out to face them. At that point men of the West Country, Wiltshire and Berkshire, their numbers swollen by Buckingham's army coming out of Wales and Henry Tudor's Breton mercenaries landing on the south coast, would fall upon Richard from behind, taking him by surprise and snaring him in a trap. There were great numbers of men willing to join the revolt and it appeared to be in good shape. It was a large and a very real threat to a government yet to firmly establish itself.

In a mysterious misfire, the men of Kent made their way to London on 10 October, eight days earlier than was planned. John Howard, Duke of Norfolk, swiftly took control of the capital while Richard was in the Midlands on his royal progress. Several of the rebels were captured and Howard extracted the details of the rest of their plan. King Richard was in Lincoln when news arrived the next day that a rebellion was underway. A muster was called at Leicester and as Richard set out south to deal with the rest of the revolt he sent men on ahead to destroy the bridges over the River Severn that would be Buckingham's only route out of Wales.

On 18 October the rest of the plan swung into action, oblivious to the fact that it was already undone. The plan was complex and this was to be its downfall. It relied on too many pieces falling into place at just the right moment. Luck, and perhaps God, was not with the rebels this time. A terrible storm ravaged England as the rebellion began, with ten days of rain leaving the Severn swollen and ferocious, bursting its banks at several spots. With the bridges destroyed, Buckingham could find no crossing and his soaked, less-than-willing Welsh levies began to desert his side in favour of the warmth of home and hearth.

In the English Channel the same brutal storm was scattering Henry Tudor's fleet as it tried to make the crossing from Brittany. Emerging, probably alone, Tudor's ship was hailed from the coast by soldiers who told him that the plan had worked perfectly, that Buckingham had been victorious and that Henry's arrival was eagerly awaited. Ever astute and suspicious, it is not hard to imagine Henry narrowing his eyes in the driving rain at the overly warm welcome. He turned his ship around and sought a way back to Brittany, his shrewd caution almost certainly saving him from capture.

Buckingham fled, taking refuge in the home of one of his retainers, Ralph Banastre. The lure of the large price placed on the duke's head broke down Banastre's loyalty and he handed over his master to Sir James Tyrell, a man loyal to Richard through a long association. Tyrell rode with the duke to Salisbury, where Richard had been dealing with the rest of the insurrection and imposing order. When Buckingham pleaded for an audience with the king to explain himself, Richard refused to allow the duke into his presence. For a man who seems to have seen the world in black and white, Buckingham's betrayal, appearing to come from nowhere, was inexcusable and unforgivable. When news had reached Richard at Lincoln of the planned revolt the king had written to his Chancellor John Russell, Bishop of Lincoln, requesting that he send the Great Seal to facilitate the raising of an army. The letter contains a postscript in Richard's own hand in which he rages against 'the malice of him that had best cause to be true, the Duke of Buckingham, the most untrue creature living', adding 'We assure you there was never false traitor better purveyed for'. Frustratingly unclear, it is impossible to determine whether Richard was furious only at the duke's rebellion or whether the fate of Richard's nephews played a part in the king's indignation. Had Buckingham killed the boys without Richard's knowledge? Had the duke counselled Richard to have it done, only to turn the act against the king? Had Richard simply expected Buckingham's unqualified support for the act? Or is any of this to read too much into the righteous vehemence of a betrayed man?

On 2 November 1483 Henry Stafford, 2nd Duke of Buckingham, was beheaded in Salisbury market square. He never received the audience that he pleaded for. The new king had dealt swiftly and decisively with the very real threat of large-scale revolt so that barely a trace remained. Buckingham was dead, Henry Tudor was back in Brittany and Margaret Beaufort, Elizabeth Woodville and John Morton, Bishop of Ely, were heavily implicated in the plot. In an age anxious for signals of God's will the inexplicably early movement of Kent and the storms that scattered Richard's enemies must have appeared clear demonstrations of God's will and Richard's right to be king. Dealing with the aftermath would be crucial and signs of Richard's political naivety are plain in his poor handling of his overwhelming victory, but it also gives the lie to the image of him as a merciless killer.

Bishop Morton fled first to the Norfolk Fens before finding a ship that would take him to Flanders. Here he hid from Richard's vengeance and continued to plot against the king, just beyond his reach. Elizabeth Woodville remained in sanctuary unmolested for her part in the uprising. Margaret Beaufort, though, was cornered, and it is the response to this lady's part that is the most remarkable. A vastly wealthy Lancastrian who slid carefully and successfully into Richard's court, she was the mother of the man who had claimed Richard's throne and probably the prime mover in the rebellion. Her punishment was surprisingly light. Placed under house arrest, she was stripped of her lands, only to have them granted to her husband to hold on her behalf, the same Lord Stanley that Richard had arrested in the Tower when he had ordered Hastings' execution. Stanley was tasked with ensuring that she made no further contact with her son and held personally responsible for her future conduct. Placing the person and wealth of a known traitor into the hands of a suspected traitor hardly seems well advised. Whether through mercy or naivety, Richard had sealed his fate.

Richard compounded the sense of alienation from his rule felt in the south by replacing those who had risen against him with men he knew from the north, transplanting them into southern estates and official posts to the exclusion of locals. This did not play well, though it is questionable whether there was any viable option at that stage other than to fall back on men the king knew he could trust. The upheavals on the throne of England had created an air of potential whenever there was a change. The sanctity of kingship was eroded each time it slipped through one set of fingers into an open hand below. Margaret Beaufort perhaps saw this more clearly than most. If she could not have her son back by peaceful means then why not take the ultimate gamble rather than settle for a life apart, her son set to die an exile devoid of land, title or prospect? This raises a tantalising but unanswerable question. How much of the events of 1483 were directed by a Tudor plot to remove the House of York altogether?

Margaret Beaufort and Lord Stanley might well have been whispering into uncertain ears in London before Richard even arrived. Did Hastings lurch from relief at Richard's decisive action to fear of his coming because his friend Stanley sowed a seed of doubt? Did Margaret feed Elizabeth Woodville the story of her sons' demise to secure her and her late husband's support for a plot to remove Richard, a side effect of which was to place Margaret's son on the throne and the sweetener for which was the promise to marry him to Elizabeth's daughter? Did Catesby drive the pre-contract story because of his family's Lancastrian links? Was the rebellion being planned even before the crown came to rest on Richard's head? The answers to these questions are frustratingly elusive. Some will never see beyond Richard's early and ruthless bid for the throne while others can see no malice in the man. Perhaps he was as much a pawn as a king, a man perfectly equipped to serve a king but ill-suited to holding the office himself, lacking his brother's subtlety.

The next two years were marked by momentous triumphs and tragic personal losses. Richard III held only one parliament spanning twenty-seven days, opening on 23 January 1484 and closing on 20 February. Like everything else touched by Richard III, his parliament is a source of passionate division. Among eighteen private statutes were the attainder of Henry Stafford, Duke of Buckingham, the return of lands to Henry Percy, Earl of Northumberland, and settlements for Richard's loyal friends Francis, Lord Lovell, and Sir James Tyrell. The most significant was *Titulus Regius*, a reproduction of the document requesting that Richard take the throne enrolled and made law. The public bills passed included the abolition of benevolences, a system of forced gifts to the crown ruthlessly exploited by Edward IV to circumvent taxation and deeply unpopular. Legal corruptions in the transfer of land titles and the compositions of juries were corrected and the system of bail was bolstered (certainly not invented) by Richard's parliament to prevent the seizure of goods of those not yet indicted, since the Parliament Rolls recall, 'Various people are arrested and imprisoned daily on suspicion of felony, sometimes out of malice and sometimes on vague suspicion, and thus kept in prison without bail or mainprise to their great vexation and trouble.' Once arrested, a suspect's goods could be seized with no guarantee that they would be returned after a not guilty verdict, creating a market in malicious prosecution and the ruining of the livelihoods of innocent people.

Polydore Virgil would write under Henry VII that Richard 'began to give the show and countenance of a good man, whereby he might be accounted more righteous, more mild, more better affected to the commonality' in a desperate bid to buy popularity. There are two main issues with this approach. As previously noted, Richard's concern for justice and its application to the common people was not new. Having formed part of his policy in the north it was merely extended on a national scale. The second point to consider is that though these moves were incredibly popular, particularly with the men in the field and the merchants of the town, they were detrimental to the interests of the very men Richard would need to win over to keep himself on the throne. The status quo benefitted the nobility and landed gentry, who were generally the beneficiaries of the corruption rife after decades of civil unrest. Upsetting the system meant upsetting the most powerful men in the land and that is hardly the way to maintain a throne.

This parliament was also the first to publish its laws in English, the language of the people rather than the French or Latin of the establishment. The law became more accessible and a law in English must have felt more like an Englishman's law. It is interesting to consider how far Richard might have gone in his reforming measures given more time, but it is more telling to ask whether this radical agenda contributed to his downfall. If his reputation for an odd flavour of justice that favoured common men over their betters caused unease in London before he arrived, his parliament sent shockwaves through the establishment and surely caused men then to wonder quite how far he might go, how they might be affected and whether they wanted this man for their king.

Shortly after Parliament was dissolved Elizabeth Woodville and her daughters emerged from sanctuary in Westminster after almost a year, but far from flying to the Continent they joined Richard's court with a public vow from the king that he would not harm them and would arrange suitable matches for his nieces. The need for a public vow assuring their safety underlines the lingering and persistent belief that Richard was responsible for the deaths of the Princes in the Tower, yet the delivery of her daughters to their suspected killer is an odd move by Elizabeth Woodville. Historians have pointed to her probable realisation that she could not stay in sanctuary forever and that she had to come to terms with an enemy to buy a future for herself and her remaining children. However stark the situation – although Henry Tudor was still at large and had sworn an oath at Rheims Cathedral that he would marry Elizabeth's oldest daughter and namesake if he won the crown – her options were not yet exhausted, so handing her daughters to the man whom she suspected of having killed her sons is an unlikely move. A more satisfactory explanation is that Richard was able to convince Elizabeth Woodville that the rumours were lies, perhaps that Margaret Beaufort had lied to her. He might have shown her evidence that Buckingham or someone else was behind the murders or even that they were not dead at all. Only this explanation can really make sense of the delivery of Edward IV's daughters to their uncle Richard and conspicuous presence at his court from then onwards.

In April 1484 the first tragedy of Richard's reign struck. While at Nottingham Castle the king and queen received the devastating news that their only son, Edward of Middleham, had passed away aged only ten. *The Croyland Chronicle* records sombrely that 'on hearing the news of this, at Nottingham, where they were then residing, you might have seen his father and mother in a state almost bordering on madness, by reason of their sudden grief'. If Richard had spent his life building a future for his son, it was all torn away now. Within a year, on 16 March 1485, Richard's wife

Anne was taken from him too, possibly by the same tuberculosis that had killed her sister Isabel, Duchess of Clarence. An eclipse of the sun marked the day of her passing and it was judged an ill omen for her husband's reign. Rumour abounded that Richard had poisoned his wife in order to clear the way for him to marry his own niece, Elizabeth of York. Richard flatly, publicly and embarrassingly denied the rumours. Stories that he had spurned his wife's bed were used against him but if she was in the final phases of the contagious and deadly consumption he might have had no choice. Certainly she would have been afflicted with terrible night sweats and violent coughing, bringing up blood and struggling to breathe, so that sharing a bed would have been impractical if nothing else.

The rumours that flitted about London pecked away at Richard's reputation at a time when he was facing another personal loss and was ill-equipped to defend himself. It was his close friends and advisors Sir Richard Ratcliffe and the lawyer Sir William Catesby who counselled Richard to make a public denial of his intention to marry his own niece. If a Tudor propaganda campaign had begun in 1483, perhaps it still bided its time in early 1485. George Buck, a seventeenth-century writer who sought to re-evaluate Richard III's dark reputation, recorded a letter which, if it was real, sadly no longer remains. This letter was sent from Elizabeth of York to John Howard, Duke of Norfolk, a close friend and supporter of Richard III, in which the eighteen-year-old Elizabeth asks Howard 'to be a mediator' for her to Richard in the cause of her marriage to the king who was 'her only joy and maker in this world, and that she was his in heart and in thoughts, in body and in all' before callously remarking that 'she feared the Queen would never die'.

Elizabeth's marriage had been used in autumn 1483 to create a cause for rebellion and Henry Tudor had sworn to make her his bride if he won the throne. If the Tudor plot still simmered perhaps the young Elizabeth, keen to be queen and urged on by her mother, wrote more than one letter unsubtly alluding to a plan between her and the king to wed once Anne was gone. If Ratcliffe and Catesby received or got news of similar letters perhaps they saw no covert motive and rushed to the king, indignant that he might be planning such a match. In fact, very shortly after Queen

Anne's death Richard sent an embassy to Portugal to negotiate a marriage for him to the Infanta Joanna, sister of the King of Portugal. As part of the arrangements, Elizabeth was to be married to Joanna's cousin Manuel, who would later become King Manuel I. The swift departure of the embassy suggests that it had been planned as Anne's illness tightened its grip and her recovery became impossible. This would negate plans by Richard to marry his niece himself and open up the suggestion that the plans were misinterpreted, or twisted, to create the myth that Richard wanted a match with his niece. Elizabeth's letter adds another dimension, suggesting her active involvement in the dissemination of the story that would discredit her uncle and paint her as an innocent in need of rescue.

In spite of Richard's best efforts, Henry Tudor had eluded him on the Continent. When the Duke of Brittany's health failed, his chief minister, Pierre Landlais, made a deal with Richard, which included a hefty bribe, to return Tudor to England. Bishop Morton appears to have got wind of the plan and warned Henry, who slipped away from his guardians' grasp and slid over the border into France. Louis XI, the Spider King, had died a few months after Edward IV, leaving his son Charles VIII to take up the throne aged thirteen. Still only fourteen, Charles' sister Anne acted as his regent and France had been as keen as England to gain control of both Henry and his uncle Jasper. Louis surely left a warning to be wary of Richard III and his martial desire, remembering the young duke who had invaded France a decade earlier, and control of a rival claimant to Richard's throne held obvious appeal. Henry himself possessed more French royal blood as a grandson of Catherine of Valois than he had English royal blood in his veins. Salic Law in France prevented inheritance in the female line, but this fact had not prevented Edward III from laying claim to the French crown and igniting a century of war on French soil. The benefits of keeping Richard's eye on Henry and Henry Tudor's eye on the English throne are obvious.

The exiled Earl of Richmond, now twenty-eight, was greeted in Paris disingenuously as the natural son and heir of Henry VI, a younger brother of Edward, Prince of Wales. Although clearly a lie, it worked, and Henry must have been overwhelmed by the lavish pageantry and conspicuous spectacle of wealth and power that always followed kings of France. The mark this experience left can be clearly seen later in Henry's understanding and deft use of the power of appearance. France set about funding Henry's plans to invade England and the earl established a faux-court, drawing those disaffected by Richard's rule, notably including men who had been at the centre of Edward IV's regime but would not work with his brother.

With his previously flagging resolve revitalised and hope rekindled, John de Vere, Earl of Oxford, burst forth onto the political scene once more. He managed to convince the garrison at Hammes Castle not only to release him but to join him in defecting to Henry Tudor's growing court in France. James Blount, Captain of Hammes Castle, and his lieutenant John Fortescue permitted Oxford to leave for France and ordered much of the garrison to go with them. Although Richard's offer to pardon all of those who returned swiftly caused most to retake their posts – a salary from the crown was too good to turn away from on a whim – Oxford made it to Henry Tudor's side, providing the pretender with a wealth of military expertise that his cause had previously missed. There was now a hungry wolf among the sheep keen to sink his teeth back into his native England. With an alternative some men spied an opportunity. Henry Tudor was both the alternative and the opportunity to anyone who disliked Richard, his methods or his policy.

Amid all of his other concerns Richard had known that an invasion was coming. After the failed attempt to land in autumn 1483 the country had been on alert throughout the campaigning season of 1484 and 1485. The danger seemed to have passed for another year when news arrived that Henry Tudor had set sail from Harfleur to test his cause once more. Richard was at Nottingham, hunting at the royal lodge at Beskwood, and was reportedly excited to finally be able to prepare to face his elusive nemesis in battle. Henry landed at Milford Haven in south-west Wales on 7 August. He fell to his knees and recited Psalm 43, 'Judge me, Oh Lord, and defend my cause'. Milford Haven was under the jurisdiction of Rhys ap Thomas, whom Richard had promoted to Principal Lieutenant in south-west Wales. Thomas had vowed to his king that 'whoever ill-fated to the state, shall dare to land in these parts of Wales where I have employment under your majesty, must resolve with himself to make his entrance and irruption over my belly'. Thomas did not resist Tudor, but joined his forces. In order to sooth his honour without being embarrassed in front of his men, Thomas supposedly stood below a bridge as Tudor passed over it. Thus Henry Tudor had made his entrance over Thomas's belly, and marched north, seeking Welsh support to swell his numbers but also heading toward the heartland of the Stanleys, his step-father's family, in north Wales and Cheshire. Turning east and south, the invaders then headed toward London. Richard sent orders for a general levy to meet at Leicester.

The two armies would meet near Market Bosworth as Richard moved to cut off Tudor's route to the capital. Henry's numbers had grown from the 2,000 that he had landed with to around 5,000, though he must have hoped for more. Richard led approximately 6,000 men from Leicester, with an additional 3,000 behind Henry Percy, Earl of Northumberland. Thomas, Lord Stanley, was nearby with 4,000 men of his own, nominally taking the field for the king. Stanley had, however, met with his step-son and supposedly promised Tudor his support in the battle. Richard held Stanley's son Lord Strange as a hostage for his father's good behaviour.

John de Vere, Earl of Oxford, led Tudor's army into the field and John Howard, Duke of Norfolk, commanded Richard's vanguard. The king wore a crown atop his helm, as Henry V had done at Agincourt, yet he uncharacteristically held himself back from the front line. After cannon fire ripped the air and hails of arrows turned the skies dark in the early dawn, the lines finally came together. The fighting was close and fierce as Oxford wheeled around to place the sun behind himself and in the eyes of his foes. Norfolk was killed and the tide began to turn against Richard, who ordered Northumberland into the fray to reinforce Norfolk's leaderless men. Henry Percy did not move. Whether this was because of impassable ground, though this would be a tactical oversight of monumental proportions, or because he backed Tudor, hoping for more Percy power in the north again, is not known. Northumberland would spend time in the Tower following Bosworth, suggesting that Tudor was not aware of any plan of the earl's, but Percy was murdered during a tax riot on 28 April 1489 in Yorkshire, his men refusing to aid him for his treacherous refusal to fight for Richard III, a man beloved in the region long after his death.

The battle was going wrong for the king. Suddenly he spied his enemy's banner fluttering across the field, a small group riding toward Lord Stanley's position at the flank of the battle where he remained stationary. Henry was possibly riding to persuade his step-father into the fray or to find out why he was not fulfilling his promise to fight for him. Stanley, characteristically, had a foot carefully within each camp, allowing him to make the decision that suited him best. Richard saw an opportunity to cut the revolt off at the head. Couching his lance and lowering his visor, the king and his household knights made a thundering charge across the field to intercept Tudor before he could reach Stanley.

Tudor's small band defended him stoutly and Richard's men were pushed back toward a marshy area. Lord Stanley saw his opportunity and ordered his brother Sir William to attack the king's forces. Lord Stanley might have mused that he would have the final victory in the long-running dispute over Hornby Castle and that he would have satisfaction for his arrest two years earlier. The king was unhorsed, but not before he had unseated Sir John Cheney, an experienced soldier at least as big as Richard's brother Edward had been. It is a mark of the king's prowess, even more striking because of the scoliosis that tests have revealed affected his spine, that he was able to defeat such a knight. Richard was so close to Henry in the end that he struck down Tudor's standard bearer, William Brandon, whose role it was to remain at Tudor's side.

Every single source, contemporary and later, would acknowledge that King Richard III, the last King of England to die in battle, met his end bravely. It might be expected that the York city records would note that 'King Richard, late mercifully reigning over us, was through great treason . . . piteously slain and murdered, to the great heaviness of this city', though to enter this in official documents when a new king, Richard's enemy, was now upon the throne was risky indeed. Crowland, no fan of Richard, wrote that 'while fighting, and not in the act of flight, the said king Richard was pierced with numerous deadly wounds, and fell in the field like a brave and most valiant prince'. Henry VII's personal historian Polydore Virgil would write that 'king Richard alone was killed fighting manfully in the thickest press of his enemies'. Even Shakespeare's famous speech has been taken out of context and misinterpreted. The whole speech runs thus:

KING RICHARD III
A horse! a horse! my kingdom for a horse!

CATESBY
Withdraw, my lord; I'll help you to a horse.

KING RICHARD III
Slave, I have set my life upon a cast,
And I will stand the hazard of the die:
I think there be six Richmonds in the field;
Five have I slain to-day instead of him.
A horse! a horse! my kingdom for a horse!

Richard asks for a horse not to make his escape, as Catesby believes, but to return to the battle. He is determined to kill Richmond (Henry Tudor), having killed five men already that he believed to be the earl. Even Shakespeare did not deny Richard his valiant end, though the passage has been misquoted to paint Richard as a coward.

Most of Richard's household and close friends perished at Bosworth with him. Sir William Catesby was captured and executed at Leicester. Catesby's will would snipe at the Stanleys, asking them 'to pray for my soul as you have not for my body, as I trusted in you' before requesting care to be given to his children, adding 'I doubt not the king will be good and gracious lord to them for he is called a full gracious prince. And I never offended him by my good and Free Will; for God I take to be my judge I have ever loved him'. These odd words open the tantalising possibility that Catesby was a Tudor agent, perhaps even from his part in the revelation of Hastings' treachery and Edward IV's alleged pre-contract. Alternatively, he was simply using the right language to see that his family was cared for after his death. Francis, Viscount Lovell, escaped into sanctuary at Colchester where he was actively courted by the new regime before he entered open rebellion.

Lord Stanley is supposed to have found the crown that had fallen from Richard's helm and placed it on his step-son's head. For his part in the birth of Tudor England, Lord Stanley would be created Earl of Derby. His family was one of the very few whose situation was improved by the Wars of the Rose and although his name is associated with duplicity his careful stewardship steered his family through the turbulent decades and out the other side. His brother Sir William would be executed during the Perkin Warbeck affair for allegedly saying that he would not fight against Warbeck if he truly was the son of Edward IV. John de Vere, Earl of Oxford, was also fully restored and served Henry VII ably and loyally.

What of all the evidence that Richard III had supposedly produced throughout 1483 to explain his actions? None of it has ever been found. Another of Richard's opponents was Robert Morton, nephew of Bishop John Morton. Robert had been Master of the Rolls between 1479 and 1483, when Richard had replaced him. Restored to that position after Bosworth, Robert would have been ideally placed to find and destroy any official evidence of Richard III's innocence. At the age of fifty-one, in 1486 Robert became Bishop of Worcester. Was this a reward for the removal of proof for the validity of Richard's rule?

The Battle of Bosworth Field ended 331 years of Plantagenet rule in England, ushering in the Tudor era. The new regime would seek to paint Bosworth as the end of the Wars of the Roses, but their neat packaging would soon unravel. Bosworth was not the end, simply the beginning of a new chapter. The House of York was not yet spent.

21

The Fate of the House of York

As early as Easter 1486 a Yorkist uprising threatened Henry's fragile grip on power. Francis, Viscount Lovell, and the Stafford Brothers, Sir Humphrey and Thomas, tried to kindle revolt. Lovell attempted to raise the north as Henry approached on his progress and the Staffords cultivated support from their power base in the south of the Midlands. The Stafford brothers managed to enter, seize and hold Worcester, but the north stuttered in the king's presence and Lovell was forced to flee. As Henry stormed southward, the Staffords fled Worcester to sanctuary in Culham, Oxfordshire, from which Henry had them dragged forcibly by Sir John Savage. This incident led to Henry procuring the Pope's approval for the removal of the right of sanctuary in treason cases. Sir Humphrey was hanged, Thomas was bound to good behaviour and Lovell fled to the court of Margaret, Dowager Duchess of Burgundy, sister of Edward IV and Richard III who was to become a magnet for Yorkist hopes.

What had been missing from this early attempted revolt was a figurehead. The rebellion was nominally in favour of Edward, Earl of Warwick, the young son of George, Duke of Clarence, and nephew of Edward IV and Richard III. Warwick, though, was under Henry's control in the Tower of London and this lack of a royal leader was to prove a death blow to the revolt. The following year an attempt was made to correct this flaw. Lord Lovell landed at Furness with a large force of professional Swiss mercenaries, paid for by Margaret of Burgundy, an army of Irish kerns supplied by the Earl of Kildare, reflecting lingering Yorkist affection in the Pale of Ireland and not one but two Yorkist figureheads.

John de la Pole, Earl of Lincoln, was the eldest nephew of Edward IV and Richard III, son of their sister Elizabeth, Duchess of Suffolk and grandson to William de la Pole. John was approaching his mid-twenties and had been working in the Council of the North under his uncle Richard. He may have been named Richard's heir following the death of the Prince of Wales and was the senior male Yorkist in terms of age. The second figure was Edward, Earl of Warwick, the twelve-year-old senior male-line Yorkist heir, who was safely tucked up in the Tower of London. This boy had been crowned King Edward VI in a lavish ceremony in Dublin before the invading army left Ireland.

The invaders were met on their landing by a handful of loyal Yorkist gentry and they headed for safe ground, marching toward York to recruit more support, but the sight of the bare-chested, bare legged Irish kerns disconcerted the authorities of York, who closed their gates. Turning south, the large army was forced to seek a confrontation with Henry without further help.

The king, no doubt slightly bemused by the appearance of the boy he thought he had locked up safely, paraded Edward, Earl of Warwick, through London before mustering an army to meet the rebels at the Battle of Stoke Field on 16 June 1487. Henry's army was around 12,000 strong and led by the Earl of Oxford, who had led Henry's own invading army at Bosworth. Lincoln had around 8,000 men.

The battle was close for some time, with a portion of Oxford's men fleeing the field, until the tide turned. Around half the Yorkist army was slain, with the Irish warriors taking the brunt of the losses, though the Swiss mercenary leader Colonel Martin Schwartz was among the casualties. Lincoln was also killed during the fighting. Lord Lovell was injured and last spied crossing the Trent as he fled. He was never seen or heard of again and vanishes from the historical record. In spite of a wealth of speculation, a safe passage through Scotland, which may or may not have been collected, and the mysterious story of a skeleton bricked up at the Lovell manor of Minster Lovell, his fate is unknown.

The boy crowned in Ireland was captured and Henry 'discovered' that he was, in fact, an Oxfordshire boy named Lambert Simnell. Holding him up as an innocent pawn of the bitter Yorkists, Henry pardoned the boy, putting him to work in the royal kitchens as a spit boy. Lambert was last heard of as a royal falconer to Henry VIII in the mid-1520s, his true identity remaining a matter for doubt and discussion.

John de la Pole had four remaining brothers, though one was in holy orders and was never to impact upon the political scene. John's younger brother inherited the Dukedom of Suffolk on their father's death in 1491, though in 1493 Henry VII downgraded the title to that of an earl; something of a slap in the face to a family no longer posing a present threat but perhaps a hint that all was not as rosy as the Tudor iconography suggested.

In the 1490s a new pretender emerged on the Continent, perhaps under the tutelage of Margaret of Burgundy. Known to history as Perkin Warbeck, he presented himself to the courts of Europe as Richard of Shrewsbury, Duke of York, younger son of Edward IV and one of the infamous Princes in the Tower. Perkin gained a great deal of support, which perhaps had less to do with his true identity than with European leaders' desire to destabilise the English king. By now, most of them owed Henry huge sums of money so had a financial interest in seeing him squirm a little. It is in the face of this threat that Henry VII took a radical step, the context of which is often overlooked.

Now, aged three and a half, Henry's second son and namesake was propelled from the obscurity of his mother's household onto the fraught playing field of politics. On All Saints Day 1494, as Warbeck proved an increasing nuisance and men of Cornwall marched on London, Henry was elaborately, conspicuously and pointedly created Duke of York at Westminster, being made a Knight of the Bath at the same time. This was a clear antidote to Warbeck's assertion to entitlement to the support of the House of York. It also served to remind those clinging to hope that the cause of the princes, Edward V and the old Duke of York was dead – certainly politically, though it carried with it the connotation of physical demise too. Henry even looked like his grandfather, the embodiment of the House of York. The old look with a new feel.

This was Henry VII's clear step onto the front foot in response to the emergence of a serious threat from the House of York. He simply created a new one. Anyone deemed safe enough was placed around the new duke to add an air of credibility to the new establishment. A side effect of this was that later betrayals by the House of York were to be viewed by Henry VIII as personal attacks and disloyalties, which perhaps exaggerated and magnified his response to those threats.

Warbeck turned out to be a prolonged threat. He wasn't captured until 1497, when he confessed to being an imposter. In 1499, Warbeck was almost certainly used by Henry VII to entrap Edward, Earl of Warwick, now twenty-four. The two were caught plotting to escape the Tower and executed. Warwick was the last of the legitimate male line of York and his removal was a requirement of Catherine of Aragon's marriage to Arthur, something she was later to believe had cursed her.

Henry VII, having secured the marriage of his heir Arthur to Catherine, now resurrected another Yorkist tradition. The extent to which he reached back in his attempts to move forward is striking. Just as Edward IV had sent his son to Ludlow to preside over a court of his own as Prince of Wales, so Arthur was despatched to demonstrate the new regime's solid link to the past. The Tudors were new, but rooted in an old stability.

Still, the petals of the Tudor rose were not without pests. Just before Arthur and Catherine's wedding, Edmund and Richard de la Pole fled to the court of Maximilian, the Holy Roman Emperor. Earlier, Sir Robert Curzon had told Maximilian that England was fed up with Henry's 'murders and tyrannies', proposing Edmund as a rival claimant. Maximilian responded that he would do all that he could to see 'one of Edward's blood' returned to the throne. Doubtless this encouragement reached Edmund and Richard and directed their flight.

The brother they left behind, Sir William, was arrested and imprisoned in the Tower of London in spite of his failure to join his brothers. For allowing Edmund to pass through Calais, Sir James Tyrell was ordered to submit to arrest. Calais was besieged when he refused, until a promise of safe passage to an audience with the king caused him and his son to emerge, only for that assurance to evaporate as they were roughly taken into custody. Tyrell was tortured in the Tower for news on Edmund, though there is no record that he was ever even asked about the fate of the Princes in the Tower, nor that he confessed to arranging their murder.

Edmund began to call himself The White Rose, Duke of Suffolk, and openly proclaimed his right to the throne. He found support from King John of Denmark, Norway and Sweden. *The Chronicle of the Grey Friars* records that on 22 February 1502 'was Sir Edmund de la Pole pronounced accursed at St Paul's Cross, at the sermon before noon'. Henry was clearly concerned by this new threat.

Things grew worse for the new dynasty. On 2 April 1502, Prince Arthur died. It is possible that the panic this fostered drove the trials on 2 May 1502 of Sir James Tyrell and others. Tyrell was beheaded on Tower Hill, with several others hanged, drawn and quartered at Tyburn for their support of the de la Poles. Henry 'put out' that Tyrell had confessed to the princes' murders during his questioning. Given the lack of any evidence of a confession it is feasible that this same panic about his own sudden dynastic fragility caused Henry to try to reinforce the notion that the sons of Edward IV were dead. It is telling that at a time of crisis for the House of Tudor, it was the House of York that was perceived as the very real threat.

In 1504, the threat Henry felt from The White Rose was again in evidence. He signed a trade treaty with the Hanseatic League so detrimental to English merchants that the only reason he could possibly have agreed was the provision that they offer no support or refuge to Edmund de la Pole. In the same year John Flamank reported to the king a discussion that had taken place in Calais among several of the town's leading figures. They reportedly spoke of what would happen after Henry's death, saying,

> The king's grace is but a weak man and sickly, not likely to be long lived ... Some of them spoke of my lord of Buckingham, saying that he was a noble man and would be a royal ruler. Others there were that spoke, he said, likewise of your traitor, Edmund de la Pole, but none of them, he said, spoke of my lord prince.

The 'my lord prince' in question was the future Henry VIII, and his father was surely disturbed that he was overlooked at a discussion of the succession. It did not bode well for Tudor security.

Matters took a turn in Henry's favour in January 1506 by sheer luck. Maximilian's son, Archduke Philip, was shipwrecked on England's south coast by a storm. Polydore Virgil wrote that Henry was 'scarcely able to believe his luck when he realized that divine providence had given him the means of getting his hands on Edmund de la Pole, Earl of Suffolk'. Philip was forced to sign a treaty resolving current trade disputes in England's favour, but was also required to give up Edmund de la Pole. The White Rose was collected from Mechlen and delivered to Calais, apparently on the promise that he would not be harmed, but that he would be fully pardoned and restored to his lands. Edmund, though, was bundled off to the Tower.

Henry VII died on 21 April 1509. For Henry VIII's coronation, John Skelton wrote 'The Rose both White and Red / In one Rose now doth grow'. Edward Hall called the new king the 'flower and very heir of both said lineages', but the White Rose had not yet been properly reconciled. On 30 April 1509, to celebrate his coronation, Henry issued a general pardon that had been provided for in his father's will, which excluded just eighty people. Top of the list was Edmund de la Pole, followed by his brothers Richard, who was still at large on the continent, and William, still languishing in the Tower.

In 1513, as Henry prepared to invade France, Louis XII offered Richard de la Pole support as a diversion. Fearing the resurgence of the White Rose threat, Henry took advantage of Edmund's outstanding attainder to have him quietly executed on Tower Green on 4 May 1513, just before leaving for France and in spite of his father's promise that Edmund would not be harmed, a vow Henry clearly did not feel bound by. Richard de la Pole now styled himself The White Rose and Duke of Suffolk, Louis recognising him as King of England. In his mid-thirties, Richard was a natural soldier and was proving his military worth to Louis in Italy in an attempt to win further aid. In 1514, Louis provided Richard with vast sums of money and a huge army. John, Duke of Albany, Regent of Scotland, agreed to take Richard to Scotland to launch his invasion. All was set. Just as Richard was about to sail, Louis signed a peace treaty with Henry and the attack was called off. When Louis died in 1515, Richard's close friend the Dauphin became Francis I. Henry seems to be have been genuinely concerned. He set Thomas Wolsey to oversee Sir Edward Poynings and the Lord Chamberlain, tasking them with arranging the assassination of Richard de la Pole. That men of such standing were appointed to this task is a mark of the threat that Henry perceived. Percheval de Matte, Captain Symonde Francoyse and Robert Latimer are all recorded as being hired to complete the task. All failed, and for a decade Richard evaded Henry's agents, moving frequently and attracting Yorkist stragglers to his court in exile until on 25 February 1525, Richard commanded the right wing of Francis's French army at the Battle of Pavia in Italy. The French army was crushed by that of the Holy Roman Emperor. Francis was captured and Richard was killed. When news reached Henry, bonfires blazed throughout London and a Te Deum was celebrated at St Paul's.

The final chapter of the de la Pole threat closed in 1538. Sir William de la Pole died, still a prisoner in the Tower of London. His thirty-seven-year incarceration remains the longest stay in the Tower's history.

Another branch of the still broad Yorkist family tree proved to be the most persistent thorn in the Tudor side. Edward, Earl of Warwick, had a sister, Margaret. Shortly after Henry VII came to power she was married to a cousin of the new king, Sir Richard Pole, to neutralise her as a focus for disaffection. Sir Richard died before Henry VII did, but Henry VIII, perhaps encouraged by a guilty Catherine of Aragorn, restored Margaret to power shortly after his coronation. She was created Countess of Salisbury, one of her parents' titles, in her own right, became a lady in waiting to Catherine and an outspoken supporter of Princess Mary in the troubles that followed. Reginald Pole was Margaret's second son, born in 1500 at Stourton Castle near Stourbridge. From an early age he was drawn to the church and Henry VIII contributed toward the cost of the young man's education, perhaps happy to see some White Rose blood soak away into the clergy. When Reginald was twenty-one, Henry encouraged and subsidised his six-year period of study at Padua in Italy. After his return to England in 1527, appointments and patronage denoted great royal favour.

Following the death of Cardinal Wolsey in 1529, Reginald was offered the Archbishopric of York, but refused it. In a private audience with Henry, he argued eloquently and firmly against the divorce from Catherine of Aragon, causing Henry to storm out, slamming the door behind him. In 1532, Reginald left England, a decision that perhaps saved him from the fate of More and other critics of the King's Great Matter. In 1535, he was again in Padua, where he received a letter from Henry asking for his opinion on the divorce again, clearly hoping that Reginald's growing influence in Rome could serve the English king. There is a fascinating series of exchanges recorded in the state papers, with Henry eagerly nudging Reginald for his response and Pole asking Henry to bear with him just a little longer. It is uncertain whether Reginald had not yet finished writing, was wrestling with his conscience or plucking up courage.

It took Reginald a year to reply. He sent back not a letter, but a book. Known as *De Unitate – A Defence of the Church's Unity*, it was written for Henry's eyes only and was very definitely not what he had been hoping for, tearing apart Henry's argument for the divorce, but then continuing to condemn a quarter of a century of poor rule and wasteful policies. Lord Montague, Reginald's oldest brother, wrote to him slamming the danger he had placed the rest of the family in and Margaret wrote to her son of 'a terrible message' that Henry had sent her.

In 1537 Reginald was created a cardinal so that he could visit England as a Papal Legate. Significantly, he was never ordained as a priest because Papist plots began to revolve around marrying Reginald to Princess Mary to unite the White Rose and the Tudor Rose and restore England to Roman Catholicism. Pope Paul III had identified Pole as the man to achieve this end. He was given 10,000 ducats to recruit men in Flanders and Germany with the aim of kindling revolt in England. Under the guise of a peaceful visit as Papal Legate, Pole was to spark rebellion, marry Princess Mary and take Henry's throne.

In France, Francis I was only put off from supporting Pole by his own desire to snatch the throne of England for himself. One thing is perfectly clear. By the mid-1530s, England was viewed as fair game. The throne was up for grabs. The only question was who would succeed in the smash and grab of Henry VIII's failing kingdom.

Reginald did not get to England, and by the end of 1537, Henry was advertising a reward of 100,000 gold crowns to anyone who brought Reginald to him, dead or alive. During the following year, the White Rose faction in England appeared to throw caution to the wind. Henry Courtenay, the Marquess of Exeter, a grandson of Edward IV, was only outdone in his criticism of the newly emerging England by Henry Pole, Lord Montague, who said that 'the King and his whole issue stand accursed'. On 29 August 1538 Geoffrey Pole, Margaret's third son, was suddenly arrested. He was, by turns, interrogated, threatened with the rack and offered a pardon to incriminate relatives. After his first interrogation, Geoffrey tried to commit suicide in his cell in the Tower by stabbing himself with a knife, but failed to do enough damage.

On 4 November Exeter and Montague were arrested. Montague was tried on 2 December and Exeter on the following day. When found guilty and condemned to death, Montague told the court 'I have lived in prison these last six years'. Montague and Exeter were beheaded on Tower Hill. Two priests and a sailor who had been accused of carrying messages to Reginald were among others hanged, drawn and quartered at Tyburn on the same day. On 28 December, Geoffrey again attempted suicide by suffocating himself, only to fail once more. Released the following year, he fled to Flanders. The Exeter Conspiracy was almost certainly a figment of Henry VIII's paranoiac fear but the king reacted savagely and it demonstrated the consuming dread he still had of the White Rose faction. In February 1539, Henry wrote to Charles V that he had only narrowly escaped a plot to murder him, his son and his daughters and to place Exeter on the throne. A few months later, Countess Margaret was included in an attainder passed against those involved in the Pilgrimage of Grace and the Exeter Conspiracy.

In the autumn of 1539, there was a further shock when Countess Margaret, aged sixty-five, was suddenly arrested and taken to the Tower. Her grandson, Montague's son Henry, was also incarcerated there at the time. She remained in the Tower until 1541, when Henry planned to visit James V of Scotland. Before leaving, he had several prisoners executed, including Countess Margaret Pole. She was awoken early in the morning on 27 May and told that she would be executed at 7 a.m. Bemused, she walked to the block and knelt. The inexperienced executioner slammed the axe into her shoulder, taking half a dozen more blows to complete his task. The sixty-seven-year-old countess later became a Catholic saint for her martyrdom and these words were found carved into the wall of her cell:

> For traitors on the block should die;
> I am no traitor, no, not I!
> My faithfulness stands fast and so,
> Towards the block I shall not go!
> Nor Make one step, as you shall see;
> Christ in Thy Mercy, save Thou me!

Henry VIII died on 28 January 1547. His son, Edward VI, died on 6 July 1553 aged just fifteen. In November 1554, with Queen Mary installed, Reginald Pole returned to England as Papal Legate, becoming Mary's Archbishop of Canterbury with the Catholic restoration. On 17 November 1558, Reginald died, aged fifty-eight, on the very same day as Queen Mary, so did not live to see Elizabeth return Protestantism to England. The White Rose threat outlasted Henry VII, Henry VIII, Edward VI and Mary I. The influence of the threat, real or imagined, is perhaps as easy to exaggerate as it is to understate. It is certain that the House of York's threat to the throne, which perhaps saw its birth in Ludlow in 1459, did not end at Bosworth, nor even at Stoke Field. It ended quietly in a bed, nearly seventy-five years after the Tudor dawn. The neat thirty-year Wars of the Roses was a Tudor construct to draw a veil over generations of failure to rid themselves of shadows cast by the House of York. Henry VIII created England as a European superpower by sleight of hand. The Tudor's security was similarly a sleight of hand, a grand trick played upon the nation to hide the desperate fears that haunted them for three quarters of a century.

22

Bones of Contention

On 6 July 1933, an urn that had stood in Westminster Abbey for over 250 years was opened and public imagination was grabbed by the examination of its contents. Professor William Wright, Dean of the London Hospital Medical College and President of the Anatomical Society of Great Britain and Ireland, along with Lawrence Tanner, a man without medical qualification or experience, set about preparing their report on these remains in an attempt to answer England's most famous murder mystery. The men had six days in which to determine whether the remains belonged to the Princes in the Tower.

Professor Wright concluded that the condition of the bones indicated that they were children but placed their ages above those of the two boys who were twelve and nine in the summer of 1483. It is to be noted that their father Edward IV was an exceptionally tall man so this discrepancy was not conclusive. The professor also noted that the jaw of the elder skeleton showed evidence of a serious bone disease consistent with a condition Edward V was believed to have suffered from. While Edward and his brother were attended in the Tower by Dr John Argentine this is by no means unusual or indicative of a serious medical condition. There is no recorded reference to Edward V suffering from any illness of his jaw outside of Sir Thomas Mores later assertion that the prince was 'sore diseased with sickness'. This same skull was also reported to display a blood stain consistent with a suffusion of blood caused by suffocation.

The bones were declared to be those of Edward V and his younger brother, Richard, Duke of York. Returned to their resting place, they have not been disturbed again in spite of continued requests for more modern examination. Westminster Abbey is a royal peculiar, meaning that it belongs directly to the crown, so the permission of the reigning monarch is required for such a testing.

A study in 1955 by several anthropologists and orthodontists questioned many of the findings of the 1933 tests. Though they were not permitted to examine the bones they had access to the photos and test results. This study concluded that the ages of the children were not sufficiently established, that the gender of neither could be confirmed, that the osteomyelitis found in the jaw may well distort the process of determining the age of the child and that suffocation was unlikely to have caused the blood stain on the same skull. The controversy was again thrown wide open.

The contents of the urn were discovered in 1674 during building work within the Tower. John Knight, Charles II's surgeon, recorded that 'in digging down a pair of stone stairs leading from the Kings Lodgings to the chapel in the white tower there were found bones of two striplings in (as it seemed) a wooden chest upon which the presumptions that they were the bones of this king and his brother Richard Duke of York' were made. John Gibbon jubilantly recalled that 'July 17 Anno 1674 in digging some foundations in the Tower, were discovered the bodies of Edward V and his brother murdered 1483, I myself handled the Bones, Especially the Kings Skull. The other which was lesser was broken in the digging.'

An anonymous source, published three years later and quoting Knight as a source, offered further detail.

In order to the rebuilding of the several Offices in the Tower, and to clear the White Tower from all contiguous buildings, digging down the stairs which led from the King's Lodgings, to the chapel in the said Tower, about ten foot in the ground were found the Bones of two striplings in (as it seemed) a wooden chest, upon which the survey which found proportionable to the ages of those two Brothers viz, about thirteen and eleven years. The skull of the one being entire, the other broken, as were indeed many of the other Bones, also the Chest, by the violence of the labourers, who cast the rubbish and them away together, wherefore they were caused to sift the rubbish, and by that means preserved all the bones.

The bones that were removed from the trench were thrown onto a rubbish heap, only to be picked from the detritus when it was decided that they might be of interest. The box was destroyed and many of the bones shattered before they were recovered, possibly mixed up with other human and animal remains. Scraps of velvet were used to suggest that the remains were royal, yet from a pile of rubbish dug out of a ten-foot pit there can be no certainty that any velvet related to the bones.

As with many historical events, context is key to the discovery and treatment of these bones. Charles II had been crowned in 1660 following the return to monarchy after the Civil War. He had ruthlessly persecuted those he deemed responsible for his father's execution, exhuming the bodies of Oliver Cromwell and two others, having their corpses hung in chains and beheaded. The heads were placed in Westminster Hall where the men had sat in judgement on Charles I and the bodies thrown into unmarked pits. In the early 1470s Charles was in conflict with Parliament over foreign wars and religious policy. In 1474 Parliament was refusing to grant Charles more funds, forcing him to seek peace where he did not want it. A set of bones discovered under a stairway might have sparked a memory of More's story of the fate of the princes. Charles may have spied an opportunity to remind his country what happens when kings are removed from their rightful throne. Just as the evil Richard III followed the deposition and murder of Edward V, so the despot Cromwell had followed the killing of Charles I. The discovery of the bones of the princes was a convenient reminder and warning.

The bones unearthed in 1674 were neither the first nor the last to be found within the Tower of London and are not the only ones identified as the remains of Princes in the Tower. In the early seventeenth century, Sir Walter Raleigh, while a prisoner in the Tower, and Lord Grey of Wilton found two children's skeletons laid out on a table in a bricked-up room within the Tower. The French chronicler Molinet had written that this was the fate

Richard had condemned his nephews to and the bones were named as those of the princes. Only a few years later another skeleton was found in one of the towers and was swiftly declared to belong to one of the princes, though it was later identified as belonging to an ape that had escaped from the royal menagerie. During the 1830s the Tower moat was drained and a wealth of bones discovered, some of which were confidently declared to belong to the princes. As recently as 1977 a child's skeleton was unearthed within the Tower. Carbon dating established that the child had lived during the Iron Age.

As the sun was setting on the Tudor era and a new Stuart dawn glowed at the rim of Shakespeare's world, he wrote his play *The Tragedy of Richard the Third*, a masterpiece in the study of evil and human nature. Richard is the ultimate anti-hero. His audience knows what he is going to do, for he tells us all, yet we do not stop him. We find ourselves liking him, daring to hope that he succeeds. William Cecil, Lord Burghley, had been Elizabeth I's closest advisor throughout her reign and had groomed his son Robert to succeed him. The Cecils favoured a Stuart, Protestant succession. It is interesting that Robert Cecil's portraits show that he suffered from kyphosis, the condition creating the curved spine Shakespeare's villain displayed rather than the scoliosis Richard III actually had. In 1588 Motley's *History of the Netherlands* described Cecil as 'A slight, crooked, hump-backed young gentleman, dwarfish in stature' and later spoke of the 'massive dissimulation [that] ... was, in aftertimes, to constitute a portion of his own character'. Motley could almost have been describing Shakespeare's Richard III. It seems possible that Richard III was a convenient villain, a man Shakespeare could denigrate with impunity with a piece of political commentary aimed to warn his audience that the country was sleep-walking toward disaster. The tale of the Princes in the Tower was possibly used as a warning in this case too.

Both the 1933 examinations and the discovery of the remains in 1674 relied heavily upon Sir Thomas More's description of the murder of the Princes in the Tower in his *The History of King Richard the Third*. More's work was penned around 1513 and is the source of Richard III's enduring reputation as a cruel murderer, upon which Shakespeare and others based their depictions. As a historical source, More's work is deeply floored. More professed to have access to people who were witnesses to the events of 1483 and whom he claimed had no reason to lie about the events.

More's account asserts that during his royal progress after his coronation, Richard decided that he could not be safe while his nephews lived. He wrote to the Constable of the Tower, Sir Robert Brackenbury, ordering him to have the boys killed. Brackenbury refused, so Richard instead tasked Sir James Tyrell with the deed. Tyrell hired two men, John Dighton and Miles Forest, and the boys were smothered in their beds. The bodies were buried beneath a staircase in the Tower and then moved to a place of more sanctity. This version presents several issues. The Tower was a busy royal palace. Digging a grave beneath a stairwell, through stone and packed earth, in the dead of night, without raising any suspicion would be difficult. To then move the bodies would require this Herculean feat to be repeated, again without discovery. Improbable, though not impossible.

The other issue is that More clearly states that the bodies were moved, meaning that the remains of the Princes in the Tower were not at the foot of a stairwell in the Tower. The initial assumption that they were the princes' remains in 1674 and the 1933 examination based their conclusions upon working backwards from More's story to decide that the remains must be those of Edward V and his brother, yet both ignored the portion of More's story that saw the bones removed. To cloud matters further, it is possible that More was mistaken in his claim that the bones were moved after their initial burial.

It is interesting that Thomas More also records that, when he wrote, Forest and Tyrell were dead but Dighton, who had been questioned at the same time as Tyrell and similarly confessed to his part in the deed, 'walks on alive in good possibility to be hanged before he die'. Dighton, a confessed regicide, was walking the streets of London causing mischief almost thirty years after he had murdered a king and a prince. This seems an unlikely fate when Henry VII would have been able to make huge political capital from the confessions of Tyrell and Dighton. There was no good reason to let Dighton go about his business after his confession.

Sir Thomas More spent time as a teenager in the house of the

Archbishop of Canterbury, who, at that time, was none other than John Morton, perennial thorn in King Richard III's side. Much of what More heard about Richard III surely came from Morton, who had no love for the last Yorkist king. More never completed his work during his lifetime, his nephew finishing and publishing it years after More's execution. Did More quickly discover that much of the story he had been told was simply untrue? Was Richard's story, even at this early stage, a political morality device? More's other great work, *Utopia*, is a political treatise, and the beginning of Henry VIII's reign had seen the judicial murders of Edmund Dudley, Richard Empson and Edmund de la Pole. It is plausible that More wrote his story as a warning to the new young king on the perils of murderous tyranny.

Sir George Buck, who completed his revisionist defence of Richard III in 1619, appears to have been certain that the reason More never published his work on Richard III was that it was not, in fact, his work. Buck believed that Morton had written the condemnation of Richard III and it had come into More's hands. The personal animosity between Morton and Richard III would explain the content of the work. Sir John Harrington, Elizabeth I's godson, also wrote that he had heard that the writings published in More's name in fact came directly from Morton's hand.

The interrogation of Sir James Tyrell dealt with the assistance that he had given to Edmund de la Pole, Duke of Suffolk, but there is no contemporary record that he was questioned about the fate of the Princes in the Tower, never mind that he confessed. Had he made a confession, Henry VII would surely have made political capital from it. Tyrell was tried and executed in short order after the death of Prince Arthur because Henry was thrown into disarray by the sudden threat to the dynasty he had been building. It seems likely that confirmation of the boys' death occurred to him as a neat side-effect of Tyrell's execution. Sir James had been a close and loyal friend to Richard III. Tyrell was granted a pardon on 16 June 1486 for unspecified offences, then granted a second pardon on 16 July, precisely one month later, also for unspecified offences. It has been suggested that these relate to the murder of the princes on Henry's behalf, perhaps as a demonstration of loyalty later pinned on Richard III, though others have attached little importance to them as nothing more than an administrative error.

One thing is certain. In the summer of 1483 Edward V and his brother Richard, Duke of York, vanished from sight and from the historical record. It is undeniable that Richard III remains the prime suspect in the mystery of the boys' fate. He had the motive and the means, and early fingers were pointed in his direction, More and Virgil naming Sir James Tyrell as his instrument. If Richard III did order the deaths of his nephews it is a singularly unforgivable act that would stain his character for all time. The mere unproven suspicion has done enough damage. They were political rivals and Richard grew up in a time when political rivalries led to war. It remains unforgivable, but Richard was undeniably a man of his times and his times were brutal, harsh, ruthless and uncertain. If he sought to impose some certainty, it may become understandable while remaining inexcusable.

There are several issues with presuming Richard III guilty of this heinous act. Even after 1485, no one ever publically, officially accused Richard of the murder. Henry VII had plenty to gain from silencing the whispered threat the boys posed to his rule. Their mother, Elizabeth Woodville, was free to condemn her brother-in-law after his death if she had felt constrained while he lived. She did not. No recorded Masses were ever said for the souls of the boys to ease their passage through purgatory and no tomb was ever erected to honour their memory. Richard was declared a child killer in the *Etats General* in France in 1484 but even this must be viewed in the context of France's own minority government, which was under threat from a relative of the young king. France had a vested interest both in painting the dangerous Richard III as an evil man and offering warnings about deposing child kings. Within a year of their disappearance, the story of Princes in the Tower was a political lesson to be taught, whatever the truth of their fate.

The single most compelling piece of evidence in defence of Richard III is that most often used to condemn him – his own silence on the matter. Just as everyone else would do, Richard made no public statement about his nephews. He did not mention them for the rest of his life. If Richard III killed his nephews it was to prevent them threatening his throne. In order to prevent this threat he would necessarily have to publicise their deaths, blaming natural causes or some other murderer, however implausible it might have been. Without informing the nation of their death, how could they cease to be a threat? Rumours that they could be dead would not do the job required. If Richard III killed the Princes in the Tower he would have had to make sure that everyone knew they were dead. In remaining silent he would have undone his own plan.

There is one scenario that offers answers to many questions yet is cynically dismissed for a lack of likelihood or evidence. In a mystery without evidence and no satisfactory explanation it seems as worthy as any other of consideration. Rather than asking who murdered the Princes in the Tower it may be more pertinent to ask whether there was a murder at all. The survival of at least one if not both of the boys allows sense to be made of otherwise bemusing events. Why did Richard III never mention the boys? They were illegitimate and needed to be forgotten. How could bodies possibly have been buried beneath a staircase in the Tower of London without arousing any suspicion? There were no bodies. How could Elizabeth Woodville emerge from sanctuary and hand her daughters over to Richard? He was able to prove to her that he had not murdered her sons. There is a Tyrell family legend that Sir James was entrusted with overseeing meetings between Elizabeth and her sons at his manor of Gipping Hall. Why did Henry VII never pronounce their deaths at Richard's hands for political gain? It was not true and could not be proven. How could pretenders threaten Henry VII well into the 1490s? The princes were not dead and Henry could never be sure whether a threat was real or not.

It is entirely possible that Edward and Richard were quietly moved to the north, where Richard III also housed his other brother's son, Edward, Earl of Warwick. Perhaps they visited their aunt Margaret in Burgundy in secret. Regular visits to their mother kept all parties content and meant that Elizabeth Woodville had no cause to condemn her brother-in-law after his death. The boys might have been well treated, as their sisters were, as Richard's kin. They might have emerged in a Ricardian future if they no longer posed a threat. Why were they never heard of again? When Richard lost at Bosworth all records relating to the boys could have been destroyed to hide them from Henry VII. If they lived, they would be a real threat to a man who planned to reverse the illegitimacy of their sister in order to marry her and harness her father's, and brother's, support. This could explain Henry's delay in doing just that after he won the throne. He needed time to be sure he wasn't making Edward V king again. If Henry didn't know that they were alive his fear that they were was very real. If he did know, then proof of their survival could have been added to the bonfire of evidence destroyed after Bosworth, perhaps by Robert Morton.

Amateur art historian Jack Leslau presented a theory that used hidden messages to reveal that the younger of the boys, Richard, Duke of York, in fact lived within the household of Sir Thomas More under the name Dr John Clement, married to More's adopted daughter. Clement was enrolled in Louvain University in 1489 and recorded as exempted from swearing the customary oath, one acceptable reason for which was living under a false name so that swearing the oath in a false name would be perjury. The entry also records Clement as being of noble birth when no noble House of Clement existed. In 1510 Clement rode in the Yorkist-dominated joust to celebrate Henry VIII's accession. At a time when the new young king was confident and vital, might he have embraced an uncle who offered no threat? Certainly. His uncle Arthur rode in the same lists. Clement was later President of the Royal College of Physicians. He was imprisoned in the Fleet Prison when More was arrested and John Dudley, later Duke of Northumberland, took an interest in the case. This is striking because Leslau also asserts that Edward V survived in the person of Sir Edward Guildford, John Dudley's father-in-law.

If this were the case, and it cannot be proved, then it adds an intriguing layer to later Tudor politics too. Dudley's son Guildford Dudley would marry Lady Jane Grey, the Nine Day Queen. Could Dudley have used the latent Yorkist blood his wife passed to his sons to pursue the throne for his family? The possibility would also impact the relationship between Elizabeth I and one of Dudley's other sons, Robert, Earl of Leicester. Accepted as the love of each other lives, something prevented them from ever marrying. Elizabeth might have feared allowing her family's arch-enemy a seat beside her if Robert Dudley was really the grandson of King Edward V.

There are other candidates who bear scrutiny as one of the Princes in the Tower. Richard Plantagenet of Eastwell was an educated bricklayer who claimed to be an illegitimate son of Richard III. Perkin Warbeck was discredited on evidence found by men working for Henry VII because Henry VII wanted evidence found. He might have forged it. The survival of the Princes in the Tower is no less likely than their deaths in 1483.

The remains contained within the urn in Westminster Abbey might be those of the Princes in the Tower, but plenty of doubt can be cast upon that assertion. With DNA available for testing they might now be conclusively identified, though permission has been refused on several occasions. It is important to consider what it might mean for those human remains if they were not the princes. Would they suddenly no longer deserve to be where they have rested for over 300 years? They are still the remains of someone's child. If they are those of Edward V and Richard, Duke of York, it would still not answer the question of who killed them and exactly when, only that they died at someone's hand.

While the mystery rages on, the remains rest peacefully within their urn. Perhaps they should remain untouched. If they cannot tell us the whole story then why should they be troubled at all? Some mysteries cannot be solved, but all should be approached with an open mind. The urn's inscription might tell you that it holds the remains of Edward V and Richard, Duke of York, and that they were murdered by their evil uncle. That does not make it true. In the absence of irrefutable evidence you can only make up your own mind, but do so without centuries of prejudice and reach a conclusion dimly illuminated by those facts that we do have.

Find Out More

Websites

British History Online: www.british-history.ac.uk. An excellent resource, which includes medieval Parliament Rolls, official papers and chronicles. It is a subscription service but is invaluable to the study of the period.

The Wars of the Roses Federation: www.wotr-fed.co.uk. The website of the re-enactment group active all over the country.

Towton Battlefield Society: www.towton.org.uk/. Devoted to the study and re-enactment of the Battle of Towton.

The Richard III Society: www.richardiii.net/. The Society is committed to the re-examination of the life, times and reputation of King Richard III. The website provides valuable resources covering the period of the Wars of the Roses.

Further Reading

Fatal Colours: Towton 1461 (George Goodwin) – A detailed study of England's most brutal battle.

The Hollow Crown (Dan Jones) – Covering the period from Richard II to Richard III, this book takes in the Wars of the Roses.

Edward IV and the Wars of the Roses (David Santiuste) – An examination of Edward IV's life, reign and military career, which defined the Wars of the Roses.

Lancaster and York: The Wars of the Roses (Alison Weir) – An account of the Wars of the Roses focussing on the human impact of the conflict.

Historical Fiction

It is crucial to remember the fiction element of these books. Some are more factually accurate than others.

Loyalty (Matthew Lewis) – The story of Richard III from the Battle of Barnet to the Battle of Bosworth, told by Sir Thomas More, who offers a twist.

Honour (Matthew Lewis) – The sequel to *Loyalty*, following Francis, Lord Lovell, after the Battle of Bosworth and charting Hans Holbein's precarious journey through Henry VIII's court.

The Wars of the Roses Series (Conn Iggulden) – A series following the diverging Houses of York and Lancaster into the Wars of the Roses, often viewed through the eyes of Henry VI's spymaster.

Rebels and Brothers Series (Derek Birks) – Follow Ned Elder and his family as the Wars of the Roses erupts about them and they are drawn into the unavoidable conflict.

Kingmaker Series (Toby Clemens) – A monk and a nun are forced to flee their sheltered lives and become embroiled in the emerging Wars of the Roses.

Warwick: The Man Behind The Wars of the Roses (Toby Clement) – The story of Richard Neville, Earl of Warwick, as he becomes a key figure in the Wars of the Roses.

The Sunne in Splendour (Sharon Penman) – The epic life story of Richard III from childhood to Bosworth as he grows up and lives through the Wars of the Roses.

The Daughter of Time (Josephine Tey) – A detective is injured in the line of duty. While recovering in hospital he turns his investigative powers to the question of the Princes in the Tower.

Films and TV

The White Queen – An adaptation of Philippa Gregory's *Cousins' War* series of novels, focussing on the women involved in the Wars of the Roses and weaving witchcraft into the story.

The Hollow Crown: The Wars of the Roses – This will be based on Shakespeare's *Henry VI* and *Richard III* plays.

The Princes in the Tower – This focuses on the interrogation of Perkin Warbeck.

The Plantagenets – A documentary telling the story of this long-lasting dynasty, presented by Robert Bartlett.

Blackadder – For an alternative history of Britain after 1485, see the first series.

Places to Visit

Fotheringhay Castle, Fotheringhay PE8 5HZ – The traditional seat of the House of York.

St Mary and All Saints Church, Fotheringhay, Northamptonshire, England PE8 5HZ – A foundation of Edward, 2nd Duke of York, designed to be a mausoleum for the House of York. Richard, 3rd Duke of York, and his son Edmund, Earl of Rutland, were reinterred here.

St Albans Cathedral, St Albans, Hertfordshire AL1 1BY – St Albans was the site of two battles during the Wars of the Roses and the abbey played an important role.

Ludlow Castle, Castle Square, Ludlow, Shropshire SY8 1AY – A mighty Marcher fortress once belonging to the Mortimer family. The Houses of York and Neville gathered behind the stout walls of this fortress in 1459.

St Laurence's Church, College Street, Ludlow, Shropshire SY8 1AN – A lovely medieval church with a Victorian stained-glass window showing the Marcher lords, including Richard, Duke of York, Edward IV, Edward V and Arthur Tudor, Yorkist symbolism and a plaque marking the spot near which Prince Arthur's heart was buried.

Ludlow Medieval Fayre, Ludlow Castle (www.ludlowmedieval christmas.co.uk) – Held in late November, the castle returns to the Middle Ages with markets, displays, food and fun.

Towton Battlefield, Towton, Yorkshire – The site of England's bloodiest battle can be walked.

Tewkesbury Abbey, Church Street, Tewkesbury, Gloucestershire GL20 5RZ – The stunning abbey is close to the site of the battle and it is from here that survivors were forcibly removed for trial. The redecoration ordered by Edward IV can still be seen in the Sunne in Splendour emblems on the ceiling, along with a plaque devoted to Edward of Lancaster, Prince of Wales, who is buried within the abbey.

Tewkesbury Battlefield, The Gastons, Tewkesbury – The site of the Battle of Tewkesbury near to Tewkesbury Abbey is still currently open.

Tewkesbury Medieval Festival (www.tewkesburymedievalfestival. org) – Held in mid-July, Tewkesbury hosts Europe's largest free medieval festival with a re-enactment of the battle, market stalls, living history camp and food.

Middleham Castle, Castle Hill, Middleham, North Yorkshire DL8 4QG – The large Neville fortress in Yorkshire that became one of the seats of Richard, Duke of Gloucester, during his time in the north.

York – A stunning medieval city at the heart of northern politics during the Wars of the Roses. The heads of Richard, Duke of York, his son Edmund and his brother-in-law Richard Neville, Earl of Salisbury, were displayed on Micklegate Bar and the city hosts a Richard III Museum and a Henry VII Museum.

Bosworth Battlefield Visitor Centre, Ambion Lane, Sutton Cheney, Nuneaton, Warwickshire CV13 0AD – A fantastic centre near to the site of the Battle of Bosworth containing a wealth of information on the battle and offering a battlefield walk. In late August the Visitor

Centre hosts the Bosworth Re-enactment Weekend, accompanied by a medieval market.

King Richard III Visitor Centre, 4A Saint Martins, Leicester LE1 5DB – Created following the discovery of the remains of King Richard III, this visitor centre tells the story of the controversy that still surrounds the last Plantagenet king.

Leicester Cathedral, St Martins House, 7 Peacock Lane, Leicester LE1 5DE – The remains of King Richard III are interred within a specially designed tomb that has seen part of the cathedral redesigned.

Windsor Castle, Windsor SL4 1NJ – An important palace throughout the Wars of the Roses, St George's Chapel houses the tombs of Edward IV, his wife Queen Elizabeth Woodville and the tomb of Henry VI, moved from Chertsey Abbey by Richard III.

Index